Praise for *Trust the Plan*

"Punchy and well-reported. . . . Sommer is the perfect person to tell this story. He traces the rise of lawless message boards like 8chan, he profiles the key players, he chronicles QAnon's influence on the January 6 attack on the Capitol, he sneaks into QAnon rallies, he analyzes Republican reactions to the blight in their fields, and he breathes deep of the madness, while staying blissfully sane himself."

—*New York Times*

"Will Sommer all but invented serious cultural reporting on the far right, inhabiting the worst corners of the internet so that the rest of us could understand them, and his new book on QAnon serves as a vital road map to one of the strangest and most disturbing movements of modern politics. Writing with insight, empathy, and historical expertise, Will masterfully documents how a random anonymous internet post on Reddit in 2017 rose up and swallowed the Republican Party."

—Garrett Graff, author of *Watergate: A New History*

"Will Sommer has established himself as the expert on America's right-wing fringe. Now he's exploring the damage that Donald Trump and the QAnon theorists who adore him have wreaked on the country. With kidnappings, murders, and Satanic rituals, this is a story so bizarre only Will Sommer could report it."

—Molly Jong-Fast, contributing writer at *The Atlantic*

"Sommer emerges to offer a close examination of the rise and continued presence of QAnon on the U.S. political landscape. Detailed and impeccably researched, *Trust the Plan* is essentially a crash course on a volatile and vocal segment of the U.S. population." —*The Guardian*

"This is an absolutely fascinating and deeply troubling book. Rage-inducing and heartbreaking, it's a rigorously researched, energetically written examination of a phenomenon laughed off for too long as fringe silliness." —*Booklist* (starred review)

"[Sommer has] turned this bizarre new world of the far right into his full-time beat. Now he's one of its most knowledgeable chroniclers—as evidenced by Sommer's new book. . . . [*Trust the Plan*] surveys the unintentional comedy and wrenching tragedy that has accompanied QAnon's infiltration into so many American brains."
—*Washingtonian*

"Investigative journalist Will Sommer has been following QAnon since it first emerged in 2017. *Trust the Plan* is an extended interrogation of the theory's genesis and roots." —*Jacobin*

Trust
the
Plan

Trust the Plan

The Rise of QAnon
and the Conspiracy That
Unhinged America

Will Sommer

HARPER

NEW YORK • LONDON • TORONTO • SYDNEY

HARPER

A hardcover edition of this book was published in 2023 by Harper, an imprint of HarperCollins Publishers.

TRUST THE PLAN. Copyright © 2023 by Will Sommer. All rights reserved. Printed in the United States of America. No part of this book may be used or reproduced in any manner whatsoever without written permission except in the case of brief quotations embodied in critical articles and reviews. For information, address HarperCollins Publishers, 195 Broadway, New York, NY 10007.

HarperCollins books may be purchased for educational, business, or sales promotional use. For information, please email the Special Markets Department at SPsales@harpercollins.com.

FIRST HARPER PAPERBACKS EDITION PUBLISHED 2024.

Library of Congress Cataloging-in-Publication Data has been applied for.

ISBN 978-0-06-311449-4 (pbk.)

23 24 25 26 27 LBC 5 4 3 2 1

For Juliana

Secrets are an exalted state, almost a dream state. They're a way of arresting motion, stopping the world so we can see ourselves in it.

—Don DeLillo, *Libra*

Contents

x   *Contents*

Author's Note

Writing about Q, the anonymous figure behind QAnon, can be difficult because so little is certain about Q's identity. We don't know whether Q is a man or a woman, or whether it's one person or many. For simplicity, and because the best investigations into Q's identity have all focused on men, I use male pronouns for Q throughout the book.

I changed the names of people who talked to me about their family members' involvement in QAnon, to protect their privacy and give them the freedom to talk about QAnon's effect on their lives. I have also used pseudonyms for minors involved in court cases.

Trust
the
Plan

Introduction: The Storm

The morning of January 6, 2021, a few hours before Congress would vote to certify Joe Biden's electoral win, hundreds of Donald Trump's most fervent supporters encircled the U.S. Capitol. Some of the protesters were setting up gallows for lawmakers who supported the "stolen" election. Others prowled in military-style body armor, zip ties in hand. Across town, Trump was giving a speech near the White House, urging tens of thousands of his voters to join the crowd already at the Capitol to "show strength."

Outside of Congress, the scene rippled with anger and open promises to commit violence if Trump wasn't reinstalled for four more years. Red hats and Trump flags featuring a muscular, armed Rambo-style Donald were popular. But there was another symbol in the swelling mob, too: a flag with a single letter. A *Q*.

Therese Borgerding, a middle-aged Trump fan from Ohio, had traveled to Washington with her own gear, carrying a giant blue cardboard *Q* on a pole twice her height, and a neck gaiter that put a large red *Q* over her mouth. She wanted to tell me something: not about Joe Biden or Donald Trump, but about the children in the tunnels.

As Borgerding told me, nefarious forces led by the most powerful people in the world—titans of Hollywood, the Democratic Party, and big business—had forced these children to live in thousands of miles of underground tunnels. Hidden out of sight, these "mole children" are terrorized by pedophiles until their bodies produce adrenochrome, a highly coveted liquid that celebrities and the world's richest financiers drink to stay young. Now Trump and the military were using the global Covid-19 pandemic as a cover to rescue the children. The Navy hospital ships deployed to respond to the virus were secretly treating the rescued mole children. For that matter, most earthquakes aren't even earthquakes—they are seismic events created when the Army demolishes the pedophile lairs underground.

Borgerding told me she was getting this information from a secretive military intelligence agent called "Q." He posited that the whole tunnel operation was run by a globe-spanning cabal of bankers, politicians, and Hollywood stars who could only be stopped by Donald Trump. Now Borgerding and thousands of her compatriots had come to Washington to make sure Trump stayed in office until his God-given mission to destroy that cabal and bring America into a new Christian era, free of war and disease, was accomplished. Rescuing the mole children was just one part of that plan, healing a symptom of a terminally sick world that only Trump could save.

"There's criminals in there that need to be arrested," Borgerding said, gesturing across the street toward the Capitol building. "The Democrat Party has done Satanic rituals on little children." For Borgerding and many others at the Capitol that day, the vote count in Congress wasn't just about who would be president. It was a physical struggle with Satan himself, a fight for the soul of the world. The Capitol was the latest battlefield in a brewing war, and they were on the front lines.

By the final days of the Trump administration, conspiracy theories abounded. Republicans concocted the lie that the 2020 election was stolen from Trump by rigged voting machines or even a rogue CIA supercomputer; for liberals, there were fantasies in the "Steele dossier" about Trump paying prostitutes to urinate on a bed Barack Obama once slept in.

Trump broke into politics by pushing conspiracy theories about Obama's birthplace, then fueled his campaign with a series of similarly bizarre claims about his fellow Republican opponents. He suggested that Senator Marco Rubio wasn't eligible to be president and that Senator Ted Cruz's father helped kill John F. Kennedy. Now Trump was the most powerful man in the world, the conspiracy-theorist-in-chief. His constant promotion of outlandish lies throughout his presidency gave his fans permission to dive headlong into conspiracy theories themselves. If the president really thought Cruz's father shot JFK, what was off-limits for his followers?

The conspiracy theory boom had practical benefits for both politicians and internet hucksters. People convinced that Democrats drank children's blood, or that Hillary Clinton ran an assassination squad gunning down her foes in the streets of Washington, came into view for Republicans as motivated grassroots activists and voters. The GOP's budding conspiracy-theorist bloc opened their wallets to buy zinc pills and meal kits to stock their apocalypse bunkers. But they also provided the raw material to keep their favorite politicians in office, donating to campaigns and the legal defense funds of Trump allies. Fearful that the lunatic fringe was no longer so fringe, most Republican lawmakers avoided attacking them.

Conspiracy theories had been gaining ground in the Republican Party since Obama was elected. But there was only one that had the power to move its supporters offline, to turn the usual online trash talk into thousands of people in the streets willing to march for their beliefs, and sometimes do worse than that. It had more resources and staying power than all the others combined. Borgerding and millions of other Americans had signed on to the biggest conspiracy theory of them all: QAnon.

In October 2017, someone calling themselves "Q" appeared on the anonymous, anarchic message board 4chan, posting a handful of cryptic messages claiming that Hillary Clinton would be arrested by the end of the month.

More messages followed, filled with unexplained acronyms and fresh warnings that a secret military operation would soon take place. Most of the people who read those first posts laughed them off. But a few 4chan users who had been obsessed for years with other conspiracy theories latched on to Q's posts. They interpreted his one-letter handle as a reference to the Energy Department's Q-level security clearance, a sign that these messages were coming from deep inside the Trump administration.

Clinton was never arrested, but Q's messages kept coming. His handful of 4chan acolytes started repackaging the clues, turning them into more accessible YouTube videos or Facebook posts. Those explanations drew in more people. QAnon believers came up with a word for radicalizing new members: *red-pilling*, like the scene in *The Matrix* when Keanu Reeves, lost in a dream world, takes the red pill and sees his life as it really is.

At first, the new recruits were Trump supporters eager for tales about how the president's enemies would be destroyed. But Q's narrative grew beyond Trump's base, thanks to social media platforms that boosted provocative content. It attracted people who had never thought of themselves before as Trump fans. They were shocked by QAnon's tales of sexual depravity, then lured in by the promise that Q could explain a chaotic world.

QAnon is still going. It has alienated thousands of people from those close to them and destroyed friendships and marriages as people red-pilled by QAnon have failed to see why their children, parents, or spouses refuse to join in the fight against the cabal. QAnon has also broken out of the United States, spreading to Canada, Europe, and Japan. QAnon has evolved since its launch in 2017, inspiring factions that include QAnon yoga groups and others that believe Trump owns medical technology that can cure any disease. It has absorbed dozens of lesser conspiracy theories, and even inspired a handful of real-world murders. That makes it hard for the average news consumer to understand just what QAnon followers actually believe. Is it that the cabal is run by lizards from another planet? Or that John F. Kennedy Jr. faked his death and is Q himself? Is it one or the other?

At its heart, QAnon has a simple message: the world is run by a cabal of Satanic cannibal-pedophiles from the ranks of the Democratic Party, Hollywood, and global finance who sexually abuse children and even drink their blood in rituals. The U.S. military, which has resisted joining the otherwise all-encompassing cabal, recruited Donald Trump to run for president to oppose this evil group of elitists. And someday soon he's going to purge all his foes in a violent, cathartic moment called "The Storm," with his opponents ending up either imprisoned in Guantanamo Bay or executed by military tribunals. All of the world's problems—and yours—will be solved forever. QAnon's dream of the Storm persisted even after Trump left office with his purge unfulfilled. Q's followers brushed off their electoral defeat and the apparent failure of Q's prophecies. Perhaps the deep state was too hard for Trump to defeat this time. But he could always try again, with help from Q and his supporters.

Q and the conspiracy theorists who support him have promised believers that a sort of utopia awaits them, if only Trump would be given free rein to deal with his enemies. The cabal has been hoarding disease cures, so even the terminally ill will be healed once Trump launches the Storm. Since the cabal causes all wars, world peace would reign once its leaders are arrested. And because the cabal controls the financial system, a post-cabal world would mean an end to credit card and student loan debt. This wasn't about policy debates or even culture wars—Trump supporters who signed up for QAnon were joining a biblical struggle between good and evil. They described themselves as divine warriors given a task from God to target specific people they saw as devils on the earth: Obama, for example, or billionaire Democratic donor George Soros.

The theory and the community that surrounds QAnon has come to encompass many things: sex, religion, politics, terrorism, and even health, as believers encourage each other to reject vaccines and refuse to wear masks. It's a symptom of the world we live in, a product of unchecked social media platforms, a crumbling education system, rampant political polarization, and the crumbling of offline communities. Q's followers have responded to modern life by retreating into a violent fantasy that exists parallel to the real world. QAnon isn't a one-time phenomenon. Instead, it's just the start of the all-consuming conspiracy theory movements to come. Unless something changes, QAnon is a glimpse into our future.

The first thing you notice about QAnon followers is the gear: clothing and posters covered in Q's, pictures of Trump, and inscrutable acronyms. They hold flags portraying Donald Trump standing victorious astride a tank. They wear shirts with a *Q* written in a fiery yellow or red, white, and blue, or motorcycle jackets with a *Q* patch. And then there's the obsession with vigilante Marvel antihero "The Punisher"—one favorite QAnon shirt is decorated with a *Q* shaped like the Punisher's skull logo, spiced up with a Trumpian blond comb-over and a message to "Keep Calm and QAnon."

Talking to QAnon supporters outside the Capitol on January 6, I was struck by how many of them were convinced the Storm was at hand that very day. But not one had the same idea of what that meant. Perhaps Trump would lead the protesters to the Capitol, bursting into the Senate right as Vice President Mike Pence betrayed the country to the cabal by certifying Biden's win. Or maybe Pence was on Team QAnon himself, and would oversee the Storm as police arrested the Democratic election-riggers in the chamber.

The believers had come to Washington to witness that epochal moment or even to carry it out if Trump called on them. In the same kind of measured, enthusiastic tone you'd expect from someone talking about their favorite sports team, they explained how Hillary Clinton eats children, and how eager they were for a new civil war. As Pence arrived at the Capitol to oversee the certification, dozens of people in the crowd began to shout the QAnon motto, "Where we go one, we go all." For years, these people had been primed with fantasies of the Storm, promised the violent executions of their political opponents and the installation of a Trump dictatorship. Now, as Pence stepped inside the Capitol, all of that was slipping away.

"The Storm is upon us," Borgerding told me.

Then the riot started.

In May 2016, I started a newsletter to try to help explain to my liberal audience how then–presidential candidate Donald Trump had taken over the Republican Party. I covered the trends and oddities of the far right, from the rise of Steve Bannon's Breitbart News to the growing influence of the racist "alt-right."

The project grew out of my unusual passion for consuming huge amounts of right-wing media. I was raised in a conservative Texas family, where road trips meant listening to Rush Limbaugh's talk radio show and Ayn Rand audiobooks. I cried over Ronald Reagan's funeral, and pored over a Bill O'Reilly book for teenagers for advice on how to handle dilemmas like smoking and premarital sex. But even after I left the party behind, I nursed a perverse appetite for Republican media personalities and the ideological struggles of the American right. For years, I spent my time at local news jobs slacking off by reading conservative columnists and blogs, tracking the outlandish personalities who were fighting for control of the conservative movement during the Obama administration.

Donald Trump's rise to the forefront of the Republican candidates stoked interest from those tracking conspiracies and far-right extremists, myself included. My wife, sick of hearing about all of the conservative pundits I spent so many hours tracking, had an idea: maybe I could write about these characters and conspiracy theories for a wider audience, instead of talking about them every night at dinner.

After five months of writing a newsletter about some of the strangest parts of Trump's base, however, I encountered something in October 2016 that made my usual topics look almost normal. Online one night, I discovered a story that would change both my life and American politics forever: Pizzagate.

I noticed that a minor alt-right figure named "Pizza Party Ben" had blanketed his Twitter feed with videos and pictures from a Washington, D.C., pizzeria called Comet Ping Pong, obsessing over its menu and decor. Ben wasn't alone—all over the right-wing internet, people were posting videos about Comet. The videos weren't sinister in themselves. Most of them just showed kids eating pizza or playing on the restaurant's Ping-Pong tables. I had been to Comet Ping Pong, too, and enjoyed it. If these guys also liked the pizzeria, I thought, at least we had that in common.

I sent Ben a message to ask why he was so interested in Comet. He wrote back, saying only that the pizzeria was involved in "many strange coincidences."

It didn't take long to realize this was not just about pizza. Ben's message piqued my interest, and I started tracing back the origins of the right's interest in Comet. A few days earlier, anonymous posters on forums like Reddit and 4chan had been discussing hacked emails from Clinton campaign chair John Podesta that had been released by WikiLeaks. Comet Ping Pong, located in a wealthy Washington neighborhood popular with political types, was mentioned a few times.

The amateur internet sleuths had seized on the pizza emails, claiming that pedophiles use "cheese pizza" as slang for "child porn." For them, it was only a small logical leap to the direst conclusion—that when Podesta and his friends were ordering a pizza, they were actually ordering a child to sexually abuse at the restaurant. As bizarre as it was, the theory, dubbed "Pizzagate," caught on with the far-right internet in the final days of the presidential campaign.

I emailed Comet Ping Pong owner James Alefantis, asking if he had seen the speculation on Reddit that his restaurant was a child rape dungeon.

"What's Reddit?" Alefantis said.

Alefantis was about to become very familiar with the online forum, and all of the other corners of the internet where he, along with his customers and staff, were seen as a locus of unfathomable evil. Death threats poured in; amateur Pizzagate detectives began wandering around the restaurant, livestreaming their investigations to viewers eager to get a glimpse into the devil's den. The theorists began to harass neighboring businesses, too, convinced that they were all connected to Comet through underground tunnels frequented by sex-trafficking Democratic leaders.

Then, in December 2016, a Pizzagate believer, Edgar Maddison Welch, stormed into Comet Ping Pong with an AR-15 rifle, convinced that he needed to rescue the children being abused in the pizzeria's basement. As customers fled, Welch fired shots into a door in an attempt to break into the dungeon. But as he searched through the restaurant, he couldn't find any tortured children. He couldn't even find a basement, because Comet didn't have one. Dejected, Welch emerged from the restaurant with his hands on his head and was arrested.

"The intel on this wasn't 100 percent," Welch said later.

Pizzagate all but disappeared from public view after the shooting, discredited by Welch's violence and the threat of defamation lawsuits from Alefantis. But online, Pizzagate never really ended—it just went underground.

A year after Welch stormed Comet, in the winter of 2017, I was back on 4chan. I had noticed a recurring conversation thread, always illustrated with a picture of a lion looking over a sunset. This tiny internet community on 4chan was a place called "Calm Before the Storm," which described itself as a place to discuss messages from someone named Q. But 4chan was full of nonsense that never went beyond the site, and I ignored those threads for a while. Whoever Q was, I felt sure we had heard the last of them.

I was wrong. Those 4chan threads were an early sign that Pizzagate had never stopped. Instead, in little-visited corners of the internet, it wrapped itself up with other conspiracy theories and internet phenomena to create QAnon, a mega-conspiracy theory that was far more compelling and dangerous than Pizzagate.

I saw more references on 4chan to this "Q" person and the Storm, even though I didn't know what they meant. Then the phrases jumped from 4chan to other places like Reddit and Facebook. Right-wing Twitter users I followed started buzzing about what Q was telling them. In the spring of 2018, I started writing about what all these people were talking about: QAnon. Soon after that, in April 2018, I watched as hundreds of QAnon believers marched in the streets of Washington, demanding an end to the Justice Department's investigation into the Trump campaign and chanting "Where we go one, we go all." That march made clear to me that QAnon was, for its believers, about much more than a weird internet rumor. A man I met there who lacked the health insurance he needed to treat his terminal cancer told me he wasn't worried about his illness. Q's predictions about the Storm would soon come true and force the cabal to release a long-hidden cure for cancer. A woman whose child was bullied in school because he was autistic said she wasn't worried about her son. Soon Trump would make the cabal release their autism cure, too.

At the time, QAnon seemed like a sad cult, but one unlikely to have a significant political impact. But as the months went on and Q's clues were woven into an increasingly elaborate narrative, I found myself writing about QAnon more. It had become a feeding ground for people looking to make money from the gullible and confused—and that meant plenty of opportunity for news stories. First for my newsletter and then for the Daily Beast, a news website I started working for in 2018, I wrote articles debunking QAnon's claims and exposing its promoters as con artists and charlatans. I thought that Washington rally in 2018 would be QAnon's largest event ever, with Q's deluded followers realizing soon that they had been fooled. But a few months later, a crazed QAnon believer driving an armored truck blocked a bridge near the Hoover Dam after one of Q's predictions about Hillary Clinton's arrest failed to come true. Q hadn't faded away. Instead, dozens of believers began to appear at Trump rallies with giant Q signs. QAnon supporters even started running for Congress.

Reporting more on QAnon turned me into a target. Leading conspiracy theorists accused me of being a deep-state operative covering up for the pedophile cabal. Q linked to my tweets in some of his posts, directing angry followers online to send me harassing messages. As I sat in the front row at a QAnon rally in September 2019, I watched as conspiracy theorist Dustin

Nemos took the stage. Apparently unaware that I was in the crowd, Nemos began to accuse another audience member who looked a little like me of being the real Will Sommer. Members of the crowd turned on their fellow Q devotee, booing and shouting at the man as he tried, without success, to convince them he wasn't me. While I couldn't miss the irony of a QAnon believer's surprise at suddenly having the mob's anger turned on him, it was also concerning because I was the guy they were really angry at. QAnon's response to the outside world was getting uglier.

As the death threats started to arrive in my inbox, it was hard to ignore the fate of other people who had angered QAnon fans. A QAnon believer murdered a New York Mafia boss, part of a botched attempt to bring him to a mythical tribunal. Another QAnon supporter murdered his own brother, convinced by theories, fringe even within QAnon, that his brother was a lizard-person.

I locked down my social media accounts, well aware of how Q's supporters could turn even innocuous photos into material for their attacks. When friends arrived to a vacation house with an Instagram-worthy pool toy shaped like a slice of pizza, I knew to stay far away. I felt like QAnon had split me in two. There was the real, mundane version of me, who was spending too much of his time reading conspiracy theories, texting with QAnon obsessives, and listening to QAnon podcasts. Then there was the version QAnon followers saw, one who was at once much more exciting, sinister, and a more acceptable target for their hate. All of this made me an uncomfortable micro-celebrity in QAnonworld. Many QAnon followers were unnervingly friendly in person, when they managed to leave the talk about executions and pedophiles behind. Some asked to pose for selfies, convinced that I was on their side and reporting on QAnon just to spread its message more widely. But then they tried to take me on in livestreamed confrontations or demanded to know whether I really thought QAnon was fake. As Q inspired more violence, I started disguising myself at pro-Trump events as much as possible.

This idea born from the internet's depths had alienated thousands of people from those close to them, destroying friendships and marriages. Whether you knew about QAnon or not, it could affect you—hurting vaccination rates in your town, or convincing a deluded man with a gun that he's carrying out Q's orders.

By the 2020 election, my own interactions with QAnon had gotten worse. I had gone from thinking of them as a disturbing, but effectively powerless, internet oddity into a growing force on the American right. QAnon wasn't a sideshow anymore. It was the main event.

By the election, though, QAnon had become about much more than just symbols in the clues and strange messages. It had become a way of life for Q's followers, a way of seeing the world, politics, and a community all at once. Q's most devoted fans abandoned their old lives to pursue their own dreams of the Storm.

Standing outside the Capitol, I was looking for an answer to a question that had pressed on me as I watched QAnon grow. What happens when a portion of a country buys into a mass delusion?

QAnon supporter Douglas Jensen came to Washington because he was convinced that Q had personally asked him to be there. He told friends back in Iowa that he thought he was communicating directly with Q, and thought every prediction would come true. He called himself a "digital soldier," a phrase Q followers had adopted as one of their slogans from a speech by Trump national security adviser Michael Flynn. Now, clad in a shirt decorated with a large *Q*, a snarling bald eagle, and the Q slogan "Trust the Plan," Jensen wanted to make sure he was out in front of the other rioters. That way, his shirt would be captured on camera and Q would get more attention.

Jensen climbed into the Capitol through a broken window, eager to help Capitol Police arrest Pence on Trump's orders. He stood out to police as one of the most aggressive rioters, egging on his compatriots to attack police and acting unfazed even as explosions went off around him. Inside the

Capitol, Jensen led a mob chasing a beleaguered Capitol Police officer up flights of stairs.

"Why are you defending these motherfuckers?" Jensen yelled at police, demanding that they detain lawmakers who had planned to certify Biden's election win. "You should be arresting them!"

Federal Aviation Administration employee Kevin Strong entered the Capitol after traveling from California, his latest step in a headlong dive into QAnon's unreality. The FBI had already been tracking him for a week ahead of the riot, alerted by an acquaintance of Strong's that he was getting deeper into QAnon. Before heading to Washington, Strong hung a Q flag outside his house and purchased a new truck, claiming that the Storm would soon absolve his debt. He told an acquaintance that January 6 would mark the start of World War III.

Once he was inside the Capitol, though, the war failed to start. Rather than helping to usher in Trump's second term, Strong was captured on MSNBC milling around aimlessly in the Rotunda. When the FBI raided his house days later, agents confiscated his QAnon flag.

QAnon believer Hank Muntzer, who was so deep into QAnon that he had painted slogans and a thunderous illustration of the Storm on the side of his Montana appliance store, breached the Capitol, too. Like Strong and Jensen, Muntzer had been motivated by QAnon, convinced that Q had inspired the American people with his clues and "awakened a sleeping giant."

Muntzer helped a surge of rioters shove through the police lines, taking pepper spray to the face as he pushed forward. Despite participating in the attack himself and posting on Facebook about how he and others "stormed the Capitol," Muntzer claimed in an interview shot on the streets of Washington afterward that any destruction shown by the media was an inside job faked by the deep state to make the rioters look bad. As of this writing, Muntzer was awaiting trial on five charges related to the riot.

Georgia resident Rosanne Boyland had been drawn into QAnon during the coronavirus lockdown, telling friends about the cabal and the mole children. A friend later said that Boyland, a recovering drug user, had become "brainwashed" by QAnon after seeing echoes of her own child-hood in its claims about crimes against children. Boyland died after a mob of Trump supporters trampled her on their way to attack police.

Air Force veteran Ashli Babbitt had come to Washington for what she claimed would mark the Storm. Babbitt had followed QAnon since February 2020, tweeting pictures of herself in a Q shirt and boasting about her skills at red-pilling new converts. Draped in a Trump flag, Babbitt was fatally shot by a Capitol Police officer as she tried to break into the Speaker's Lobby.

But maybe no rioter summed up the growing derangement QAnon had set off in the United States more than Jacob Chansley, the self-proclaimed "Q Shaman."

Chansley, a failed actor who had reportedly been kicked out of the Navy after he refused to take an anthrax vaccine, had transformed himself after discovering QAnon, draping himself in animal pelts and horns, painting his face in red, white, and blue, and wielding a spear wrapped in an American flag. By embracing QAnon in its most outlandish form, Chansley took on a new identity, turning from an unemployed actor living with his mother into the Q Shaman.

The shaman became a familiar figure in the QAnon hotbed of Arizona, bellowing outside the courthouse when a QAnon believer was released on bail and riling up angry crowds outside of polling places with allegations of voter fraud.

Many Q supporters describe themselves as warriors, but Chansley actually donned a QAnon battle costume, putting on what he called his war paint to carry out "war that is of a spiritual nature." He wore a hat made of coyote fur, in a nod to indigenous beliefs about a coyote trickster god, topped with buffalo horns. The message of the horns, Chansley explained, was less complicated: "You mess with the bull, you get the horns."

On January 6, Chansley rushed into the Capitol, using a bullhorn to encourage other rioters to confront congressmen. Chansley even breached the Senate chamber, posing for pictures with his spear in the chair recently vacated by Pence himself.

Chansley left a note for the vice president. "It's only a matter of time," Chansley wrote on a piece of paper, then added a QAnon slogan that doubled as a threat. "Justice is coming."

As flashbangs went off and tear gas drifted over the crowd outside the Capitol, I ran into Borgerding again, just as a man waving a giant Q flag rode by the Capitol's broken doors on a scooter.

"It just happened," she said. "We're taking our country back."

Chapter 1

The Genesis

In late October 2017, an anonymous poster on a bustling, chaotic online message board called 4chan made an announcement to the world. Most of 4chan's tens of millions of users spent their time on the site exploring the internet's darkest or most frivolous corners, talking video games, swapping racist memes, or teaming up to troll other websites. But this user had a much more serious message: former presidential candidate Hillary Clinton would soon be in jail:

Hillary Clinton will be arrested between 7:45 AM - 8:30 AM EST on Monday - the morning on Oct 30, 2017.

In a follow-up message, the user claimed that the Trump administration was coordinating with American allies to prevent Clinton from fleeing the country. Her arrest would trigger civil strife, setting off riots and inspiring anti-Trump elites to also flee. If anyone doubted something big was coming, they should ask National Guard members if they'd been called up for duty on October 30.

For QAnon believers, those two posts from the figure who would become known as Q mark the start of their sacred text, the first of the "Q drops" that reveal the true state of the world. But at the time, many 4chan users were just annoyed. Plenty of people before Q had played on the site's culture of near-universal anonymity to impersonate unnamed government officials. Starting in 2016, 4chan had witnessed a multiyear procession of self-proclaimed law enforcement and intelligence whistleblowers purporting to spill the country's most sensitive secrets. They often called themselves "Anons," short for anonymous.

"Oh god, not another one," one 4chan user wrote after Q posted for the first time.

In 2017 alone, there had already been "CIAAnon" and "WH Insider Anon," each of whom promised that an explosive revelation about Clinton was just around the corner. A poster who called himself "Anonymous5" revealed more allegations about the Clinton family, while insisting that he personally had lived to be 120 years old through the power of secret technologies. A character named "High Level Insider Anon" told Trump supporters that Clinton used her private email server to sell American secrets to the Chinese government. 4chan users thrilled to the stories of FBIAnon, a supposed FBI insider with confidential dirt on the federal investigation into Clinton. Sometimes the anonymous personas would set up question-and-answer threads, holding forth on space aliens and bitcoin's investment prospects.

This parade of leakers seems to have found few followers, even on 4chan. For most users on the site, the whistleblower game was a way to pass the time, to focus their hate on Clinton, and to rev up their enthusiasm for Trump. When one poster complained that an insider was obviously "FAKE FAKE FAKE," others chimed in to quiet the skeptic.

"Who cares?" one 4chan poster wrote. "Fuck off."

At first, few on 4chan took the character who would become known as Q seriously, either, especially after the October 30 deadline passed without any Clinton arrest.

Paul Furber, a South African computer programmer who would become one of Q's most devoted early followers, watched as Q unfolded his outrageous initial claims and felt just as skeptical. After all, Furber thought, this was 4chan. Anyone could say anything. Q's allegations that Hillary

Clinton would be arrested were "utterly outrageous," Furber thought. But as Q ramped up his posting, releasing as many as thirty new messages a day, Furber began to reconsider. He noticed a string of what QAnon followers call "Q proofs"—irrefutable evidence that both Q and his ideas are legitimate.

Those proofs gave Q credibility among 4chan users in a way that the whistleblowers that preceded him failed to do. Some of those earlier leakers talked about UFOs and eternal life, ideas that were hard to take seriously. But Q's clues, at least initially, seemed to be grounded in some sort of reality. Even better, he appeared to get things right. First Q said something cryptic about power players making moves in Saudi Arabia. Then the Saudi monarchy really was convulsed by an internal purge two days later.

Q posted a picture from an airplane window that 4chan users became convinced could only have been taken from Air Force One, suggesting that Q was a Trump insider posting on the president's behalf. The skeptics started to come around on Q. There were fewer insults directed at Q on the board, replaced by requests for users to work together to research his claims.

After the Air Force One photo, Furber recalls, "we took him very seriously indeed."

Furber and other early acolytes started contacting YouTube conspiracy theorists, urging them to make videos promoting QAnon. Soon the clues wouldn't be limited to people with the patience to wade through hundreds of anonymous posts. QAnon was about to escape its birthplace.

Years after Q first appeared, 4chan users aren't the only ones falling for his claims. Belief in QAnon and its tenets has become relatively mainstream. A March 2021 poll of 5,149 adults conducted by the Public Religion Research Institute found that 15 percent of respondents believed the core QAnon belief that the world's top institutions are run by "Satan-worshipping pedophiles who run a global child sex trafficking operation."

Even more respondents approved of the idea of the Storm, with 20 percent saying they believed that "[t]here is a storm coming soon that will sweep away the elites in power and restore the rightful leaders." A poll of over 2,000 people conducted by the American Enterprise Institute in January 2021 after the Capitol riot found that 15 percent of respondents believed Trump was engaged in a secret war with pedophiles in Hollywood and the Democratic Party.

Support for QAnon rises among more conservative groups. Twenty-seven percent of white evangelical Christians in the AEI poll, for example, said QAnon's claims were at least mostly correct.

Other polls that ask respondents directly whether they support QAnon, rather than its beliefs, have found lower levels of support. Between September 2020 and April 2022, a running poll taken online by survey company Civiqs that received more than 55,000 responses found only between 4 and 7 percent of respondents describing themselves as QAnon supporters. While that number is smaller than other polls, it would still amount to millions of Americans endorsing a crazed, violent ideology.

The polling shows that QAnon believers don't always look like the wild-eyed mob at the Capitol. They could have a conversation with you about the weather, then casually mention that the government controls that weather. They could be parents at your children's school, fellow customers in the grocery store, or politicians—all of them divorced from reality by a conspiracy theory that began with a few much-mocked posts on 4chan.

QAnon has a unique ability to recruit people who have never considered themselves conspiracy theorists before. Pulling people in through the journey to understand the QAnon clues, it creates a community where people radicalize one another—or as Q has put it, to see how deep the rabbit hole goes. It comes with an entire religious and political agenda, a call for a world cleansed of everyone standing in the way of Trump and his supporters.

QAnon is a dark dream about sanctioned violence against political and cultural enemies. It threatens to undermine democracy, laying the groundwork for an authoritarian takeover justified on the grounds that Democrats and other liberals are child-eating pedophiles. How, QAnon believers ask, can we coexist with people like that?

To understand where QAnon is going, you must understand where it started: 4chan, the unruly online message board where Q first found his flock.

4chan began in 2003, when a lonely New York teenager named Christopher Poole needed more anime porn. Poole, who went by the name "moot" online, had already discovered a trove of anime on the massive Japanese image-sharing board 2channel, but he didn't speak Japanese.

Poole copied 2channel's code to launch 4chan, an English-language clone of the Japanese site, originally intending it as a place to swap anime with his friends. 4chan began with just two subforums: "/a/," devoted to Poole's anime interests, and "/b/," the "random" section of the website.

Poole borrowed more than code from 2channel. On the Japanese site, users were anonymous, all going by the Japanese term *Nanashii*, which translates into English as "nameless." As he set up 4chan, Poole plugged the Japanese term into an online translator, where it was transformed into English as "Anonymous." Poole wrote 4chan's code so every user would show up by default with the name "Anonymous." Fourteen years later, this choice would become the name taken by Q's followers: "Anons."

4chan's anime section thrived, but /b/ took on an outsize life of its own, becoming the site's best-known section to the wider internet. The forum's anonymous users created a string of blockbuster memes that went on to become ubiquitous online, inventing "LOLcats"—the hungry meme cats who asked to eat "cheezburgers"—and "Rickrolling," the concept of tricking other internet users with a misleading link to singer Rick Astley's 1987 hit, "Never Gonna Give You Up."

The anonymous hordes on /b/ soon began to flex their muscles off the site, invading online children's games with racist messages or bruising Apple's stock prices by spreading hoaxes about founder Steve Jobs's death. By

2008, the more politically minded users had coalesced into "Anonymous," a loose-knit online movement based around "hacktivism," the idea that internet activists could change the world for good, through massed online actions or hacks. Supporters of Anonymous protested outside branches of the Church of Scientology in Guy Fawkes masks inspired by the movie *V for Vendetta* and attacked websites connected to Middle Eastern governments during the Arab Spring.

As the rest of the internet became aware of 4chan, so did neo-Nazis, who began flooding into the site after 4chan's "Anons" trolled racist website Stormfront by spamming it with violent and obscene images. The white supremacist newcomers found a receptive audience on 4chan, where racial slurs and jokes about Black people having AIDS were already popular. Rather than let the white supremacists roam freely across 4chan, Poole decided to quarantine the neo-Nazi influence from the rest of the site by creating a new forum, "Politically Incorrect," or /pol/, in 2010.

Instead of cutting the neo-Nazis off from the rest of 4chan, author and 4chan expert Dale Beran notes, /pol/ began to pull in all the site's worst elements, inviting them into a place where the neo-Nazis held forth for a captive audience. The white supremacists had been given a home to mingle with other insidious groups of 4chan users: the involuntarily celibate "incels," who raged against women for not having sex with them, and the garden-variety conspiracy theorists who had been drawn by 4chan's reputation as the internet's Wild West.

On /pol/, all those groups could radicalize one another with their beliefs, then reflect them back out onto the rest of 4chan. The forum's anonymity meant that every user looked the same, giving them the chance to couch their extremist ideas as normal in a way that a neo-Nazi rally in real life never could. In an early example of the forum's power, angry /pol/ users teamed up with members of 4chan's video game forum to help drive Gamergate, the backlash to the rise of feminism and other social justice movements in the gaming industry.

Donald Trump was a dream candidate for /pol/. In debates, he trolled his debate opponents with taunts as mercilessly as they did to their foes online. Both Trump and /pol/ users had the same concerns, calling Mexican immigrants "rapists" and sharing a sense that the United States needed a strong leader to arrest its decline. They dubbed him the GEOTUS—the "God-Emperor of the United States," in a nod to an ancient, pitiless galactic dictator from the military strategy game *Warhammer 40,000*. While /pol/ wasn't large enough to sway any election with their own votes, its users became an online engine for Trump, pumping out viral meme images to support his campaign. On election night in 2016, the forum exploded as Trump's unlikely win became reality. When Trump carried Florida, one /pol/ user predicted Clinton's impending arrest: "bitch is going to jail."

By the time Q first appeared on the forum on October 28, 2017, Trump had failed to deliver on his /pol/ supporters' hopes. Construction had not begun on the border wall, and Mexico wasn't paying for it. Special Counsel Robert Mueller had been investigating ties between Trump's campaign and Russia for five months. Worst of all, Hillary Clinton was still not in jail.

Q's posts offered Trump's fans an explanation for all the president's woes. The issue was that the world's problems were far worse than they had even imagined. Forget bringing jobs back from China or repealing ObamaCare—this was a life-or-death battle with Trump and his supporters on one side and decadent elites who drank children's blood on the other. The wall would have to wait.

Three weeks before Q first appeared on 4chan, Trump summoned reporters to a surprise press event in the White House, where he posed for a picture with military leaders.

"You guys know what this represents?" Trump asked reporters. "Maybe it's the calm before the storm."

"What's the storm?" one journalist said.

"Could be the calm before the storm," Trump repeated.

By November 2017, enough 4chan users were interested in QAnon that /pol/ featured a regular thread devoted to QAnon called "Calm Before the Storm," citing a reference Q made in a post early that month about a coming military operation. Those early Q threads became the first hubs for QAnon activity. Q would occasionally pop into the threads to offer more clues, which were instantly dissected by a growing army of QAnon believers.

"You're a great patriot and we got your back," wrote one new supporter.

But Q's followers had no idea who their new hero was. While most users on 4chan and other chan sites are anonymous by default, users can choose to identify themselves. On any other website, this would mean logging on with a screen name and password. But 4chan doesn't have an account system, a decision Poole made when he created the site to keep data costs low. Instead, 4chan users who want to establish continuity between their posts must rely on something else: a "tripcode," a password-style concept popular on chan sites that lets other users know that a group of posts are all from the same person. To post as Q, whoever controls the account enters a password, which is then transformed by 4chan's coding into a publicly displayed random hash of letters, numbers, and symbols. Anyone who saw that tripcode across every Q post would know that this was Q—or at least someone with access to the password.

Able to track Q's messages across the forum, believers built up an entire language around the clues. They came to instantly recognize the meaning of the most common phrases and acronyms in the same way that crossword enthusiasts know to expect short words with plenty of vowels. They pored over the QAnon crumbs and revisited older clues years later with new events in mind, convinced the earliest QAnon clues could reveal some secret knowledge about the present. Every QAnon follower knows "the MB" is the Muslim Brotherhood, for example, while "AW" is disgraced former congressman Anthony Weiner.

Consider Q's second message on 4chan, from October 28, 2017:

Mockingbird
HRC detained, not arrested (yet).
Where is Huma? Follow Huma.

This has nothing to do w/ Russia (yet).
Why does Potus surround himself w/ generals?
What is military intelligence?
Why go around the 3 letter agencies?
. . .
They never believed for a moment they (Democrats and Republicans)
*   would lose control.*
This is not a R v D battle.
Why did Soros donate all his money recently?
Why would he place all his funds in a RC?
Mockingbird 10.30.17
God bless fellow Patriots.

To the uninitiated, this post is gibberish. But to believers, it's a foundational text for the QAnon worldview, a hopeful message that Trump was on the verge of defeating his foes. At the top of the post, Q alludes to "Operation Mockingbird," a real CIA program during the Cold War to manipulate media outlets. Here the implication is that the media has been infiltrated by intelligence agencies working for the cabal and, unlike Q's anonymous posts, can't be trusted. "Huma" is Huma Abedin, the close Hillary Clinton aide who Q claimed had flipped against Clinton to cooperate with the patriots involved in the Q operation.

The lines about "Potus," "generals," and "3 letter agencies" lay out the QAnon belief that many of the traditional institutions of American government, like the media, have been undermined by shadowy forces. "Three-letter agencies" like the CIA and FBI have been compromised by the cabal, so Trump has to work with generals and military intelligence to bring on the Storm.

The average QAnon follower would understand the second half of the clue, "this is not a R v D battle," as a message that the cabal controls both political parties, meaning that only Trump and the military could break its control of the government. After that, Q pulls a random event from the news—billionaire Democratic donor and Republican bogeyman George Soros donating much of his fortune to his charity, or, in this telling his "RC" or "Registered Charity"—to suggest that Soros is either preparing to hide his assets and become a fugitive or resigning himself to death.

Then Q repeats "Mockingbird" in reference to October 30, 2017—the day Q has promised believers Clinton will be arrested. The implication of the Mockingbird mention is that the media can't be trusted to tell you whether Clinton has really been arrested on October 30. Finally, Q closes with a salute to "fellow Patriots."

Not every post was so dense. As Q grew more influential, he started directing his followers to potential targets: journalists or Republicans critical of Q. Other posts featured a picture of an American flag or a pro-Q meme. The constant drum of Q posts kept followers enthralled, always ready to tune into 4chan for a new update.

QAnon users don't just rely on the clues, which they call "breadcrumbs." Instead, whenever a new post drops, they start elaborating on them with their own internet research, a process called "baking." In the replies under each Q post, QAnon believers tell each other about how many hours they spent "baking" new proofs by surfing the internet. Armed with even more conjecture, they spin off their own theories. Q might pick up some of those fan-theories in a later post, the highlight of a QAnon supporter's baking career. Working together, believers think, they can decode the clues and uncover the truth about the world as Q wants them to see it.

For those who didn't have the time to bake for themselves, dozens of QAnon websites sprang up in the movement's first months with annotated collections explaining what the breadcrumbs were supposed to mean. On one QAnon baking site, for example, the "R v D" line in the Q post is explained as proof of a "declaration of war between the Patriotic Factions of the US Government and the Swamp," a symbol of the corrupt Washington establishment.

The first test of Q's predictive powers came just two days after the initial posts appeared, the day Clinton was supposed to be arrested. But rather than ending that day in a prison cell, Clinton signed copies of her campaign memoir in Chicago.

Instead of giving up on QAnon, the days-old conspiracy theory's supporters looked for more proof that Clinton had actually been arrested. They zeroed in on Clinton's billowing pantsuit legs at public appearances, claiming her clothes had been cut large to avoid showing the silhouette of a court-ordered ankle monitor. Or perhaps Clinton had been executed and replaced with a clone to avoid causing a public panic.

In late November 2017, a month after the first clues appeared on 4chan, Q gathered up his flock: it was time to move on. They were headed to 8chan, a less-popular chan-style board whose users behaved even worse than 4chan's denizens. 4chan, Q declared, had been "infiltrated" by his enemies. It was time to move QAnon to a place that was solely his own.

Even as QAnon moved to 8chan, his followers still didn't know his identity. Q did a lot of talking about the world, but said nothing about himself. Believers could only rely on Q's tripcodes to know which posts to trust. His supporters felt sure that Q was someone at Trump's right hand—the head of an intelligence agency, perhaps, or a trusted aide or a Trump family member. To skeptics, the list of suspected Q culprits was much shorter. They suspected Paul Furber, the early Q acolyte from South Africa, or the owners of Q's new home on 8chan.

To Anons, though, Q's real name didn't matter at all when compared to their fascination with Trump. Every permutation of QAnon to come would have Trump at its core, the god-emperor who would solve their problems. That devotion would pose both a challenge and an unusual opportunity for Trump and his administration, because QAnon believers were about to enter the real world.

Chapter 2

"Ask the Q"

Roman Riselvato and his girlfriend, a fellow QAnon supporter named Cassidy Bailes, set out with their infant daughter one day in July 2019 to see Donald Trump at a rally in North Carolina. Bailes had written TRUMP with a marker on the front of her daughter's onesie, adding "Q" on the back because it was July 17—an important number for QAnon believers, since Q is the seventeenth letter of the alphabet.

During the rally, Trump pointed at the couple's daughter in the crowd.

"Wow, what a baby," Trump said. "What a baby! That is a beautiful baby! That's like from an advertisement, perfect! Look how happy that baby is! So beautiful, thank you, darling. That's really nice."

For Q believers, it was the kind of providential acknowledgment they had been waiting for since QAnon began two years earlier. "Q Baby" started trending on Twitter, mentioned more than 38,000 times. For some, Trump pointing at the baby became a moment of near-religious gratification. His gesture meant there was no more "plausible deniability" that QAnon was real, one blogger wrote. *The Q Baby is a symbol of Good prevailing over Evil,* a Q fan tweeted. *The baby represents the dawn of a new era.*

Never mind that Trump couldn't have seen the *Q* marked on the back of the baby's shirt.

QAnon emerged in 2017 as a coping mechanism for Trump voters troubled by his stalled presidency. It was a fairy tale for people wondering why

Trump hadn't fulfilled his promises, recasting the struggling president as a hero of biblical proportions. But QAnon is also incredibly weird, and, to anyone outside of its influence, clearly delusional. That put Trump and his retainers in a bind as QAnon grew: How could they avoid alienating Q supporters and costing Trump votes in the process, while also making sure Trump didn't become known more broadly as the QAnon candidate?

As long as Q's message was restricted to the internet, the Trump administration could avoid confronting that inconsistency. But there was one place where that contradiction couldn't be avoided: a Trump rally.

The rally is the ultimate expression of Trumpism, an interactive experience with the Donald and his family, soundtracked to his favorite oldies. It was only natural that QAnon, another expression of utter devotion to Trump, thrived there. Rallies became a place where followers could encounter fellow believers in person, receiving validation that they weren't the only ones who thought this Q guy might be on to something. As Trump crisscrossed the country on his permanent reelection campaign, each new row of red Q shirts and round of "Where we go one, we go all" chants announced that QAnon had successfully planted itself in another corner of America.

QAnon believers started showing up at Trump rallies in the spring of 2018, just months after Q's first posts. At first, their numbers didn't stand out, and few outside the movement bothered to investigate the meaning of all these signs saying "WWG1WGA"—the acronym for QAnon slogan "Where we go one, we go all." A senior Trump campaign official said the campaign tried to avoid bringing up QAnon at all—to avoid "pissing off the crazy." Then Trump traveled to Tampa, Florida, on July 31, 2018. After months of treating QAnon like an internet sideshow that could be safely ignored, the American political and media establishments couldn't look away from it that night. QAnon followers coordinated their outfits, appearing in stark white shirts illustrated with a red *Q*. They carried identical "We Are Q" signs on printer paper. As Trump began speaking, the believers lifted up their signs and revealed that there were dozens of them spread throughout the crowd.

No one watching the Tampa rally could unsee it. A giant Q sign blocked

Trump from view, leaving TV viewers to wonder why the president had been blotted out by the seventeenth letter of the alphabet.

Reason magazine called the Tampa rally QAnon's "coming out party." Liberal late-night talk show host Bill Maher donned a hood and claimed that he was Q, issuing a top-secret directive for followers to stay home on Election Day. NBC News reporter Ben Collins summed up QAnon for baffled newcomers, comparing it to a dangerous drug known to cause psychosis: "Pizzagate on bath salts."

QAnon's Trump rally debut was a disaster for Republicans looking to win over moderate voters. A few days before the rally, a Florida Republican observer had complained to a local website that the increasingly visible presence of Q believers in the state meant the Florida GOP was becoming seen as the party of QAnon—and that was before dozens of followers stole the show at a rally ostensibly meant to promote Republican candidates, not Q.

For Trump allies, the smartest response to the party's newest faction had been to stay quiet. Florida politician Ron DeSantis pioneered this response after QAnon believers crashed the Trump rally in Tampa that was meant to promote DeSantis's campaign for the governor's mansion. A few weeks after the Tampa rally, DeSantis claimed ignorance about the Q-emblazoned rallygoers that appeared there and at many of his other events.

"I'm not sure what that is," DeSantis told a reporter.

For Republican officials, maintaining a polite distance from Q had some benefits. It meant they wouldn't come off like lunatics to voters not already soaked in 4chan mind games. But it also meant that Q supporters wouldn't be antagonized, either.

After the Tampa rally, Anons became both a grassroots army and a source of embarrassment for Trump's campaign. Campaign staffers struggled to hide an increasingly obvious fact from both cable news cameras and swing voters: a growing swath of Trump rallygoers had become obsessed with adrenochrome, cabals, and the Storm. The campaign was faced with the challenge of separating the QAnon brand from Trump, a problem made even harder by Trump's curious refusal to come out and say QAnon wasn't real.

Some Trump allies claimed QAnon was a trap meant to make Trump supporters look like buffoons. Former White House adviser Sebastian Gorka called QAnon a "cult" and a "con," saying QAnon believers had no place in the Republican Party. In response, Q encouraged his followers to report Gorka to the FBI, while followers published his home address. To Q's fans, Republican opponents like Gorka were, at best, RINOs—feckless "Republicans in Name Only" best shoved aside by true Trump loyalists. At worst, they were agents of the cabal.

The Trump campaign never publicly announced a crackdown on QAnon symbols at rallies, perhaps because a confirmed ban would run the risk of alienating Q's supporters. Instead, the rules went into effect without a press release. A few weeks after the Tampa rally, believers began complaining that Trump campaign staffers were telling them to turn their Q shirts out and fold up their signs. As attendees filtered into rallies, campaign workers standing outside announced that no Q clothing would be allowed inside.

The T-shirt saga consumed QAnon for weeks, raising a difficult question for the faithful. Q has tasked believers with evangelizing their movement ahead of the Storm, raising awareness of the cabal and its crimes to avert a civil war when the mass arrests happen. QAnon supporters call that duty to preach about Q "The Great Awakening." But if Trump wanted believers to spread the word, as Q told them, why was he embarrassed to see them at his rallies? Anons blamed false-flag provocateurs bent on making QAnon look bad. In a post, Q himself claimed that sinister forces made threats to commit violence at Trump rallies while posing as QAnon believers, scaring the Secret Service into cracking down on their signs and shirts.

QAnon followers failed to grasp the more obvious explanation: their movement was making their hero look bad. Everyone around Trump knew that it was fake, and that it turned off voters who didn't want to hear ravings about "breadcrumbs" or "the cabal."

Instead of grappling with Trump's attempt to distance himself, Q's flock became more resourceful. They altered campaign signs, adding a slash to turn the zeroes in "Trump 2020" into *Q*'s. Some of those signs made it into footage for Trump campaign ads, convincing Anons that Trump was secretly on their side. Defying the ban on QAnon merchandise, other supporters smuggled their shirts into rallies by turning them inside out or layering them, covering them up with official Trump shirts until they could be revealed when the cameras came on.

For those who persisted in the face of the prohibition, it was about spreading the QAnon message on one of the biggest stages in American politics. Lisa Thornburg, a Q devotee who attended a West Virginia rally in 2018, told me the Secret Service stopped her husband from wearing his Q shirt into the arena.

"I ended up holding the shirt up high and waving it during the rally so it could be seen," Thornburg said.

Even if the Trump campaign could have confiscated every shirt and sign, though, they couldn't stop his base from talking about Q. The movement's growth in the Trump grassroots became clear outside a rally in Grand Rapids, Michigan, in March 2019. As a camera panned down blocks of Trump supporters waiting to get into the rally, the man behind the camera held up a Q sign. Among a line of hundreds of people, roughly one in four reacted to the sight of the Q sign, shouting "QAnon!" or jumping up and down with excitement or pointing to their own Q shirts.

Believers were starting to show up at Trump rallies everywhere. Campaign press secretary Kayleigh McEnany couldn't even film a feel-good story about some Trump supporters without running into them.

A Trump rally in Phoenix in February 2020 had just exploded in cheers at the sight of two men carrying a one-hundred-year-old World War II veteran to his seat. Trump mentioned the moment in his speech, and the trio posed for pictures with Donald Trump Jr.

McEnany wanted to interview Jason Frank, one of the men who had carried the veteran down the stairs, for a campaign video. As reporters and Trump fans milled around outside the stadium where the rally was held,

McEnany gave Frank a mic and asked about the viral moment. But Frank only wanted to talk about Q.

As McEnany struggled to get Frank to focus on the rally, he expounded on the deeper, unifying meaning of QAnon. Behind him, a crowd shouted "We Are Q!"

"I'm one of the digital soldiers General Flynn talks about," Frank said. "That's why I don't sleep, that's why all I do is share information."

"If you could say one thing to the president, what would you say?" McEnany asked.

"Who is Q?" Frank said.

"Okay, I will pass all of this along," McEnany said, swiftly cutting off the interview.

For QAnon believers, the promise to "pass all of this along" wasn't an abrupt end to the conversation, but was instead proof that one of their own had reached the president. Frank's request would get them one step closer to a key QAnon goal: a blessing from Trump himself. Like Riselvato, the father of the "Q Baby," Frank wanted someone to "ask the Q." Supporters' beliefs had earned them ridicule, both online and sometimes in person from their friends and family members. But if someone would just ask Trump whether QAnon was real, they felt confident he would confirm it. Their ideas would be validated by the most powerful man in the world. Trump might even use the occasion to launch the Storm.

The McEnany interview turned Frank into a Q star. He had been the latest supporter to recognize a Trump rally as a national opportunity to push the movement. Frank refused to go on Fox News' morning show, claiming they wouldn't let him mention the conspiracy theory. Instead he appeared on a QAnon livestream where commenters begged to know whether he had used his photo op with Don Jr. to "ask the Q."

For Anons, Trump is a figure of messianic proportions, sent to destroy the pedophile cabal, usher in a thousand-year peace, cure diseases, and absolve their debts. To mark his primacy in their canon, they call him "Q+"—an even bigger deal than Q.

So what does Donald Trump actually think of QAnon?

For anyone else, the prospect of leading a global cult premised on lurid tales of sex and violence would seem overwhelming. But Trump seems to treat belief in QAnon like membership in a patriotic Trump fan club, no more outlandish than someone who rides in a Trump boat parade or owns MAGA hats in both their red and camouflage varieties.

There isn't much evidence about what Trump thinks privately about QAnon. In July 2020, Trump met with White House aides and then–Senate majority leader Mitch McConnell, according to an Axios report, ostensibly to discuss Senate elections. Instead, Trump just wanted to talk about how much QAnon believers liked him.

Trump brought up QAnon backer Lauren Boebert, who had just pulled off a surprise primary win in a Colorado race for the U.S. House. Boebert, Trump said, believed in "that Q-an-uhn."

"People say they're into all kinds of bad things and say all kinds of terrible things about them," Trump told McConnell. "But, you know, my understanding is they basically are just people who want good government."

Stunned White House aides laughed "in terror."

As the central figure of the conspiracy theory, Trump could have destroyed the movement with just a few dismissive words. He never did. Instead the president and his allies went from knowing nothing about QAnon at the start of his term, to winking at QAnon supporters, to openly defending them by the end of his 2020 campaign. He pulled the rest of the Republican Party along with him, gambling America's electoral sanity for QAnon's votes.

The first sign that Trump's administration would be willing to tolerate QAnon as part of its coalition came in August 2018, shortly after the Tampa rally. Asked to respond to QAnon's increasingly visible devotion to

Trump, White House press secretary Sarah Huckabee Sanders sidestepped the question.

"The president condemns and denounces any group that would incite violence against another individual, and certainly doesn't support groups that would promote that type of behavior," she said.

Sanders didn't explicitly condemn QAnon. Still, this wasn't the confirmation believers craved. They were left to scrutinize every gesture Trump made for evidence that Q was real. One popular tactic relied on tracing Trump's swooping hand motions during speeches to discern whether he had made a "Q" or a "17" in the air. His tweets doubled as a supplement to the QAnon clues themselves, offering an endless number of odd capitalizations and quickly deleted typos that could hold greater meaning. If Trump included the number "seventeen" in a tweet or posted during the seventeenth minute of any hour, believers had all the evidence they needed to launch a days-long investigation.

But as the prospect of Trump taking the podium to launch the Storm remained distant, QAnon believers decided they might hear from Trump in other ways. When the Federal Emergency Management Agency prepared to test a nationwide alert system in October 2018, Q supporters became convinced Trump would use the message to announce the Storm. Relying on an old clue, they concluded the message would read, "My fellow Americans, The Storm Is Upon Us."

On message boards, believers braced for the day their phones would buzz with personal orders from Trump, calling themselves "the next generation Minutemen." The anticipation around the emergency alert broadcast and the idea of being pressed into service at Trump's behest to purge the cabal seemed to give QAnon followers a sense of drama and purpose in their lives.

"SO HAPPY!" wrote one supporter. "THANK YOU 45!"

When the message came, however, it really was just a test of the emergency alert system. Once again, there had been no Storm—but there was always next time.

One afternoon in May 2018, a woman from Kentucky walked up to the White House fence. She had driven five hundred miles, she told Secret Service officers at the fence, for a meeting with Q.

"I'm where Q told me to go," she said.

The woman claimed she had been in communication with Q. He gave her orders to visit the White House to find out who would be charged under forty thousand sealed indictments prepared for the Storm. When officers told her no one named Q worked at the White House, the woman wandered off, confused by their insistence that Q didn't have an office there.

That QAnon believer appears to have been the first to try to make it inside the White House to "help" Trump and Q. But she wouldn't be the last.

In December 2018, a Virginia man stole his sister's car, drove to the White House, and tried to get a meeting with Trump, saying he needed the president's help to end human trafficking. A month after that, he filmed himself making a snowman late at night in the park in front of the White House, uploading the video to YouTube with the caption "QAnon." A few days later, he tried to scale the White House fence, scraping his hands on anti-climb spikes. As officers dragged him away, the QAnon believer asked for First Lady Melania Trump to put a bandage on his wounds. Eleven months later, he returned to the White House and was arrested again.

Q's themes of patriotic espionage seemed to inspire some believers to try their hand at spy craft to get inside the White House themselves. In June 2018, a woman in Florida met with congressional staffers working for staunch Trump defender Representative Matt Gaetz, offering to be the one to "ask the Q."

Clearly, she said, no reporters in the White House press corps had the guts to ask Trump the question that would launch the Storm. But she had once been a nanny for high-powered people, earning a security clearance in the process. Why, the woman asked, couldn't she either use that clearance or steal a reporter's identity to get inside the White House, pose as a journalist during a briefing, and ask Trump if QAnon was real?

All she needed was help from Gaetz. To win the staffers over to her plan, she told them about QAnon.pub, a site that aggregated Q clues. Gaetz's chief of staff, dismayed by an offer to join a scheme to breach White House security, called the Secret Service instead.

"The meeting was rather uncomfortable," one Gaetz staffer remembered in an email.

As some believers were throwing themselves at the White House fence, others were invited in through the front gate. Less than a month after QAnon made its numbers felt in Tampa, New York talk radio host Michael Lebron leaned over Donald Trump in the Oval Office and smiled for a picture. Lebron had latched on to QAnon early in its growth. A bearded dandy whose self-proclaimed specialties include "monology, extreme thinking, and bluegrass," Lebron had become the movement's avuncular court jester.

Now he was in the White House, smiling with the president and posing self-seriously in the hallways for a picture he captioned on Twitter with the hashtag "WWG1WGA." When I saw the picture of Lebron grinning over the presidential Resolute Desk, I couldn't square it with what I knew about him. How could someone like that get into the White House, even in the Trump era?

"This president is a president for all Americans," quipped one White House source, as I tried to find an explanation for how Lebron got in the building.

The White House claimed that Lebron had visited the White House on a group tour. But White House sources disputed that, pointing out the obvious: the average tourist doesn't get a chance to pose for pictures with the president. In a video describing his visit, Lebron claimed that he had received a personalized note from Trump. As for the big question of whether he asked Trump about QAnon, Lebron said he had demurred, assuring his audience only that Trump knew about Q.

Lebron's White House appearance grabbed some headlines, but it seemed like an aberration. Q believers could flock to Trump rallies and hold bizarre stunts to try to get Trump's attention, but aside from Lebron's visit, Trump hadn't made moves to embrace QAnon as part of his base.

By June 2019, though, QAnon had grown large enough to earn a spot in Trump's coalition. He invited two QAnon promoters, including one known for her Q earrings, to his White House "Social Media Summit." The event was a gathering of Trumpian internet characters collected to share memes and gripe about their suspicions that social media giants were biased against them. Invites to the White House meant that the Trump administration didn't see QAnon as unacceptable anymore. But for many of Q's fans, Trump's most important encouragements came through his own Twitter feed.

Until Twitter banned him in January 2021, Trump was the site's biggest promoter of QAnon accounts, often retweeting Q promoters multiple times a day to tens of millions of his supporters. Just a month after QAnon first appeared on 4chan, Trump retweeted his first Q account, a poster called "MAGAPill." Trump praised a list MAGAPill had posted of his accomplishments, adding that he wished the "Fake News would report" on the document. But the account was also filled with conspiracy theories, including rumors of "ancient occult magic" at the Vatican and child-sacrifice rituals featuring Hillary Clinton and pop star Lady Gaga. The MAGAPill retweet was just the start. Trump eventually retweeted QAnon supporters at least 315 times between 2017 and 2021, according to liberal watchdog group Media Matters.

Not even the FBI could stop the Trump campaign's flirtation with QAnon. On August 1, 2019, Yahoo News reported that the FBI considered QAnon a potential source of domestic terrorism. In a memo circulated to other law enforcement agencies, the FBI wrote that QAnon and other conspiracy theories would drive "both groups and individual extremists to carry out criminal or violent acts."

A day later, a speaker for the Trump campaign promoted QAnon at a rally. Now the conspiracy theories weren't coming from the crowds, but from the podium. Speaking at the rally in Ohio, Trump warm-up speaker Brandon Straka amped up the crowd with a loud "Where we go one, we go all!" to cheers.

A gay former hairdresser, Straka had launched the "Walkaway Movement" in 2018, urging LGBT people and other traditionally Democratic constituencies to "walk away" from the Democratic Party. Until his Q moment, I considered Straka to be, at worst, a huckster who used his identity to grift Trump supporters in a Republican Party where racial or sexual minorities stood out. Straka was someone who fumed to me when he didn't score an invite to the Social Media Summit, not an extremist pushing dreams of bloody purges.

How had he, in the space of a year, come to riff on QAnon to rile up thousands of people—and apparently earned the Trump campaign's sanction to do so?

Straka later insisted he didn't mean to make a QAnon reference during his speech by deploying the most famous QAnon slogan, a phrase that has not existed in American culture outside of Q since the 1996 sailing movie *White Squall*, from which it's borrowed. Even then, though, Straka couldn't bring himself to denounce QAnon.

"If people are now inspired to search for the truth, that's a positive thing," Straka told the *Washington Examiner*.

Two years after his speech, Straka was arrested for trespassing during the U.S. Capitol riot. Dressed in sunglasses and a houndstooth coat, Straka choked on tear gas as he urged rioters to wrestle a shield from a Capitol Police officer.

Straka's speech was just the start. As the movement became more powerful and the 2020 election inched closer, Trump's circle dropped the pretense of not knowing what QAnon was. In January 2020, Trump social media guru Dan Scavino posted a meme featuring an animated clock going "tick tock," which Anons took to mean the time was ticking down toward the Storm. Trump son's Eric posted and later deleted a Trump meme with a giant *Q* in the background to his Instagram account.

Trump himself shifted from quietly signaling to Q believers to defending them in public. After QAnon believer Marjorie Taylor Greene won a primary runoff in Georgia, Trump praised her on Twitter, then all but embraced QAnon supporters as a segment of his base during a White House press conference.

"During the pandemic, the QAnon movement appears to be gaining a lot of followers," a reporter said to Trump in August 2020. "Can you talk about what you think about that and what you have to say to people who are following this movement right now?"

This was the question both QAnon believers and their critics had been waiting for. In a moment, Trump could either legitimize QAnon or devastate its recruitment prospects.

"Well, I don't know much about the movement, other than I understand they like me very much, which I appreciate," Trump said. "But I don't know much about the movement. I have heard that it is gaining in popularity."

Across the country, QAnon believers cheered at his remarks. It wasn't quite the Storm, but it was almost an endorsement. Then Trump went further.

"At the crux of the theory, is this belief that you are secretly saving the world from this Satanic cult of pedophiles and cannibals," the reporter said. "Does that sound like something you are behind?"

"Is that supposed to be a bad thing or a good thing, you know?" Trump said. "If I can help save the world from problems, I'm willing to do it, I'm willing to put myself out there. And we are, actually, we are saving the world from a radical left philosophy that will destroy this country, and when this country is gone, the rest of the world will follow."

Backing QAnon after so long offered another benefit for Trump, aside from the votes of Q supporters: it satisfied his ego. In his simplistic view of the world, in which everything broke down as either pro- or anti-Trump, the president seemed to see QAnon as essentially a die-hard Trump fan club. They liked him, so they must be good.

In a televised town hall event two months later, NBC anchor Savannah Guthrie tried, finally, to get Trump to admit that QAnon's fantasies were just that.

"Let me ask you about QAnon," Guthrie said. "It is this theory that Democrats are a Satanic pedophile ring and that you are the savior of them. Now, can you just once and for all state that that is completely not true and disavow QAnon in its entirety?"

"I know nothing about QAnon," Trump said.

"I just told you," Guthrie said.

"You told me, but just telling me doesn't necessarily make it fact, I hate to say it," Trump said. "I know nothing about it. I do know they are very much against pedophilia. They fight it very hard. But I know nothing about it."

"They believe it is a Satanic cult run by the deep state," Guthrie said.

"I'll tell you what I do know about," Trump said, pivoting away. "I know about Antifa and the radical left."

Later in the town hall, Trump defended his decision to retweet a QAnon account pushing an idea that was bizarre even for Q followers: that Biden had conspired to murder Navy SEALs and fake Osama bin Laden's death. In his response, Trump summed up his approach to QAnon: he didn't care if they were right or wrong. They were out there, and he'd promote them when it was advantageous to him.

"You retweeted to your eighty-seven million followers a conspiracy theory that Joe Biden orchestrated to have SEAL Team Six—the Navy SEAL Team Six—killed to cover up the fake death of bin Laden," Guthrie said. "Now, why would you send a lie like that to your followers?"

"I know nothing about it," Trump said.

"You retweeted it," Guthrie said.

"That was a retweet," Trump said. "That was an opinion of somebody, and that was a retweet. I'll put it out there. People can decide for themselves. I don't take a position."

Chapter 3

Q's Priests

On October 18, 2018, film executive Franklin Leonard's phone started vibrating and would not stop. His eyes grew wide as his screen filled up with Twitter alerts from strangers hurling vicious, baffling insults at him, hundreds of tweets at a time. He was a rent boy for billionaire Democratic donor George Soros, they said, or he ran the Muslim Brotherhood alongside Huma Abedin. Some said they were eager to see him killed.

Leonard was no stranger to threats: in 2005, he launched "The Black List," an annual publication highlighting Hollywood's most popular unproduced scripts. It drew attention to the then little-known screenplays that would become Oscar-winning movies like *Spotlight*, *Argo*, and *Slumdog Millionaire*. As his profile as a Hollywood tastemaker grew, Leonard periodically faced down a few furious screenwriters who felt he had snubbed their work, but he always got an apology in the end.

Leonard had never experienced anything like this Twitter storm before, though. It seemed this time, through no fault of his own, a large group of people on the internet had decided to try to destroy his life. But these weren't failed screenwriters coming for him. Leonard had no idea at all why they had chosen him as their target.

"Clearly, somebody has this fixation on me," Leonard thought.

Leonard quickly noted that the people attacking him on Twitter were all using the same hashtag, one he had never seen before: WWG1WGA. After a little online research, Leonard realized that the acronym meant he had become a target for QAnon, but he still had no idea why. He knew other Hollywood figures were harassed by QAnon. Thousands of believers on Twitter had mobbed model Chrissy Teigen and her husband, singer John Legend, convinced that they abused children in Satanic rituals. Tom Hanks, once the universal ideal of a nice guy, had been transformed by QAnon into a ghoul who drank children's blood to keep up his boyish good looks.

"But they're famous," Leonard said. "I'm not. I'm just some random guy."

At first, Leonard told me, he treated the internet attacks on him like a big joke. They insisted that he was a sort of sexual plaything for Soros, or a CIA operative, two allegations Leonard couldn't take seriously. But as the death threats continued to pour in, Leonard started to worry about his safety. He remembered Pizzagate and the gunshots at Comet Ping Pong two years earlier. Not wanting to panic, but well aware of the risk, Leonard had to admit to himself that a single crazed QAnon supporter might make an attempt on his life.

It was a feeling I knew well. Q would post one of my tweets or articles, giving the signal for their followers to descend on me. First they'd come in the form of thousands of menacing tweets and messages.

"Hopefully one day you die via mass shooting or pressure cooker bomb," one Q supporter wrote to me on Facebook. "Dumb pedo supporter."

Then, more worryingly, some pro-QAnon accounts published my address and the names of my family members. As long as the more dangerous threats stayed on fringe social media platforms, I didn't want to take any action against them for fear of drawing attention to them and encouraging more harassment. And besides, what could I really do?

I knew the likelihood that anyone would try to hurt me in person was small. But it's hard to ignore the fact that many people had said, directly to me, that they wanted me dead. I had to adjust in ways that felt scary and foreign, but necessary. When I moved to a new house, I installed a security system and worked to scrub my new address from online databases. When I reported on QAnon events in person, I wore hats and sunglasses to make it harder for people to recognize me from across a crowd. Those precautions could seem overdramatic, even to me, but I spent my days reading these people's violent fantasies. I knew what they thought themselves capable of.

After sifting through more messages from QAnon supporters, Leonard realized that the mysterious online attacks weren't directed by Q himself. Q had never posted anything about him. Instead, they were inspired by just one person: a popular QAnon promoter whose legions of fans knew him only by the alias "Neon Revolt."

Hundreds of thousands of accounts on Twitter and Facebook have promoted QAnon online, but only a few of them can match Neon Revolt's reach. He writes rambling essays about QAnon targets like Facebook CEO Mark Zuckerberg and gun control activist David Hogg, assuring his followers that the world will soon be rocked by revelations only hinted at by Q. For instance, Neon Revolt once predicted that a long-hidden video of Barack Obama wielding an AK-47 and dressed in "full Muslim garb" would soon hit the internet, showing Obama either shredding an American flag with bullets or executing a captive American soldier.

Now Neon Revolt was obsessed with Leonard. On his blog, Neon Revolt portrayed Leonard as a globe-spanning puppet-master, running the Muslim Brotherhood with an attachment of Iranian allies, in between visits to a "Cabal-affiliated" hotel in Los Angeles. Leonard's Black List wasn't just an industry cheat sheet and a hot topic on the Beverly Hills cocktail party circuit, Neon Revolt wrote; it was a tool to weaken America's social fabric by highlighting the most divisive, demoralizing movies. Among the films implicated in Leonard's plot: the children's science fiction film *A Wrinkle in Time* and Benedict Cumberbatch's Alan Turing biopic, *The Imitation Game*.

"The man is a Rabid Marxist/Leftist, with deep, subversive instincts, Radical Islamic sympathies, and a profound Anti-white bias," Neon Revolt wrote in the blog post where he first sicced his fans on Leonard.

Leonard wondered about his security as Neon Revolt kept up the attacks. He reconsidered whether he was safe in his ground-floor apartment, and worried that someone might attack his fiancée to get to him. Leonard became more nervous walking on the street in Los Angeles, fearing that each stranger he passed on the sidewalk was a QAnon believer coming to kill him in Q's name.

If you're a QAnon supporter who wants to thank Q, or yell at them, or give them a hug for showing you the truth about the world, you can't find them. There isn't a public Q whose YouTube channel you can subscribe to, whose nutrition pills you can buy, or whose convention you can pay thousands of dollars to attend. There also isn't an official Q who can tell you what on earth the breadcrumbs actually mean. An Anon who manages to seek out Q's posts on one of the chans is met with a blizzard of cryptic references to baking, *Alice in Wonderland*, child sacrifice, pizza, and late billionaire pedophile Jeffrey Epstein that, when combined, often amount to nonsense. Q also tends to disappear for months at a time, leaving eager Q followers hungry for their next update on the Storm.

That void where a singular figurehead, the actual Q, should be, has created an opening for thousands of QAnon entrepreneurs, who push their own individual versions of the theories that make up the fabric of QAnon. In countless YouTube videos and social media posts, they explain Q's clues in an accessible, exciting way—and they're happy to take donations for their services.

QAnon stands out among new religious and political movements, according to Canadian extremism and religion expert Amarnath Amarasingam, because its head is totally uncharismatic. The Branch Davidians in Waco, Texas, had David Koresh, and Jonestown had Jim Jones. But Q is totally invisible outside of the chan posts. While their leader might be nowhere to be found, Q followers are easy to spot in a crowd. And their shirts are not emblazoned with the names of their favorite YouTube channels: they all have a *Q*. But the QAnon promoters are really to blame for QAnon's spread—maybe even more than Q himself. Few people actually appear to have been drawn into QAnon directly through Q posts on the chans. When I interview believers, they'll name a YouTube channel they watch, or a hoax-riddled website that first drew them in. If QAnon is a house, Q just laid the foundation—the QAnon promoters built the structure.

"QAnon's like, 'Here's a bunch of incomprehensible things, you guys do what you want with it,' which is unheard-of for a movement like this," Amarasingam told me. Promoters amount to a "priestly class" in QAnon's hierarchy, interpreting the Q clues for believers like clergy for a congregation, Amarasingam said.

"They themselves have become celebrities, and quite important for the movement," he told me. "Jonestown never did that. Waco never did that."

While a number of people have tried to distinguish themselves from the hordes of "Anons" and make their name in the movement, only a few dozen Q personalities have successfully built their own brands within the conspiracy theory. For QAnon interpreters who do succeed, though, there is money to be made.

QAnon promoters, like the often-contradictory ideas that coexist within QAnon, come in a sweeping variety of options. Some take basic pro-Trump ideas from Fox News and talk radio and shape them around Q, offering relatively mundane tales of Trump foiled by duplicitous intelligence agencies and federal prosecutors. On the other end of the spectrum, other QAnon promoters allege that the world is controlled by reptilian aliens from another planet.

When I talk to QAnon leaders, there's a question in my mind: Does this person really believe what they're saying? They might be in it for the money, or they might really think QAnon is real. For most, I think it's a mix. They think QAnon is genuine, and they're happy to profit while they lead people to Q. But whether a Q promoter is a true believer or a cynic, there is, again, plenty of money to go around.

A pro-QAnon book published by twelve decoders in early 2019 proved to be a surprising hit, reaching the top ten on Amazon's bestseller chart. One of the book's authors, a Florida conspiracy theorist named Roy Davis, claimed that roughly 200,000 copies were sold at around $15 each—a massive success for any book, much less a little-anticipated anthology of internet screeds. Even after the split between the twelve authors and their publisher, each author would likely have received hundreds of thousands of dollars from the book. Davis used his money, in part, to paint a fiery *Q* on the hood of his Corvette.

In July 2018, Q went silent for twenty days, the longest that the flock had gone without their shepherd. Seizing the opportunity, a Q wannabe named "R"—the letter in the alphabet after *Q*—stepped up, suggesting that Q was really JFK Jr., who hadn't died in a 1999 plane crash off Martha's Vineyard after all. Instead, JFK Jr. faked his death to avenge his father's assassination by the deep state. While many QAnon believers rejected that idea because it didn't come from Q himself, a splinter group embraced it. They awaited the day that Mike Pence would soon resign, to be replaced as vice president by JFK Jr.

If JFK Jr. was alive, he had to be someone QAnon believers could identify, they reasoned. So much of QAnon is premised on the idea that both Q's plan and the cabal's misdeeds are taking place in plain sight, if you only know where to look. A star in the Democratic convention logo? That's a Satanic pentagram. At the same time, the cabal has grown so arrogant after centuries of power that they feel comfortable celebrating their villainy publicly through coded Instagram posts or notable articles of clothing. Wearing red shoes, for example, is supposedly a telltale sign of being a cannibal-pedophile. As one popular QAnon aphorism goes, "Symbolism will be their downfall."

QAnon believers looking for JFK Jr. settled on Vincent Fusca, a then-little-known Trump fan. Fusca, who drives a van emblazoned with Trump's face, had enough connections to the Trump campaign that he often earned VIP access to the rally seats behind Trump's podium at Pennsylvania events. All it took to turn Fusca into JFK Jr. were a few image comparisons that put pictures of Fusca at rallies next to pictures of JFK Jr. QAnon believers began to focus on his rally appearances, claiming that he was close to Trump because JFK Jr. needed to protect the president from the deep state that had killed Kennedy's father.

Of all the maddening, incomprehensible things I've encountered in QAnon, Fusca might be the thing that drives me craziest. He shows up at as many QAnon and Trump events as he can in his signature outfit—a fedora, a suit jacket, a permanent salt-and-pepper scruff, and a T-shirt with a cover of JFK Jr.'s *George* magazine printed onto it. He relishes the attention when he's surrounded by Kennedy devotees, but he doesn't seem to be making any money from the ruse. At a November 2020 pro-Trump rally in Washington, fans asked him if he was really JFK Jr., only for Fusca to smile and move on. Later that day, he soaked up more of the adoration owed to a QAnon celebrity—singing karaoke from a portable machine on the street to cheering crowds, signing hats and copies of a pro-Trump newspaper. It's clear to me that Fusca doesn't believe he's actually JFK Jr., even though he's never acknowledged that people think he's Kennedy. But his position of power means that he can make QAnon real with just his presence, and his silence. It's too disturbing, even for QAnon believers, to imagine a man letting people think he is JFK Jr. just because he enjoys taking selfies with his fans. The only solution has to be that Fusca really is JFK Jr.

While QAnon mobs typically focus on harassing innocent people caught up in their conspiracy theories, they can also transform random people into stars. Fans dress up as Fusca for Halloween. They perform elaborate numerological calculations on his van's license plate, speculating about what the numbers and letters could mean about the QAnon plan. One fan tried to launch a congressional campaign in his name. For $4.95 a month, subscribers to the YouTube channel for pro-Trump cable channel One America News could use a custom emoji of his face. A QAnon supporter arrested near a Philadelphia vote-counting site with a gun made a comic book about him.

The QAnon obsession with the Kennedys seems to play on believers' longing for a lost golden age—the same halcyon period the cabal took from all of us. For older Q supporters, the John F. Kennedy assassination marked the most traumatic national event of their childhoods. The idea that Kennedy was murdered by the cabal gives his death meaning, and a way to set things right by embracing Q. In their eyes, JFK Jr.'s own tragic demise is redeemed if he instead faked his death to avenge his father and one day team up with Trump.

At a pro-Trump rally filled with Q gear and flags outside the Supreme Court in December 2020, Fusca parted the crowd as people turned their heads to get a look at him, convinced that they were witnessing John John himself. I tried to intercept Fusca to ask him the one question on my mind: Why does he play along with this? It wasn't easy to catch him, as a knot of his supporters closed in around him. As usual, he said he would talk to me later that day. This time, Fusca's renown had grown so much that he even had an amateur publicist with him who assured me he would set up an interview. I never heard back from either of them about an interview after the rally.

"JFK Jr!" one man shouted after Fusca, as the JFK Jr. impersonator pulled away from me.

A group of women from Buffalo, New York, posed for a selfie with Fusca. As the QAnon star moved on, I asked one of them, a Fusca fan named Susan Parisi, how she could think Fusca is Kennedy in disguise. The answer, she said, was special effects.

"Have you never seen in Hollywood, the Grinch, or Madea?" Parisi said.

Few people have done more to lay the groundwork for QAnon than Alex Jones, the conspiracy theorist turned mogul who was ranting about cabals decades before Q. As QAnon grew in its first months, an encounter with

Jones was inevitable, setting the stage for a showdown that pit old-style conspiracy theorists against a new generation.

Jones launched his budding conspiracy theory empire in the 1990s, shouting about Bill Clinton and black helicopters on an Austin, Texas, community TV station. At first, Jones came off as merely a colorful local character, but he won enough of an audience that he was able to create a syndicated talk radio show that appeared on radio stations across the country. Jones was obsessed with the New World Order—the idea that shadowy forces were conspiring to make a single world government and turn ordinary people into serfs. Jones grew to become the country's leading conspiracy theorist during the Obama administration. He prepared his audience for the explosion of a conspiracy theory like QAnon by claiming that a plethora of news events, including the 2012 mass shooting at Sandy Hook Elementary School in Newtown, Connecticut, were "false flags" intended to make conservatives look bad. You couldn't trust the news media, Jones said—you had to do your own research by watching his online video channel, InfoWars.

Jones reached the peak of his prominence in the first years of the Trump era. As a candidate, Trump appeared on InfoWars in 2015, praising Jones as "amazing." But by 2017, there was a force competing with Jones on the more extreme edges of the Trump movement: Q.

In December 2017, QAnon was moving off the chans and into more mainstream platforms like YouTube and Facebook. It was also getting big enough to interest some of the right's biggest conspiracy theorists. Just two months after Q first started posting, two early QAnon promoters appeared on an InfoWars show hosted by one of Jones's underlings. After the appearance, searches for QAnon exploded online. The budding movement started to attract attention from two of the biggest names in conspiracy theories: Jones and his Washington "bureau chief," Jerome Corsi.

A partnership between InfoWars and QAnon would benefit both sides. For Jones and Corsi, it meant latching on to an energetic movement that generated fresh content for their broadcasts. For QAnon, InfoWars represented a direct pipeline to an enormous audience of the conspiratorially minded. But that initial partnership between Jones and Q would soon turn sour as they fought for control of QAnon.

After years of promoting 9/11 conspiracy theories, Jones had suddenly gained a surprising measure of credibility on the right after Trump's appearance on his show. But while selling pills and survival supplies to his viewers had built Jones a media empire in Austin, his hoaxes were starting to catch up with him.

By the time QAnon launched, Jones had become radioactive even among many Republicans for promoting conspiracy theories about the 2012 shooting in Newtown, Connecticut, that left twenty-six people, including twenty children, dead. Jones had also promoted Pizzagate, only averting a lawsuit from Comet Ping Pong's owner with a last-minute apology.

Jones's disastrous earlier forays into conspiracy theories didn't stop him from promoting QAnon. Shortly after the QAnon personalities appeared on InfoWars, Jones's network united behind QAnon, even cooking up another deep-state whistleblower of their own who came on the show to confirm that Q's breadcrumbs were true.

While Jones boosted QAnon on his network, Corsi became InfoWars' official liaison to the Q faithful. Corsi is one of the fathers of modern American conspiracy theories. He helped demolish John Kerry's 2004 presidential campaign by smearing him with a group called "Swift Boat Veterans for Truth," a group aimed at undermining Kerry's reputation for heroism in the Vietnam War. Corsi was also one of the most outspoken promoters of "birtherism," the idea that Barack Obama was born in Kenya and therefore not eligible to be president.

Corsi is deep in the Trump movement's underbelly, locked in an often-fractious relationship with Trump operative Roger Stone. Both men were targeted by former special counsel Robert Mueller's investigation, exchanging emails as Corsi allegedly acted as a cutout between Stone and WikiLeaks.

Given his ties to Trump and his position as a sort of conspiracy-theorist elder statesman, Corsi's endorsement of QAnon amounted to an anointing for Q's upstart promoters. After struggling to win credibility for their theory in the backwaters of the internet, they now had one of the right's most venerable conspiracy theorists on board. Corsi was invited to join a chat room where other QAnon promoters planned the next steps for promoting Q.

Just as QAnon began taking off, its leading figures started to grapple for control. In January 2018, Corsi claimed in the chat room with other QAnon leaders that a handful of recent Q clues were fake. When a less prominent booster who went by the name Tracy "Beanz" Diaz, a key early YouTube conspiracy theorist backing QAnon, disputed Corsi's claim that the posts were not from the "real" Q, she was banished from the discussion—and a role in influencing QAnon's future.

But Corsi's own position in the movement was tenuous, too. With as much influence as promoters like Corsi wielded over the QAnon faithful, they still couldn't stand up to Q. As InfoWars began to co-opt Q, with Corsi as Jones's chosen Q interpreter, the earlier QAnon promoters feared they would be displaced by their more established rivals.

QAnon believers came to fear the influence of "paytriots"—QAnon slang for false "patriots" who were only interested in their own "pay." Suddenly, in May 2018, Q addressed the split in a series of 8chan posts, warning believers to not "fall victim to con artists."

"This is NOT about a single person," the post read. "This is NOT about fame, followers, or profiteering."

It says something about the reputation Jones and Corsi had within QAnon that believers instantly thought that the references to fame-hungry QAnon leaders were aimed at them. As the InfoWars duo began to be pushed out of QAnon, they turned on it, with Corsi accusing the Q account of being hijacked.

Q's attack on Jones and Corsi pitted the upstart Q and the little-known internet personalities spreading his message against two of the grandfathers of internet conspiracy theories. Surprisingly, Q more or less won.

QAnon continued to grow, while QAnon believers who had once supported Jones now saw him as an agent of the deep state.

After being exiled from QAnon, Jones started to attack it. QAnon was no longer a reliable source of truth, he said—it might be a cabal plot itself. But Jones's final break with QAnon didn't come until after the January 6, 2021, riot, when the conspiracy theory was inextricably linked to the violence. As federal prosecutors closed in on the rioters, Jones, who was outside the Capitol during the attacks, stressed in a broadcast that he was not part of QAnon.

"I'm sick of all these witches and warlocks!" Jones said.

To the people who knew him in the real world in the spring of 2018, Robert Cornero seemed to be going nowhere. In his early thirties, he lived with his parents and had just lost a position as a grocery store clerk in the same New Jersey strip mall where he got his first job in middle school. The height of drama in Cornero's life had been a feud with his bosses over whether he could run the store's frozen food section. He met a woman online who lived thousands of miles away in Canada, but she dumped him after her father called him a loser.

When Cornero turned on his computer, though, he was a star. Tens of thousands of people were waiting to hear what he had to say. Just by setting up a website in February 2018, Robert Cornero had become Neon Revolt, a powerful QAnon blogger able to shape how millions of people saw the world.

Before, Cornero's life had been in a long-term decline. His troubles began in his last months at a prestigious medical high school in 2004, when he tried to impress a girl by listing the ways he would murder his classmates. Police raided Cornero's locker; he was banned from prom.

In his final years in high school, Cornero developed a fascination with movies. The passion grew, Cornero claimed, after a doctor told him he was too handsome to work in medicine, urging him to go to Hollywood instead. After narrowly avoiding prosecution in the shooting threat incident, Cornero moved to Los Angeles to sell his screenplays.

But as with so many hopefuls before him, Hollywood success eluded Cornero. He scored some minor accolades, winning second place in an online screenwriting contest with an action-comedy script he billed as "*Clerks* meets *Army of Darkness*." But Cornero felt like a failure in a town that, as far he could see, was full of winners. While rival screenwriters earned mentions in Leonard's Black List, Cornero was stuck in L.A. traffic driving a car with a broken air conditioner.

Leonard, who often spoke about using the Black List to promote diversity in Hollywood, was a symbol of the forces that Cornero thought had stopped him from succeeding, even though the two men never had any direct interaction.

"The industry, even during that time, had grown increasingly hostile to 'straight, white men,'" Cornero recalled later.

In time, Cornero gave up on Los Angeles and moved back to his New Jersey hometown. But he still seethed at the industry that had rejected him—at one point, he tweeted that someone should *BURN THE WHOLE DEGENERATE TOWN DOWN!*

With seemingly endless amounts of time to spend on the internet after his grocery store shifts, Cornero began to cycle through political ideologies. He embraced Ron Paul's libertarian presidential bids, then moved on to Gamergate. All of his rage at his Hollywood failures pushed him onto 4chan's /pol/ in 2014, frequenting a place where users attempted to radicalize one another into extremist ideologies with "redpills." They would show each other a depressing, often skewed statistic—say, the long odds millennials faced to buy a house or figures purporting to show that the deck was stacked against white men. The posts were meant to make people angry, and they worked on Cornero.

"I was surrounded by a vampiric culture of death, knee-deep in the dead, and I was determined to fight my way out, even if I had to slog through the bowels of hell itself to get there," Cornero recalled later.

Inspired by 4chan, Cornero launched a Facebook page to share more negative memes. Soon, Cornero recalled, he had 70,000 followers and 4chan's nihilism "coursing through my veins." Cornero was delighted by how quickly he had seized some level of internet prominence, and devoted himself to making more memes.

A frequent /pol/ user, Cornero encountered Q in its early days, shortly after losing his job at the grocery store. Cornero started posting on Facebook about QAnon, attracting more Q fans to his page. When Facebook banned Neon Revolt, Cornero moved to a group on the far-right social network Gab and launched the Neon Revolt blog, which soon became a hub for QAnon activity online.

As his fame grew, Cornero started crowdfunding to publish a book about his QAnon ideas. His eager fans donated nearly $160,000 to the cause, expecting to hear his proof that QAnon was real and that the Storm would soon arrive. What they may not have anticipated were dozens of pages about Cornero's own life and his radicalization from little-known frozen food clerk to QAnon figurehead.

Cornero stood out among QAnon promoters because he could write more than a few dozen words at a time. His Neon Revolt persona succeeded where his Hollywood scripts had failed. While others relied on YouTube videos or barrages of tweets, Cornero could hold forth at essay length, tying globe-spanning events and Q clues together in a tenuous logic that nevertheless appealed to QAnon fans. If most Q promoters relied on tweets and short YouTube videos, Cornero's blog posts, which often ran into multipart series, felt like settling in for an episode of *60 Minutes*. He described the blog as a "pressure valve" unleashing his "years of pent-up thoughts and emotions like a torrent upon the world."

As Cornero grew into his Q-world fame, he became convinced that his Hollywood failures were a blessing in disguise. After all, he recalled in his book, succeeding in the entertainment industry would have meant joining the cabal and participating in unspeakable acts against children. Better to fail there, and spend his time blogging and deciphering Q's breadcrumbs with fellow 4chan Anons—people with "genius-level" intelligence—than cut deals for Tinseltown success in the way he imagined Leonard had.

In October 2018, Cornero posted his first "investigation" into Leonard, titled "Soros' Hollywood Rentboy." Cornero posited that Leonard wasn't just a Hollywood tastemaker—he was tied into Satanic forces, and using the Black List to undermine humanity. Cornero returned to the theme in later posts and his crowdfunded book. As his armies of fans slammed Leonard online, Cornero rejoiced that Leonard and his other targets couldn't avoid the masses of Neon Revolt readers harassing them. Cornero had spent more than a decade being picked on everywhere—at school, in Hollywood, even at his grocery store job. Now QAnon gave him the power to be the tormentor.

"They just had to endure it for days and weeks on end," he wrote.

Cornero didn't seem to care if his harassment mobs were serving any larger purpose. Instead, he appeared to just delight in attacking people whose politics he didn't like. The best part of sliming his targets, Cornero wrote, was that "there was really nothing they could do about it."

Nick Backovic, a researcher for a disinformation research company called Logically, discovered Cornero's double life in January 2021. Using corporate registration details for the company selling the Neon Revolt book, Backovic traced the account to Cornero. In a blog post on Logically's website, Backovic tied the Neon Revolt persona to Cornero, identifying him as a failed screenwriter who had often raged against the movie industry online before adopting his QAnon persona. Cornero has never publicly acknowledged or disputed the identification. He did not respond to emails, phone calls, or a letter I sent to his parents' house.

For Leonard, it suddenly made sense. As he puzzled for years over why so many QAnon believers wanted him dead, he had ignored the most obvious explanation: a vengeful screenwriter fuming over his failed Hollywood dreams.

"If he spent half the time working on his craft of screenwriting as he did on this stuff, he might have had a successful screenwriting career," he said.

The Neon Revolt blog hasn't been updated since Cornero was tied to his online alter ego. But other QAnon promoters took his place, picking up the conspiracy theories he had crafted about the cabal's influence on Hollywood. The people Cornero indoctrinated into QAnon didn't suddenly leave the movement when his identity was exposed; they just went looking for another Q leader to follow. Cornero's interpretations of Q's clues are still referenced on QAnon websites and social media pages. His legacy in QAnon lives on even after he went silent.

As influential as he was, though, Cornero was just one part of an enormous radicalization machine. Leaders like Cornero could take QAnon in their own directions, but they were all just building on the work of its originator: Q himself.

Chapter 4

Who Is Q?

Q is a prank played by Italian leftists who all share the name of a hapless soccer player. Q is the creation of dozens of Trump allies, from Roger Stone and Steve Bannon to Michael Flynn. Q is a pig farmer in the Philippines.

Or maybe it's all of them at once.

For people outside of QAnon, the question of Q's identity is the biggest unresolved question about it. Someone decided to sit down at a computer, write all these clues, and fool millions of people. Q is still out there, his continued anonymity a challenge to those of us who have kept our connection to reality.

Q's followers have their own theories about Q's identity—that it's Michael Flynn, Trump social media guru Dan Scavino, the former head of the National Security Agency, or JFK Jr.

For Q's supporters, his identity might be the least interesting thing about their movement. They assume it's someone close to Trump, and they're happy to leave it at that. But for everyone else, it's a challenge. While QAnon believers follow Q's clues down internet rabbit holes, the rest are left to wonder who started this twisted treasure hunt in the first place. Just as there are dozens of people promoting their own take on QAnon, there are shadowy agendas and self-interested actors at play behind any allegation about who runs QAnon.

After believers flooded the Tampa rally in August 2018, I tried to figure out who was behind QAnon. What I found instead was a thriving parallel conspiracy theory community devoted to finding Q.

As I looked into Q's identity, I found a semi-reformed conspiracy theorist who was trying to move on from his beliefs by discovering Q's identity. As he laid out his ideas, he appeared to have some genuinely good leads on Q's name. Then he claimed that the target of his Q obsession received secret messages every day at 4 a.m. on a server controlled by the global cabal. This was the same server, he explained, that QAnon believers themselves think controls the media's agenda. And it was real.

In that moment, it became clear to me that this guy had no idea who was behind Q. But then, neither did anyone else. Any attempt to find Q's identity will mean falling over and over for red herrings. As I began my hunt for Q, I followed another thread involving Cicada 3301, a mysterious, devilishly difficult online puzzle game that has been dogged by unproven rumors that it's an intelligence operation meant to recruit genius-level operatives. An internet troll named Manuel "Defango" Chavez, who claimed to be associated with Cicada, would tell anyone who listened that his former Cicada partner turned rival was behind QAnon. That man, an eccentric composer named Thomas Schoenberger, shot back that Chavez himself might be involved in QAnon. They had no proof of their allegations, but they were more than happy to waste my time and suck me into their games. Like most people pushing ideas about who was behind Q in 2018, they came up empty.

There are theorists who claim that Trumpworld characters like Bannon and Flynn are behind it, again, without much evidence. In 2018, onetime Pizzagate promoter Jack Posobiec, in an apparent attempt to quash QAnon before it became a more visible embarrassment to the Republican Party, claimed he had chat logs proving a white supremacist troll who used the alias Microchip was behind QAnon. Microchip had become notorious for his efforts to elect Trump, and it wasn't impossible to imagine that he had resorted to concocting a whole conspiracy theory universe to boost the president. But the logs could have been easily faked, and were never corroborated by other evidence.

And then, there are the Italians.

In August 2018, as QAnon reached a new level of media prominence, BuzzFeed News declared that it was "extremely likely" that QAnon was a stunt on Trump supporters inspired by a group of Italian leftists collectively named Luther Blissett. When I first read the story, I was stunned—I had been scooped on the biggest story on my beat. But the article quickly fell apart. The connection seemed to rest entirely on the fact that both Blissett and Q used the seventeenth letter of the alphabet. Given that Q is just one of twenty-six letters, that wasn't exactly a smoking gun. Still, I had to see if it was true.

Twenty years earlier, an amorphous collective of Italian pranksters had all started to go by "Luther Blissett," after a British soccer player who had a disastrous run in Milan. The group began to pull political pranks around Italy. They stole Jesus statues from churches, only ransoming them back for hefty donations to the local poor. The pranksters duped art critics into covering the debut of a painting chimp named Loota, who, in the story circulated by Blissett operatives, had been rescued from a lab by environmental terrorists and would now display her art at an international fair in Venice. In truth, Loota existed only in their imaginations. They tricked a state-run Italian TV station into hunting across Europe for a missing British artist named Harry Kipper, who had been attempting to trace out the word *ART* in a bike ride across Europe. Like the monkey, however, Kipper was a fake. When a Satanic panic swept Italy in the late 1990s, Luther Blissett concocted a lurid outbreak of Satanism in one region of the country to fool the media, staging a demonic ritual complete with devil worshippers and witch-hunters.

In 1999, the Blissett collective released *Q*, a hulking novel about the Protestant Reformation and European religious wars. The book pits an Anabaptist rebel against a mysterious Catholic Church agent named Q, who taunts his foe with messages. The book became an unlikely hit and was translated across the world.

Q was what prompted BuzzFeed and other QAnon-watchers to suspect that Luther Blissett might be involved in QAnon, or had at least inspired it. There were some similarities between Q and the authors of *Q*, including the cryptic messages, the clue-giver's name, and the Blissett group's toying with Satanic imagery.

Roberto Bui, a former Blissett member, agreed there is some overlap between QAnon and the story in the *Q* novel. Bui speculated that the first person to post as Q could have been inspired by the book, but said the collective was not involved in the conspiracy theory.

"Of course, we're not behind QAnon in any way," Bui told me.

To me, the Blissett rabbit hunt represented how slippery Q had become by 2018. He was an increasingly powerful figure who had already amassed tens of thousands, if not millions, of followers. Yet so little was known about his identity that a media outlet could claim some artsy European pranksters were behind QAnon, and that explanation could seem as likely as any other.

The best lead on Q's identity centers on 8chan, the forum where QAnon landed after fleeing 4chan in November 2017. And understanding 8chan means understanding Fredrick Brennan—the onetime Q believer and ringmaster who turned on the movement he helped create.

Brennan was born in 1994 in Albany, New York, with osteogenesis imperfecta, or brittle bones. The disease meant that, for Brennan, an otherwise minor fall or bump could turn fatal. It shriveled his limbs, stunted his growth, and caused him to break his bones more than one hundred times.

With his access to the world outside his upstate New York home limited by his genetic disorder, Brennan turned to the internet after getting access to his first computer at six years old. Brennan's parents had divorced a year earlier, leaving him with little supervision over his online activities. When he was twelve, 4chan users raided a *Sonic the Hedgehog* forum Brennan was reading by posting obscene images on the page, exposing him for the first time to the imageboards that would take up nearly the entirety of his teenage years. He became fascinated by the chans, a passion aided by his disinterested parents.

"My dad did not really care what I did on the computer," Brennan said.

Brennan spent most of his adolescence on 4chan, soaking up the forum's atmosphere of trollish pranks and hateful politics. After Brennan's father surrendered custody of his son to the state of New York when Brennan was fourteen, Brennan was sent to a series of foster homes. He escaped his grim new circumstances by burrowing deeper into 4chan.

As 4chan grew less anarchic amid a push for some kind of respectability, Brennan plunged into other chan sites. He befriended the owner of Wizardchan, a chan-style site devoted to male virgins who expected to stay that way for the rest of their lives, claiming they accrued "magic" by avoiding sexual contact with women. But Brennan's friend soon lost his virginity, enraging the "wizards"—Wizardchan users who had turned thirty or older without ever having sex—and was forced to sell the site to Brennan for a pittance.

Brennan's own reign as the virginal king of Wizardchan didn't last long, either. After a night of passion, Brennan, too, had to move on.

At nineteen, Brennan moved to Brooklyn, thrusting himself into a world that wasn't built for a wheelchair-bound young man whose major life experiences up until then had often taken place in the online company of trolls and adult virgins. At one point, Brennan took nearly $5,000 in cash on a trip that passed through New York City's Port Authority Bus Terminal; he was confident that no place called the "Port Authority" could be that dangerous. He was robbed almost immediately.

While Brennan struggled in the offline world, he was on his way to stardom online. One night in 2013, coming down from a mushroom trip, Brennan loaded up 4chan. As the psilocybin throbbed in his brain, Brennan started to see fractals spread out across the 4chan home page. He imagined combining a new site similar to 4chan with a function borrowed from Reddit that would let users make their own subforums. Years later, that feature would prove key for QAnon users looking for an online home.

Inspired, he finished coding the first version of 8chan two days later. Brennan launched 8chan with remarkably permissive rules, even by the standards of chan sites. While 4chan might boot groups that engaged in high-profile online harassment or other unsavory activities, Brennan didn't have those concerns. Under Brennan's rules, anything legal under U.S. law was allowed on 8chan.

At first, 8chan's few users created just around one hundred posts an hour, many of them in languages Brennan didn't speak. That didn't bother Brennan, who intended to use the site as a sandbox to practice his programming. But his hands-off approach to moderation began to pay off, in both traffic and notoriety. Brennan had launched 8chan just a few months before the start of Gamergate, the right-wing backlash and harassment campaign aimed at women working in video games. After being banned from 4chan, as QAnon would be years later, Gamergate found a home on 8chan. To its advocates, Gamergate was about protecting a gaming industry they saw as overrun by liberal activists. In practice, Gamergate "activism" often amounted to organizing online harassment mobs that targeted female video game journalists and developers.

Brennan welcomed 8chan's new position as a safe harbor for Gamergate. After mainlining 4chan's ethos since he was in middle school, Brennan had come to embody them. Brennan wrote a blog post for a neo-Nazi website arguing for eugenics, citing his own genetic disease as a reason to support forced sterilization. When a reporter asked him whether imageboards like 8chan had become known for "misogyny" and "nihilism," Brennan said that was just the price of free speech.

"That's exactly what makes them such wonderful places," Brennan replied. "I wouldn't change a thing."

Brennan's role as Gamergate's protector made him a hero to some of the internet's angriest young men, who had affectionately dubbed him "Hotwheels." 8chan's traffic exploded as the forum became Gamergate's new home in September 2014, with a nearly 4,000 percent increase in hourly posts.

Brennan soon realized that he couldn't maintain the site at that level on his own. Help arrived from Japan in the form of a private message from a young man named Ron Watkins, who used the screen name "Codemonkey." Watkins was the administrator of 2Channel, the massive Japanese imageboard that had inspired 4chan and, indirectly, Brennan's creation of 8chan.

Watkins and his father, Jim Watkins, wanted to buy 8chan and hire Brennan to run it for them. They urged Brennan to join them at the headquarters of the Watkinses' tech network in the Philippines, where a live-in nurse for Brennan would cost less than $300 a month.

Brennan agreed. The night before he left for Manila in October 2017, Brennan partied with roughly two dozen Gamergaters at a strip club, where a dancer presented him with a cake marking 8chan's first birthday. The group posed for a picture in Brennan's apartment, with Brennan clutching a handle of vodka. By embracing some of the internet's worst people, Brennan had found his community.

Jim Watkins was a U.S. Army veteran with a Filipino pig farm and a number of online businesses. He seemed like an unlikely person to travel across the world for, especially given Brennan's disability. But for Brennan, Watkins seemed like someone he would have no trouble dealing with.

"I viewed him as perhaps something of a foster father that I could maybe control a little bit more," Brennan said.

By the time QAnon began in October 2017, however, Brennan and the elder Watkins were on the outs. Brennan had stopped running 8chan for Watkins in 2016, growing concerned about the white supremacists and other hate groups that were finding a home on his site. But he continued working for Watkins on his other websites.

As Brennan and Watkins were growing apart in the fall of 2017, QAnon was in its infancy on 4chan. But Q needed a home of its own. Q moved to 8chan, with Paul Furber, the South African programmer, as the moderator of Q's home on the site.

Furber's apparent control over the Q persona has made him one of the leading suspects for who originally controlled the Q account on 4chan. In the first weeks of QAnon, Furber boasted on 4chan about the special connection he claimed he had with Q—braggadocio that some QAnon fans found irritating, but others took as a sign that he was hinting that he really was Q. Furber actually managed one of Q's first boards on 8chan, effectively giving him control of Q's public presentation.

Perhaps the only thing that is clear about Q's identity is that multiple people have controlled the name "Q" at different points.

The first person behind QAnon could be anyone who logged on to 4chan one day in late October 2017 and decided to start making up stories about Hillary Clinton. But the suspicion about who first started Q often lands on Furber himself, because of his close affiliation with QAnon in its early days. While Furber denies publishing as Q, the *New York Times* reported in 2022 on a linguistic analysis report of Q drops that suggested Furber was a close match to be their author.

On January 5, 2018, Furber lost whatever control he had over Q. The fight over the Q identity lasted for just a few posts. Now the moderator of the 8chan board where Q made his posts, Furber started seeing what, in his telling, didn't seem like legitimate messages from Q. They had the Q name, but they didn't read to him like "real" Q posts. Furber made a post announcing to the faithful that the latest round of Q drops shouldn't be trusted. Q's account, Furber declared, had been hacked.

Before that moment, Q and Furber had moved in concert, working together to build QAnon. But this time, Q turned on Furber. The Q account shot back that it was Furber, not Q, who was suspect.

"Did they get to you?" Q asked Furber, suggesting that the loyal programmer, too, was an agent of the cabal. "Board compromised."

After months as the ultimate Q insider, Furber was now on the outside. With Furber cast out, whoever now controlled Q's alias wrote in a follow-up 8chan that there was only one man who could verify that this was really Q: 8chan administrator Ron Watkins, Jim Watkins's son. Q asked the younger Watkins to confirm him as the legitimate Q, and create a new board outside of Furber's control. Watkins agreed, and Q moved to the new board. That's the moment, some Q-watchers say, that Ron and Jim Watkins became Q.

From his apartment in Manila in November 2019, Fredrick Brennan watched as some of the most anticipated Q posts yet went live.

The drops were a string of cryptic commands that looked like computer code, but meant nothing in practical terms. But they appeared in November 2019, after 8chan had been down for three months. Now, with 8chan finally back online and rebranded as "8kun," these new posts were proof that Q wasn't done yet.

QAnon believers rejoiced at their leader's return. But for Brennan, nothing about Q's homecoming on the rebranded 8kun made sense. For one thing, Q appeared to have a unique ability to post on the reopened forum, even as other 8kun users struggled to make their own posts. That suggested that Q wasn't getting the same access as every other 8kun user; he was somehow operating from inside the site's internal controls. Even Brennan, who had written 8chan's code, couldn't post yet on the new site. Like 4chan, 8chan was founded on a principle of anonymity, yet Q seemed to have some kind of special internal access. And if Q was leading a global movement to save the world from unspeakable evil, with help from the American president and military, why was he staking everything on a website that could barely manage to stay online?

As the sole source for verified Q messages since January 2018, 8chan had become the center of the QAnon universe. But it went down for months starting in August 2019, after a gunman in Texas posted his racist manifesto on the board before murdering twenty-three people in an El Paso Walmart. That shooting followed two other white supremacist massacres, at mosques in Christchurch, New Zealand, and a synagogue in Poway, California, which were also announced beforehand by their perpetrators on 8chan.

The Christchurch gunman even posted a link on 8chan to a livestream of the shootings.

Brennan felt sick as he watched his brainchild become a stage for some of the world's most depraved, violent minds. He had quit 8chan in December 2018, tired of working for the mercurial Jim Watkins and being affiliated with the increasingly toxic site 8chan. Now on the outside, he launched a campaign to push it offline, pressing the tech companies whose services 8chan required to stay online to blacklist it.

After the El Paso shooting, though, Brennan had become a serious opponent for Watkins. Armed with just his Twitter account and a comprehensive knowledge of 8chan's technical underpinnings, Brennan helped convince companies like internet infrastructure provider Cloudflare to pull their services from the site, taking 8chan offline.

While Brennan grappled with his conscience, Watkins wasn't as conflicted. Just days after the El Paso shooting, a rumpled, mustachioed Watkins addressed his critics in a video, denouncing Cloudflare for pulling support for 8chan, which he described as a "peacefully assembled group of people talking."

Three months later, as Brennan watched the Q drops pile up on the newly resurrected 8kun, it wasn't adding up. Q had tethered himself for no clear reason to Watkins, a political pariah best known outside of QAnon for running 8chan as a neo-Nazi hangout. It wasn't even certain that Watkins could keep a website up, much less play a key role in a global intelligence operation.

"If Q were a third party, they would want a way to post that is not controlled by Jim Watkins, obviously, because nobody in this situation would really put all their eggs in one basket," Brennan said.

Brennan started to think that Watkins—the man who had taken him halfway around the world, and who would soon help turn Brennan into an international fugitive—had become Q.

He thought back to the January 2018 fight where Furber was ousted as Q's moderator. The writing style on Q posts changed, suggesting a new author had taken over. Brennan claims, based on his own knowledge of the 8chan code, that Ron Watkins would have been in a position as 8chan's administrator to easily take control of the Q name. Brennan has also stated that, while he was still working at 8chan, Ron Watkins was excited about the influx of traffic to 8chan from QAnon adherents, and that Jim Watkins had told his son to make sure Q couldn't leave the site. If Ron Watkins did seize the QAnon account, from Furber or someone else, that goal was now accomplished.

"I knew that Ron Watkins was very happy about all of these users coming to his board," Brennan said.

Furber, who insists that the original Q really was a legitimate intelligence insider, also claims that Jim and Ron Watkins stole Q that day to hand the identity to someone else.

"Ron Watkins and his father Jim Watkins, had deliberately hijacked the Q operation in order to drive traffic to 8chan," Furber wrote in his memoir about the early days of QAnon.

For Furber, that alleged heist marked the end of his belief in Q. But to the wider QAnon community, it barely meant anything. QAnon was less than three months old. Q supporters hadn't flocked to Trump rallies, or murdered anyone, or taken elected office. Whatever the dispute about Q's identity meant, it was barely noticed in the broader QAnon universe, which was rapidly growing on platforms far larger than 8chan. New Q recruits hardly visited 8chan and, later, 8kun. The Q content on sites like Facebook and Twitter was much more exciting and easy to read. As Brennan and the Watkinses brawled over Q's identity, QAnon believers were moving on without Q.

After the El Paso shooting in August 2019, the House of Representatives summoned Jim Watkins to Washington, D.C., for an interview about 8chan's role in the massacres. I interviewed Watkins in Washington shortly after his interview with congressional investigators. As we sat outside at a cafe a mile from Congress, Watkins held forth on his bizarre interests as his lawyer looked on, occasionally wincing at his client's remarks.

Watkins proudly announced that he had worn a Q pin and pizza-themed socks to his congressional interview. But when I asked Watkins why he was promoting Pizzagate, which had inspired both a shooting and an arson attack at Comet Ping Pong, Watkins hedged in a downright Trumpian style.

"I personally don't believe that the pizzeria had a basement and all of these horrible things happened there," Watkins said. "But people talked about that. I don't believe that. But it was spoken about and some people think that they were actually speaking with keywords, using pizza as keywords. Who knows? But they talked about it, and it was sweet, and it was okay."

"Well, there's a lot of things people talk about," I said. "But I think the decision to wear the pizza socks suggests—"

"Let them talk," Watkins said, cutting me off.

Watkins seemed incapable of giving a straight answer about anything. When I asked him about Q, his board's most famous member, Watkins wanted to talk instead about a *Star Trek* character named Q. When I asked him about a recent *New York Times* article in which Brennan called for 8chan to be shut down, Watkins insisted he hadn't read it.

He said he had only recently learned that QAnon had taken up residence on 8chan, more than a year after his son intervened in the Furber/Q clash.

"You're being a little cagey on whether you believe in QAnon or not," I said, pointing to his Q pin.

"I didn't even know about QAnon on our servers until a few months ago," Watkins said. "You know, it's a big website. It's not the size of Twitter or a Facebook, but it's a big website."

"You didn't know that?" I said. "You didn't know that's one of the main draws?"

"I'm busy," Watkins said.

Watkins dodged my questions about QAnon, but he's saying even less now. When I emailed him in March 2021 to ask for another interview, he refused and threatened to sue me.

Both Ron and Jim Watkins did sit for interviews, however, with director Cullen Hoback for his HBO documentary, *Q: Into the Storm*, which chronicled Hoback's efforts to find out Q's identity amid the growing feud between the Watkinses and Brennan. Throughout the documentary, Watkins and his son gave wildly varying stances on their relationship to QAnon. Ron initially claimed to not even know what QAnon is, then spent another interview with Hoback rehashing niche QAnon-world gossip. He said he rarely posted on 8chan, only writing posts to offer dry technical updates as the site's administrator. At the same time, he provided Hoback with internal 8chan data that seemed to suggest Steve Bannon was behind Q—data Hoback suspected had been faked to convince him Ron Watkins wasn't actually Q.

In the documentary's climax, Ron Watkins appears to boast that he's been the driving force behind 8chan's QAnon board all along.

"So thinking back on it, it was basically three years of intelligence training, teaching normies how to do intelligence work," Watkins said. "It's basically what I was doing anonymously before."

Watkins was using the same language QAnon believers use to describe the purpose of their movement. But then Watkins smiled and said that whatever he had done, it was "never as Q."

Still, Watkins appeared to have slipped up. If what he said amounted to a confession, it meant that QAnon wasn't about fighting the deep state or creating a better world. It would mean that QAnon was about two men in Manila, messing with people an ocean away to accumulate money, power, and a few laughs.

Ron Watkins backed away from Q after the Capitol riot, when interest in Q's identity reached a new height. Two weeks after QAnon believers helped breach the Capitol and two QAnon supporters died in the riot,

Watkins said, effectively, that the election fraud hunters should respect the transfer of power and "go back to our lives as best we are able."

"Please remember all the friends and happy memories we made together over the past few years," Watkins wrote in a social media post.

Brennan was stunned to see Watkins wash his hands of QAnon, just as people had started fighting and dying in Q's name.

"Bye everybody, we tried," Brennan said, parodying the tone of Watkins's farewell post. "Let's all just go back to this world where deep-state cannibals are eating everybody."

Brennan succeeded in publicizing his suspicions about the Watkinses. Thanks to a media blitz from Brennan and Ron Watkins's own semi-admission of guilt in Hoback's documentary, the Watkinses appear to be the most likely suspects behind the current iteration of Q. But Brennan hasn't emerged from his feud with the Watkinses unscathed. Because of a legal dispute with Jim Watkins that culminated in a criminal indictment for libel, Brennan fled the country in February 2020 ahead of his potential arrest. He broke up with his wife and will likely never be able to return to the Philippines because of the indictment.

"I've lost my marriage, the place I've lived," Brennan said. "Everything except my dog."

Q's identity still hasn't been definitively proven. The linguistic analysis reported by the *New York Times* named Ron Watkins as Q's second author, after Furber, but the report focused only on known suspects, meaning that an anonymous Q creator no one knows of wouldn't have turned up in the analysis. Unless someone confesses to it, it's likely that we'll never know for sure.

For many QAnon believers, though, Q's identity doesn't matter.

For years, they had been laying the groundwork to move on without Q. Supporters already had dozens of QAnon influencers to direct the movement, and plenty of forums beyond 8chan to discuss the clues. But most important, they had decided that QAnon was less about Q, and more about the beliefs Q and his followers had created together: their shared understanding of a world controlled by a Satanic pedophile cabal that could only be vanquished violently by Donald Trump.

The bickering over 8chan's future had consumed both the Watkinses and Brennan, but it was barely known outside of hard-core Q-watchers like myself. QAnon believers had moved on. Based on conversations with Anons, I'm confident that the vast majority of Q believers didn't interact with Q posts on 8chan. Even if Q wasn't real, the argument went, what he taught them was real. They could also leave 8chan behind, with far more compelling sites available to them. As the 8chan feud simmered, Q's army was growing elsewhere. YouTube, Facebook, and Twitter were the new homes for QAnon.

Chapter 5

Plan to Save the World

In 2019, a North Carolina woman named Carol created her first Facebook account. She favorited the pages for Fox News and Donald and Melania Trump, and liked memes making fun of Democrats.

Facebook's algorithm—the programming that determines what recommendations users like Carol receive—wanted her to go further.

Two days after joining Facebook, Carol received recommendations to like a page called "Q WWG1WGA," which used a fiery *Q* as its profile image. A few days after that, Facebook recommended she check out another QAnon page illustrated with a screenshot of a Q clue. The page's slogan: "Do you believe in coincidence?"

Carol wasn't a real person. She was the creation of Facebook employees testing how the site's algorithm would nudge a woman fitting Carol's profile—a conservative southern mother—toward conspiracy theories and disinformation. By populating the Carol account with "likes" for only mainstream conservative figures, they were able to see how the site's algorithms encouraged users to check out QAnon and other conspiracy and fringe theories even when they had shown no interest in them in the first place.

But even without a sophisticated algorithm, Facebook was becoming a recruitment tool for Q worldwide. Existing QAnon believers figured out on their own how to leverage Facebook to spread their ideas. By 2020,

Facebook had thousands of QAnon groups and tens of thousands of believers on its site. QAnon fans boosted its growth on the site with bulk invites to their Facebook communities, with one pro-Q user blasting potential recruits with nearly 400,000 invites in just a few months. Once inside private QAnon groups, new members were brought up to speed on QAnon lore and invited to help terrorize the movement's victims.

Facebook whistleblower Frances Haugen leaked a report on the Carol experiment in 2021 as part of a huge cache of internal documents she had taken from the company. Haugen's leaks revealed that Facebook had known for years about its role in fueling the movement's growth. The leak revealed that Facebook, far from being a neutral platform, had accidentally turned itself into a major QAnon recruiter in its quest for more users and activity.

In 2018, Chief Executive Officer Mark Zuckerberg made the decision to prioritize content that drove reactions from other Facebook users. That change benefited QAnon, a movement based entirely around emotionally charged content that provokes responses. By encouraging content that sparked reactions, Zuckerberg inadvertently made his platform into fertile ground for QAnon.

QAnon started on the chans, but it would never have become the force it is without major social platforms like Facebook, YouTube, and Twitter. The social media networks were easier to use than the chan sites and had far larger user bases, enabling the movement to grow exponentially.

In early 2018, Reddit became QAnon's first major online hub on a mainstream social media site. While Q himself continued to post on 8chan, his first acolytes moved much of the action to Reddit. The site's top two QAnon communities—"subreddits," in Reddit parlance—had more than 90,000 combined users, with the largest receiving more than 10,000 comments a day. Reddit's communal structure, where the most popular comments receive votes that give them more visibility, made it perfect for the kind of obsessive group sleuthing QAnon believers love. While QAnon continued to drive new users to see Q's messages posted on 8chan, the more obscure site receded in the Q imagination in favor of Reddit.

In a seven-month period in 2018, Reddit administrators launched a series of purges that eliminated QAnon from its platform almost accidentally. When they banned the largest QAnon subreddit in October 2018, administrators said the community had broken Reddit's rules against "inciting violence, harassment, and the dissemination of personal information."

Reddit's ban stamped out QAnon on the site, putting the lesser-known social media network years ahead of its larger rivals in getting a handle on its QAnon problem. But Reddit's bans didn't come as part of a concerted policy against QAnon. Instead, the banned QAnon subreddits ran afoul of more general Reddit rules against harassment and "doxing," or publishing personal details. "I don't think we've had any focused effort to keep QAnon off the platform," Reddit's chief technology officer told *The Atlantic* in 2020.

The Reddit crackdown scattered QAnon's growing online community, leaving new recruits scared or otherwise unable to post on 8chan with nowhere to go. But Anons soon found their way to sites that had both more potential recruits and more complacent executives. Social media platforms offer some obvious benefits for anyone looking to spread a conspiracy theory. Before the internet, a lone crank pushing strange ideas might have struggled to find allies in his neighborhood, or even his town. But on social media, conspiracy theorists can search the world for people who agree with them.

And so Reddit's QAnon exiles landed on YouTube, Facebook, and Twitter. Each platform would play a different role in QAnon's development. YouTube hosted a vast archive of QAnon material, offering supporters a chance to convert someone just by emailing a link to a ten-minute clip. The videos ranged from rambling screeds shot in dimly lit rooms to twenty-four-hour livestreams with dozens of people on staff.

QAnon videos could be surprisingly compelling. In 2018, an early pro-Q upload to YouTube called "Q: The Plan to Save the World" became a kind of calling card for the movement. "Plan to Save the World" evokes the feeling of watching a Marvel movie trailer, a military recruitment ad, and a video game intro all at once. A growling narrator rants about "criminal presidents" and an unseen cabal. Only Trump can stop the evildoers. The video's logo, a *Q* combined with the skull symbol of vigilante comic book hero "The Punisher," became a popular symbol for QAnon believers awaiting the Storm.

The video has racked up millions of views, becoming an easy way for QAnon believers to red-pill their friends. Even former Boston Red Sox pitcher Curt Schilling, a potential future Hall of Famer, was a fan.

"You will not be able to stop watching once you start," Schilling wrote on Facebook.

The upload spawned more pro-QAnon videos with faux-documentary trappings, some of them even more popular than "Plan to Save the World." They had ominous names like "Out of Shadows" and "Fall of the Cabal," and received millions of views each.

By 2018, QAnon had established growing bases of support in Facebook, Twitter, and YouTube. That year, one study discovered that tens of thousands of Q believers were active on Twitter alone. Researchers tracking the spread of disinformation online started to investigate QAnon's rapid growth on the sites.

The Facebook employees behind the Carol test account weren't the only people noticing how the site's algorithm was helping to grow QAnon. In 2015, Stanford University disinformation researcher Renée DiResta set up a dummy Facebook account of her own to track antivaccine groups. Facebook's recommendations initially pushed her account to conspiracy theories like "chemtrails," the idea that planes spray mind control chemicals from the air. The algorithm also introduced her to a world of quack medical cures like colloidal silver, which turns users' skin permanently blue. As DiResta tracked where the groups overlapped, she noticed that joining one conspiracy theory group meant Facebook would prompt her account to join a group devoted to an unrelated, but equally false, belief. Facebook was pushing the conspiracy theory communities together, setting the stage for a superconspiracy like QAnon to take them all over.

Right as QAnon started to infiltrate Facebook's network in 2018, DiResta noticed prompts urging her dummy account to join QAnon groups. But the Facebook algorithm wasn't just promoting QAnon to her antivaccine test account. It was also pushing people interested in other fringe movements toward Q. Facebook's algorithm had turned into a massive funnel pulling people from unrelated conspiracy theory communities around the site into QAnon. Facebook's QAnon groups turned into radicalization swap meets where antivaccine activists could trade extreme ideas with militia members and flat-earthers.

Facebook's recommendation engine relied on a user's previously expressed interests on the site, setting up a conspiracy theory rabbit hole for users to explore. Express interest once in anything conservative or pro-Trump, and you had a good chance that Facebook's algorithm would introduce you to QAnon.

"Let me push this into your field of view, and you can choose whether or not to click on it," DiResta said, describing how Facebook introduced users to QAnon. "But if you click on it, we're going to show you the next one, and the next one."

Facebook took QAnon to membership levels it never would have reached if it had remained on a far smaller site like 8chan. Unlike Facebook, 8chan lacks the kind of hyper-engineered algorithm aimed at ensuring that users stay logged in and posting. When Facebook finally banned QAnon in October 2020, the movement was widespread enough on the site that cleaning up QAnon meant deleting more than 5,600 groups and 50,000 Facebook profiles.

"QAnon would not have existed in its present form but for Facebook," DiResta said.

As QAnon established its recruiting methods on YouTube and Facebook, Twitter became the place where QAnon went to inflict pain on the outside world. In Twitter's information free-for-all, QAnon believers were able to blend in and push their ideas. Some pro-Q figures amassed hundreds of thousands of followers on the site, decoding Q's posts and connecting current events to their vision of the world. Because of the size of the QAnon community on Twitter, its accounts could easily dominate the site's "Trending" page, putting QAnon hashtags in front of millions of people. People working in politics or media also love using Twitter, meaning that the site was an easy way for QAnon users to reach them. After an apparently oblivious Fox News host on the *Fox & Friends* morning show read a tweet from a major Q account on-air to show that Trump's latest executive order was a hit with the public, believers rejoiced at their newfound respectability, declaring, "We are the news now."

More than anything, though, Twitter was a place for QAnon followers to harass their targets. Their methods for deciding who was an enemy of Q were often indecipherable to outsiders, relying on a mix of amateur cryptography and ambient paranoia.

The worst I received on Twitter for my reporting were some threatening messages. Others had it much worse. In May 2019, QAnon's Twitter ire fell on a previously little-known elementary school in California, putting children in harm's way.

The spark for this new QAnon pursuit was an odd one: former FBI director James Comey was participating in a Twitter hashtag game called #FiveJobsIveHad, where he posted the titles of jobs he had once held: a grocery clerk, for example, or a chemist. But QAnon's Twitter investigators thought Comey was actually talking about old summer jobs to send a signal to a terrorist sleeper cell. "Five Jobs I've Had"? If you squinted, it might read like "Five Jihad" instead. And if you added up the first letter of each job Comey listed, they formed an acronym: "GVCSF."

And so Grass Valley Charter School in Northern California fell into Q's crosshairs. The school had a related nonprofit called the Grass Valley Charter School Foundation, which was holding a festival as a fundraiser in a few days. The message was clear: Comey was ordering a terrorist attack on innocent schoolchildren.

The school was deluged with warnings from QAnon believers, sharing frantic messages about an impending shooting or terrorist attack at the fundraiser. Organizers canceled the event, suddenly fearful that the strangers ranting about impending violence at their festival could inspire a lone-wolf gunman.

The Grass Valley story might be most notable because of how few Anons were needed to derail life at a school for weeks. The idea that Comey was plotting a false-flag attack on a fundraiser unfolded on QAnon's edges, never reaching anything close to Comet Ping Pong levels of notoriety. The Grass Valley conspiracy theory originated with a no-name Q supporter, not a major Q promoter or Q himself. But that anonymous user managed to use Twitter to sow chaos, quickly turning hordes of Q believers onto their theories and weaponizing them against the school.

Twitter also became an engine for QAnon believers to push their claims about arrested celebrity pedophiles to millions of people. In the first days of the pandemic, QAnon users on Twitter spread a rumor that talk show host Oprah Winfrey had been arrested and charged with abusing children. They focused on a supposed bulge in Winfrey's pants leg during an interview with Meghan Markle and Prince Harry, claiming it was proof that Winfrey was wearing an ankle monitor after being arrested by Q's allies.

Oprah is a witch and was part of a child sex trafficking cult, one Twitter user wrote, in a typical post about Winfrey.

The claims against Winfrey were ridiculous. But QAnon users were able to use their presence on Twitter to turn the allegations against Winfrey into the top trending topic, introducing the idea of Satanist Oprah to unsuspecting Twitter users. Winfrey even responded herself, tweeting that her mansion had not been raided and that the pedophilia claims were *NOT TRUE.*

QAnon's Twitter conspiracy theory machine became so powerful that it didn't need Q himself to operate anymore. The movement had brought together enough freelance conspiracy theorists and given them enough social media clout that they could self-generate conspiracy theories on their own.

The QAnon mob's ability to grow mostly undisturbed by administrators on Twitter helped create a conspiracy theory that spread far beyond QAnon: the Wayfair sex-trafficking plot.

In June 2020, a prominent QAnon leader who went by the name "The Amazing Polly" tweeted that she was suspicious of the online furniture retailer Wayfair. She noted that some cabinets on Wayfair were being sold at astronomical prices, roughly $15,000 each. The cabinets were often sold under female brand names like "Yaritza" or "Samiyah."

My spidey senses are tingling, she wrote. *What's with these "storage cabinets"? Extremely high prices, all listed with girls' names.*

The Amazing Polly didn't spell out her exact concerns, but other QAnon supporters stepped in to puzzle out the connection between the furniture names and their absurd prices. The conspiracy theory they created held that the furniture model names represented real children who had been abducted.

QAnon believers searched for girls who had been reported missing and matched their names with the furniture on sale. In this telling, Wayfair served as an online marketplace for pedophiles to buy those exact children, under the cover of buying furniture named directly after them.

Despite its lunacy, the Wayfair conspiracy theory spread beyond QAnon's corner of Twitter. The husband of an Instagram beauty influencer in Arizona filmed himself calling Wayfair's customer service line and attempting to order one of the $17,000 cabinets. That video helped push the Wayfair hoax into Instagram lifestyle communities, where hundreds of thousands of followers picked up the story and demanded that Wayfair explain itself. Tip lines meant to stop actual sex-trafficking were suddenly overwhelmed with calls about Wayfair. The furniture company hired extra security guards to protect its corporate headquarters.

In reality, the inflated prices were just a function of the site's algorithm. If a price for an item hasn't yet been entered, Wayfair will assign an exorbitant price by default to prevent an item from being sold before its real price has been confirmed.

One of the "missing" girls, a nineteen-year-old named Samiyah Mumin, wasn't missing at all. Mumin had briefly been reported missing two years earlier, after she ran away from home for a day. Now Mumin found herself in the unusual position of insisting to strangers online that she wasn't trapped in a cabinet. In a Facebook video she posted to prove that she wasn't being trafficked, Mumin jousted with QAnon investigators in her comment section and threatened to stuff them in cabinets themselves if they kept it up. But Mumin's video also revealed the power of the life-upending tornado QAnon could bring down with social media on an innocent person's life.

"Let me get a picture of *you* and say *you're* missing," Mumin said. "Let's see how you feel."

Eccentrics ranting about the powers-that-be aren't unusual on the streets of Hollywood. But they don't usually herald the arrival of an entirely new conspiracy theory movement. One day in July 2020, roughly one hundred people picketing on the streets of Hollywood represented a younger, hipper take on QAnon—one cooked up entirely on social media.

At the march's climax, the protesters entered the lobby of CNN's Los Angeles headquarters, which they saw as a stronghold of the cabal. As they waved signs about Pizzagate, the marchers chanted one message in unison: "Save the Children!"

Many of the people at the protest didn't look like the kind of people who supported QAnon before. Before QAnon's explosion on social media, the average Q believer looked a lot like a Trump voter. They were more likely to be evangelical Christians, white, and older. They wore plenty of Trump red.

Outside of QAnon, they had mostly conservative opinions about guns, immigration, and abortion.

The people toting QAnon signs in the Hollywood march were younger and less white than the stereotypical QAnon fan. Some dressed like they were on their way to an organic grocery store. These unusual QAnon believers were the new face of the "Save the Children" group, a fast-growing social media movement recruiting a new type of person into QAnon.

Save the Children's origins began earlier that summer, when Facebook started deleting some QAnon content. To avoid the ban, believers organized around a hashtag used by Save the Children Fund, a child welfare charity founded in 1919. By operating under Save the Children's name, they figured, they could dodge Facebook's rules. But "Save the Children" came to encompass more than just a way to hide from Facebook's moderators. Instead, it became a rallying cry for a social media–centric trend that embraced QAnon's tenets about widespread Satanist abuse of children but had nothing to do with the Q drops or orthodox QAnon.

Save the Children played on old QAnon tropes, but it arrived at a time of especially high interest in child sex-trafficking. The suspicious 2019 jailhouse death of wealthy pedophile Jeffrey Epstein, officially a suicide by hanging, prompted new public interest in the idea of powerful elites abusing children. That created an opening for a kind of QAnon that reached beyond its usual base of Trump supporters.

Save the Children overlapped with the rise of other new QAnon brands on social media. There was "Pastel QAnon," so named because of its style of QAnon promotion: images couched in a soft Instagram aesthetic filled with friendly colors and cursive fonts. There was also "QAmom," named after its appeal to mothers concerned about children's welfare. All three trends represented a change for QAnon. It had managed to morph on social media from the bloodthirsty Punisher-skull image of its first months into something less intimidating.

Save the Children's leaders were different, too. While the average QAnon promoter in the past emerged from other conspiracy theory internet communities and ranted like a wannabe Alex Jones, Save the Children's most recognizable faces were aspiring musicians, yoga instructors, and New Age Instagram influencers.

Save the Children was a cooler, more approachable version of QAnon.

Rather than grappling with stories about secretive assassins and space lasers causing wildfires, Save the Children played on a basic human desire to protect children. Its initial pitch was often vague about who exactly was doing what to "the children." Only later, when the new member was fully on board and researching Q, would the more shocking revelations be revealed. Matthew Remski, a podcaster who covers the intersection of spirituality and conspiracy theories, told me that Save the Children "provided a layer of bourgeois respectability" to QAnon.

Save the Children also helped QAnon-style conspiracy theories grow on new social media apps like TikTok. QAnon blossomed on the app, in clips of worried-looking teens rehashing old Pizzagate posts. TikTok's QAnon explosion focused on teen issues like whether a particular Justin Bieber music video included nods to child sex-trafficking.

But not everyone in QAnon was thrilled that the movement had established a successful new recruiting outpost online. For traditional QAnon enthusiasts, the new recruits—young, often people of color, and more liberal on other issues—were exactly the kind of people they didn't want to join QAnon.

New Save the Children believers might believe in the cannibal-pedophile cabal, but many were also still liberals. Save the Children activists in Portland, Oregon, for example, paired a "Hang pedophiles" sign with an obscene sign attacking U.S. Immigration and Customs Enforcement, infuriating QAnon's conservative old guard.

As Save the Children marches proliferated in the United States and Britain, QAnon leader Jordan Sather tweeted that these couldn't really be QAnon supporters. After all, where were the MAGA hats? He'd only believe these were genuine QAnon fans when there were "more American flags and Q swag."

Save the Children demonstrated QAnon's ability to shapeshift online into different communities, hijacking them under the idea of protecting children. Starting in 2017, QAnon had worked mostly on Trump supporters. But by 2020, QAnon was able to exploit a new kind of person's suspicions about world elites and the abuse of children. Thanks to social media, QAnon's ability to grow was no longer restricted to Trump and the Republican Party.

QAnon expanded steadily on the major social media platforms between 2018 and 2020. The sites might occasionally ban individual users or groups for breaking long-standing rules, like making threats or posting personal information about their targets. But there was no blanket ban on their content. Even as QAnon's followers began committing terrorism in Q's name, the platforms didn't coordinate a larger response to QAnon.

After discovering how Facebook's algorithm pushed users toward QAnon, DiResta had tried for years in meetings with social media companies to convince them to crack down. But she found the tech giants afraid of stopping QAnon because of the potential for political backlash from Republicans. For years, the companies found it easier to ignore QAnon than to be accused of censorship.

"If we do nothing, then we're maintaining the status quo and nobody can get mad at us," DiResta said, summing up the excuses she encountered.

QAnon's free ride on the platforms finally came to an end a few months before the 2020 presidential election. The bans came right as QAnon's presence on the platforms grew too big for Silicon Valley executives to ignore. QAnon had set its eyes on more ambitious targets, pursuing corporations like Wayfair and celebrities like Chrissy Teigen. When people and businesses with actual power started to be attacked, the social media giants finally took action. In July, Twitter banned seven thousand QAnon accounts, a decision that came right after the Wayfair conspiracy theory exploded on the site. A month later, Facebook added QAnon to a list of sanctioned groups that posed "significant risks to public safety," a change that made it harder to find QAnon Facebook groups.

Facebook launched its more serious crackdown on QAnon a month before the election, declaring that any Instagram or Facebook accounts "representing QAnon" would be deleted from the site. YouTube followed a few days after Facebook, announcing a ban on Pizzagate and QAnon videos.

The final crackdown came after the Capitol riot. In its aftermath, Twitter and Facebook announced that they had deleted thousands more QAnon accounts on their sites.

The social media platforms had finally acted against QAnon. But by then, it was too late. The tech giants had allowed QAnon to proliferate on their sites at the most crucial moment of the movement's growth: the coronavirus pandemic.

Chapter 6

Viral Load

When the United Kingdom entered its coronavirus lockdown in the spring of 2020, college student Leila Hay thought that for her it would mean at most a few weeks back at home with her parents. Hay had fantasies of monkish productivity. She dreamed of epic study sessions, emerging from lockdown ready to become a top student in her next semester at the University of Hull, in northern England. With her offline life put on hold by social distancing, Hay had enormous blocks of time to spend alone. But she barely cracked her books. Instead, Hay fell headfirst into QAnon when her boyfriend posted an article to Facebook claiming that Tom Hanks was a pedophile. Hay's boyfriend thought it was funny. She thought it was horrifying.

Two years earlier, a Hollywood D-lister named Isaac Kappy had vaulted into the QAnon pantheon by accusing Hanks and other celebrities of being pedophiles. QAnon believers soon came to see Hanks, once as uncontroversial and universally beloved as an actor could hope to be, as a pillar of the cabal's Hollywood wing. Hanks's youthful good looks had persisted into his sixties, something that conspiracy theorists pointed out could be the sign of an addiction to adrenochrome, an invigorating substance QAnon believers think is derived from torturing children. When Hanks went public with his Covid diagnosis, QAnon promoter Liz Crokin announced that Q's operatives, dubbed the "white hats," had "tainted their adrenochrome supply with the coronavirus."

Hay was uniquely vulnerable to QAnon's magnetic pull. At nineteen years old, Hay had recently emerged from adolescence herself, and the possibility of powerful people abusing children chilled her. She had been diagnosed with an anxiety disorder and had a habit of obsessing over things that were out of her control. The idea of the world's most influential people worshipping Satan in pedophile occult rituals was the definition of something that was out of her control, and she couldn't stop reading about it. A few weeks into the lockdown, Hay believed that everything she thought she knew about the world before she discovered QAnon was a lie.

Hay was joining a new generation of QAnon believers created by the pandemic. As people around the world found themselves with more time to spend online and as their lives grew more uncertain and the world more foreign-seeming than ever, interest in QAnon boomed. For new Q recruits like Hay, that meant entering a scary new world where it was hard to tell what was true.

Hay saw friends on Facebook mentioning "Frazzledrip"—a video that QAnon supporters believe shows Hillary Clinton and aide Huma Abedin torturing a young girl in a Satanic ritual. At one point, the two women even wear the girl's face. The mythical video has achieved a totemic power in QAnon circles. Believers claim that "Frazzledrip" is so vile that just watching it might be fatal to the viewer. According to this campfire tale, several New York police officers who watched the "Frazzledrip" video on a laptop seized from Abedin's husband, former congressman Anthony Weiner, were so disturbed by the gruesome footage that they took their own lives.

"Nothing else in my life mattered after that news," Hay said. "It was like my education didn't matter, my friends, my family. Because at the end of the day, these children were being murdered in these rituals."

Hay was terrified and, owing to the pandemic, practically alone. She stopped talking to her friends and burrowed deeper into QAnon, spending at least six hours every day researching new clues.

Hay's life split in two. There was the one she led in the real world, where she argued with skeptical friends and family members who refused to believe her claims about the pedophile cabal. There was the life in which she pretended to be interested in the mundane aspects of her existence, from online schooling to relationships with her family, until she could make it back to the world of QAnon, where she could start her research anew. Q's revelations about the Satanic sexual abuse of children became a weight that pressed on her in every moment. Reflecting later on her pandemic-fueled conversion into QAnon, Hay said that it took over her life: "It becomes who you are."

"I didn't want to believe in QAnon," she said. "I believed in it the same way I believe in climate change. I don't want climate change to be true, but I recognize that it is true."

Hay spent her lockdown summer in a fugue, depressed by the gruesome images QAnon crammed into her head but unable to stop researching to find more. Instead of studying for her upcoming semester back at college, Hay studied the ins and outs of cabal depravity. When she did finally log into her first online class back at college that fall, Hay realized she had no idea what her professor was talking about.

Hay's pandemic brush with QAnon did eventually end. While other Anons had incorporated Q into their identities, Hay was desperate to convince herself it wasn't real. She scoured the Twitter feeds of journalists and academics covering QAnon, but nothing convinced her it was fake. Then she found a Twitter thread that listed dozens of Q predictions that had failed to come true. For Hay, the thread broke through to her in a way that so many arguments with her exasperated friends and family couldn't. She finally realized QAnon wasn't real.

Looking back on her anxious, panicked months as an Anon, Hay thought it was lucky that she was so desperate to get out of the movement, even when she believed in it. She was struck by how many QAnon supporters who she saw join during the pandemic seemed happy to live in the world Q had created for them.

"It just consumed me," she said.

As the spread of Covid-19 washed over the world, the perfect scenario for the spread of misinformation emerged as well. Suddenly tens of millions of people in the United States alone started working from home. Millions more lost their jobs. And everyone had more time to spend on the internet. QAnon was near death when the coronavirus arrived. With 8chan down after the El Paso shooting, Q was homeless. His followers had no leadership and no way to get the Q spin on current events.

The months of silence before Q reappeared on "8kun" had hurt Q's credibility. Getting Q's message out to his followers was supposed to be a mission of staggering importance and patriotic sacrifice, powered by the American military's best technology. Yet the 8chan outage demonstrated that Q was totally reliant on the technical capabilities of Jim Watkins, a mustachioed oddball who seemed far more interested in trolling his critics than saving the American republic.

After two years of covering QAnon's spread, it seemed we might finally be nearing an end. All that time, I expected QAnon to be just one failed prediction or outrageous headline away from utter collapse, only to see it keep growing. But at the end of 2019 it was finally petering out. QAnon shirts weren't as ubiquitous at Trump rallies, and referencing QAnon had fallen out of fashion for pundits aspiring to any kind of mainstream Republican success. It felt like last season's trend. In September 2019, I went to a Trump rally in North Carolina to interview Q believers, expecting to see at least one struggling to sneak a sign past the Secret Service. But I didn't see any open QAnon supporters at the rally at all—not even a Q pin smuggled in a purse, or a "Where we go one" chant.

The Trumpian love affair with Q seemed to be over. After two years of failed predictions, believers were drifting away. Understanding the cabal seemed less pressing, too. Q had appeared a few months into the Mueller investigation, when Trump's presidency was in doubt and his supporters were desperate for good news. By the fall of 2019, though, Mueller's investigation was over. There was no need for Trump's most devoted fans to escape into a fantasy world.

As Q's home came back online, a new virus was spreading throughout the Chinese city of Wuhan. The Covid-19 pandemic plunged the entire world into a crisis unprecedented in living memory, transforming what people everywhere thought about their jobs, their health, and their politics. That chaos launched QAnon to a new level of prominence, accelerating its growth outside the United States and winning new adherents who had never before considered themselves to be conspiracy theorists. As schools and offices shut down, QAnon had just reopened for business.

Before the pandemic, a budding Anon needed to devote a good chunk of their life to getting thoroughly radicalized. They might spend hours and days sorting through cryptic Q posts, and even more time keeping up with the evolving thinking on the latest decodes. They had to learn the hundreds of personalities, good and evil, who made up QAnon's dramatis personae, information that might be doled out only sparingly in rambling YouTube videos. Keeping up-to-date on QAnon was a full-time job.

As QAnon's popularity grew exponentially during the early days of the pandemic, Q himself barely acknowledged the virus. Q had promised for almost three years that globe-shaking events were just around the horizon. But when one arrived, Q fell silent. That left QAnon leaders and their followers a void in which to invent their own response to the pandemic. The result was a web of conspiracy theories that would become jumbled and contradictory even by QAnon's standards. Masks were meant to test the population's compliance with the rise of a global dictatorship, or to cover up human trafficking by making it impossible for kidnapped children to ask bystanders for help. The virus was a hoax, no more harmful than the flu. Or it was incredibly deadly, cooked up by China and the U.S. government's Dr. Anthony Fauci to sabotage Trump's reelection. The vaccines came with microchips for tracking citizens, or they would cause a mass die-off to ensure that tech mogul Bill Gates and his associates could finally rule the world.

The details of who created the virus might have been hazy, but QAnon believers were united around the idea that something suspicious was going on, that the virus indeed was man-made, with the end goal of empowering the world elites and enslaving the average person. As Michael Flynn put it, "This is all about a one-world order."

The fear and anger that surround pandemics have always made fertile ground for conspiracy theories. In medieval Europe, fear of the Black Death inspired widespread violence against Jews, who were blamed for propagating the disease. Mass pogroms during the plague exterminated more than one thousand Jewish communities across Europe, while judges ruled that Jews had spread the disease by poisoning wells. During cholera outbreaks in the 1830s, rumors spread that doctors and other government agents were spreading the disease to cull the number of poor people reliant on welfare programs. In Russia, mobs broke into cholera hospitals to attack medical staff, while rioters in Great Britain targeted doctors over rumors that cholera patients were being murdered so their bodies could be sold to medical schools.

But no one who lived through the Black Death was on Twitter.

QAnon content exploded on major social media platforms in the tumultuous first months of the pandemic, as people everywhere suddenly found themselves desperate for answers about the state of the world. Between March and July 2020, QAnon activity grew significantly on social media, rising by more than 77 percent on Instagram, 63 percent on Twitter, and 175 percent on Facebook, according to a report from the Institute for Strategic Dialogue, a British think tank. Google searches for QAnon-related terms like *WWG1WGA* and *adrenochrome* rose as well, giving the conspiracy theory its biggest spike in search engine traffic since the 2018 Trump rally flooded by QAnon believers and the mysterious 2019 death of billionaire pedophile Jeffrey Epstein.

Some of the pandemic's most iconic places became fodder for QAnon theorizing. After a Christian charity set up a field hospital in New York's Central Park for overflow Covid patients, QAnon personality Timothy

Charles Holmseth claimed the tents were really being set up for a far different purpose. The pandemic was a cover for military attacks on the cabal hidden deep underground in their pedophile bases, Holmseth explained. Once the battles were over, the rescued "mole children" would be rehabilitated in those Central Park tents.

Navy hospital ships dispatched to New York City and Los Angeles drew conspiracy theorists' attention, too. The ships were part of the mole children rescue effort, or played some other covert role in the pandemic response. In Los Angeles, a train engineer who had spent late nights reading QAnon websites deliberately derailed his train near one hospital ship. He described it as an attempt to draw media attention that could uncover the ship's true nature, which he suspected involved a plot to "get rid of" healthy people. Spouting QAnon-style language after his arrest, the engineer told FBI agents that he thought the derailment would "wake people up."

QAnon social media campaigns also sent believers scrambling to their local hospitals—but not to help anyone. In April 2020, less than a month after the shared trauma of Covid's emergence seemed to galvanize and unite most people around the world in support of its victims, Anons began urging one another to #FilmYourHospital. Armed with their smartphones and under the impression that the pandemic was either overblown or entirely fake, they filmed empty hospital lobbies and parking lots. At least one Film Your Hospital ringleader even bypassed security in a hospital to storm a coronavirus ward to prove the virus wasn't so deadly. If the situation was so serious, Film Your Hospital proponents asked, where were all the patients? The empty parking garages could, of course, be explained by the fact that hospitals banned visitors and canceled most non-Covid-related procedures to avoid spreading the disease. But the videos became more grist for the QAnon content mill.

Q's social media power made the conspiracy theory a powerful machine for pumping out disinformation about the virus, even serving as a vector for conspiracy content that wasn't branded explicitly as pro-QAnon. And just two months into the pandemic, QAnon played a key role in the dissemination of a video that would introduce millions of people to coronavirus conspiracy theories.

In May 2020, a well-produced video called "Plandemic" rocketed across Facebook, receiving eight million views in a week. The video starred Dr. Judy Mikovits, a scientist with a history of making bizarre claims. Her reputation as a researcher had been badly damaged in 2011 by a controversy over a paper she wrote positing that chronic fatigue syndrome was caused by a virus. Mikovits's paper on the mysterious illness had initially seemed to be a breakthrough, but the journal that published it retracted her findings after other labs failed to replicate them. Rather than grappling with the failure, Mikovits turned her back on the mainstream scientific community entirely. When Covid started, she began alleging that Fauci had concocted high-level plots against her.

Mikovits threw out a mess of new crackpot ideas in the video, suggesting that the coronavirus might have been cooked up in an American military lab as a bioweapon, that the virus could be cured with a trip to the beach, and that wearing a mask somehow "activates" Covid-19. Despite the outlandishness of her claims, the video's documentary-style production made Mikovits look like a credible whistleblower. Even as Facebook and YouTube tried to ban the video, Mikovits's new fans kept it alive by rapidly uploading copies as quickly as the last ones were deleted.

"Plandemic" starred Mikovits but was the creation of Mikki Willis, a little-known fifty-two-year-old filmmaker in California. Willis had met Mikovits through friends before Covid-19 began to spread in the United States. In the pandemic's first days, Willis asked Mikovits her thoughts on the virus and was impressed. He decided to record Mikovits's unorthodox ideas on the pandemic for a production that he claimed would cost only $2,000.

"We made the video to go viral," Willis boasted to the *Los Angeles Times*.

Ensuring "Plandemic"'s success online meant getting QAnon on board. Willis introduced Mikovits to Zach Vorhies, a prominent Q supporter and former Google employee. Vorhies hatched a plan to turn "Plandemic" into a hit. In a video sent to other right-wing influencers, Vorhies urged them to promote "Plandemic" as soon as it was released, promising that it would be "part of the Great Awakening." He helped Mikovits set up a Twitter account before the video blew up, creating a central place for her fans to find her. One pro-Q Facebook group with almost 25,000 followers posted "Plandemic" early in its momentous launch, declaring it "a must watch."

More than 1,500 people reposted the video from that one group, according to a *New York Times* analysis, ensuring that "Plandemic" would spread into their own individual networks and far beyond its original QAnon context. "Plandemic" attracted attention across Facebook, vastly outpacing the view-counts of similar must-watch footage like a Pentagon video of possible UFOs. Mikovits's name began to appear on protest signs at rallies pushing for an end to lockdown restrictions. Opponents of pandemic measures had a new hero, courtesy of the Q machine.

The coronavirus gave QAnon new life. But as Q followers on every tier of the movement refused to take the vaccine, their beliefs turned fatal. At its core, QAnon is about distrusting institutions. The media, the government, and big business are all out to get you and your kids. The only people you can trust are Q and Trump. That deep-rooted suspicion would make QAnon an obstacle in a public health crisis that required people to trust government officials and pharmaceutical companies. It also drove QAnon believers to seek alternatives.

From the pandemic's first days, QAnon was a clearinghouse for coronavirus treatments that were, at best, useless and, at worst, potentially lethal. QAnon leaders and social media groups first embraced hydroxychloroquine, the inexpensive antimalarial drug that Trump promoted as a quick cure for the pandemic. Hydroxychloroquine's promise faded, and was all but abandoned by QAnon after Trump didn't take it himself while hospitalized with the virus. But the miracle potion pushers didn't stop there. Q's base pivoted quickly to ivermectin, a drug typically used to eliminate worms. Again, there was no solid evidence that ivermectin successfully treated the virus. But it was also cheap, giving believers what they saw as a loophole to avoid Big Pharma's Covid regime. The drugs were a revelation for Q's flock. They didn't have to accept a cabal vaccine filled with microchips or a fatal chemical cocktail brewed by Bill Gates. They could take ivermectin and hydroxychloroquine instead.

Most doctors refused to prescribe either drug for Covid-19, citing their unproven effects. The physicians who were willing to write scripts to anxious believers seized on that opening—for a price. Some doctors promoting ivermectin united in a group called America's Frontline Doctors, which they used to promote the drug as a Covid treatment. They also charged roughly $100 for an online consultation. Online, patients complained the group directed them to pharmacies that overcharged them by hundreds of dollars.

QAnon's embrace of the equivalent of internet folk remedies put believers on a collision course with the virus. The very real risk to QAnon supporters who refused the vaccine became apparent in the summer of 2021. Capitalizing on their new pandemic popularity, prominent QAnon figures hit the road for conferences and even nationwide tours. By their nature, the events drew people who were less likely than the general public to be vaccinated or wear masks. QAnon rallies were bound to become superspreader events.

Hundreds of unmasked QAnon fans packed a Pennsylvania gym one day in July 2021 to see a tomahawk-toting QAnon leader named Scott McKay—or, as he's known to his fans, the "Patriot Streetfighter." McKay sliced the air with his ax and gushed over the idea of executing Democrats. But as McKay shouted and his fans cheered, the air at the rally turned into a coronavirus soup that would sicken McKay and his entourage and eventually kill his elderly father.

Robert David Steele, a conspiracy theorist and self-proclaimed former CIA agent who had been an early QAnon backer, also toured the country that summer. Steele too became sick from the virus. Even from his hospital bed, though, Steele refused to take the vaccine or even acknowledge that Covid-19 was a real illness. In a blog post illustrated with a picture of Steele wearing an oxygen mask, though, he admitted that his outlook wasn't good.

"The bottom line is that my lungs are not functioning," Steele wrote.

A week later, Steele was dead. Rather than take his death as a sign they should get vaccinated, his paranoid followers alleged Steele was murdered to stop him from revealing more explosive truths about the virus.

Rank-and-file QAnon followers began to die, too. Elderly Chicago resident Veronica Wolski was known as a sort of beloved grandmother figure in Q circles, thanks to her practice of posting signs with QAnon messages on a freeway overpass. Wolski refused to get the vaccine and flouted coronavirus mandates, filming herself entering a store in a Lone Ranger–style eye mask to meet a store's "mask" requirement. Her budding following even earned her a meeting with Michael Flynn.

But eventually, the coronavirus came for her. After Wolski was hospitalized, QAnon believers besieged her hospital with phone calls demanding that she receive ivermectin. When Wolski died of the virus, QAnon followers claimed she had been a victim of "medical murder."

In the spring of 2021, I flew to Oklahoma to see the collision between Covid denialism and QAnon in person. A little more than a year after lockdowns began, pro-Q leaders, antivaccine activists, and the head of the state's Republican Party were meeting at a megachurch outside Tulsa for the "Health & Freedom Conference," an event that promised to be a coming-out party for the union of Covid skepticism and Q.

Hundreds of Americans were still dying every day from the coronavirus, and vaccines had only recently become available to the entirety of the adult population. That didn't stop conference organizer Clay Clark, a rising far-right figure and failed local politician, from packing thousands of people from across the country, all of whom hate both masks and vaccines, into one room. After a weekend of swapping conspiracy theories, the conference would culminate in a celebratory mask burning.

But Clark's event wasn't just about Covid. There weren't any Q symbols on his promotional materials, but his speaker's list was filled with QAnon promoters. Ann Vandersteel, a prominent Pizzagate and QAnon leader with an internet radio show, would be there. Gene Ho, a former Trump photographer who had been deeply red-pilled, was touted as one of the biggest names appearing at the event. But Clark had also invited comparatively obscure QAnon leaders, like David Nino Rodriguez, a former boxer who dabbled in QAnon's fringiest corners.

All these Q personalities appearing at one event wasn't an accident. The Tulsa conference would mark QAnon's new guise as a mainstream conservative movement opposed to pandemic restrictions. I knew I had to see it for myself. But security was tight. In the lead-up to the conference, organizers had talked a lot about the need to look out for attacks from left-wing antifascist "Antifa" activists—a threat that seemed remote in an exurb a half-hour drive from Tulsa, and a thousand miles away from anything that might be called an Antifa hotbed. Organizers had also announced that they would keep all but the most right-wing reporters out.

While I used my real name to buy my ticket, I knew I needed a disguise to avoid the chance that some irate QAnon devotee would recognize me and get me kicked out, or worse. Just a few months earlier, I had seen an Associated Press photographer beaten by angry January 6 rioters when one of them accused the photographer of being Antifa. An hour before the conference, I bought a disguise at an outdoor supply store: aviator sunglasses and a baseball cap. I was ready to thrust myself, then only partially vaccinated, into pandemic QAnon. Approaching the conference, I fully expected to contract the coronavirus that day. The night before the January 6 riot, after all, Clark had given a speech in Washington where he urged his audience to embrace strangers, declaring the rally "a mass spreader event!"

Getting my ticket to the conference, I made a friend—a woman who told me how she had quit her job because she refused to wear a mask. Now, more than a year into the pandemic, she was still unemployed, but unconcerned about her dwindling finances. God, she said, had provided for her.

Behind us, two other women who had just met one another swapped Q's latest conspiracy theories at a rapid clip. Biden wasn't really the president, and the White House we saw on TV was just a set at entertainment mogul Tyler Perry's studios in Atlanta. The massive container ship that had recently blocked the Suez Canal was carrying child slaves for the cabal.

"Supposedly, Clinton's foundation and Walmart owns that ship," one woman said. "Supposedly, there were 1,200 children on that ship. Just disgusting!"

The second woman said she was thrilled that her adult son wasn't going to vaccinate his children. Her new friend wasn't so lucky.

"I'm going to lose my family and most of my friends," she said.

Clark was at the mic as I filed into the church, where roughly five thousand people were already waiting. Judging by his remarks, he was still passionate about spreading the virus.

"Hug somebody you don't know," Clark said. "Covid won't kill you!"

The church vibrated for two days with the strange passions set off by a year of pandemic life. A leading lawyer for antivaccine groups pulled a pair of pantyhose over his head, to demonstrate some point about masking. It wasn't clear exactly what his point was, since the pantyhose muffled his remarks, but the crowd loved it. After a New Jersey gym owner took the stage to boast about how he had flouted that state's masking laws, members of the audience started passing up donations to keep his gym afloat. After his speech was over, he left the stage with two sacks of cash, each near bursting.

The people in line with me to get into the conference had been excited about Q. But at first, even Q-friendly speakers didn't mention the movement. Michael Flynn appeared, but didn't even drop a perfunctory "Where we go one, we go all." I thought I would definitely get a QAnon mention out of Vandersteel, a blond-helmeted online video personality known for ersatz Fox News–style "reporting" on conspiracy theories. But when Vandersteel took the stage, she focused instead on her pet theory that the

British Crown spread the coronavirus to get revenge for the American Revolution: "They want their colonies back!"

It would take pro-Trump lawyer Lin Wood to finally unleash the pent-up enthusiasm in the audience. In two speeches at the conference, Wood gave the audience what they wanted all along: permission to show that they were still devoted to Q. Wood had once been a star defamation lawyer, rising to fame working for wrongfully accused Atlanta Olympics bombing suspect Richard Jewell, so legal observers were surprised when, in 2020, Wood added "WWG1WGA" to his Twitter profile. Wood didn't entirely embrace QAnon at first. I called Wood before the election to ask him about whether his Twitter profile change meant he was a QAnon guy now. He insisted he had just watched a video of Flynn taking the QAnon oath with his family on the Fourth of July, and added the phrase to his profile in Flynn's honor.

"I'm not sure exactly what QAnon is," Wood said.

By the time he appeared in Tulsa, though, there was no question that Wood knew exactly what QAnon was. Since we had last talked, Wood had detonated his career by embracing conspiracy theories about the 2020 election. He became a kind of surrogate Q to followers after Q went silent, alluding to dark conspiracies against him and calling for Mike Pence's execution. He suggested that Chief Justice John Roberts was a Satanic pedophile—a convenient idea for Wood to promote since, according to his former legal partners, Wood was obsessed with taking Roberts's spot on the Court. Wood was estranged from his adult children and facing a disbarment investigation in Georgia over his attempts to overturn the election.

Taking the stage on the first night of the conference, Wood came off as a mix between a stand-up comedian and a tent revival preacher. He shambled and capered across the stage, alternately joking and raging against the medical establishment and Bill Gates. And then, for the first time of the conference, he mentioned QAnon.

"Watch out for this next move," Wood told the audience, then waved his hand in a *Q* over and over. "There's your *Q!*"

It was like Wood had pulled the pin out of a grenade. Thousands of people in the audience shot up and cheered just for the idea of the letter *Q*. The real pandemic, Wood said, was child sex-trafficking. The conference might be about "Health and Freedom," but nothing was more important to Wood than "the health of the little children."

"Q does not like child sex-trafficking, Q does not like the Illuminati, Q does not like Satanic worship," Wood thundered in his southern accent.

The crowd exploded. After days of sitting politely as they heard about unlawful school mask mandates and the like, someone was at last giving them something they could bite into: the blood of the cabal and a chance for ultimate revenge on their enemies. It was fine to talk in public about vaccines and masks, the policy issues of the real world. But this was what they really wanted to hear.

Wood's speech was pure lunacy, but it was a collective delusion shared by thousands of people in the room, and many more watching the conference online. This audience might have initially been attracted to QAnon because they opposed lockdown orders, or just because it explained the pandemic state of the world to them in ways that the media, government, or doctors on TV never could. But as I watched them cheer Wood on for nearly an hour, applauding him and egging on his call for Democrats to face firing squads, it became clear that they were ready to move on to something far more ambitious and dangerous than protesting mask laws. QAnon had adapted to the pandemic and grown its base in the process. But as the pandemic receded, QAnon was returning to its origins and bringing those new recruits along to a darker place. Covid had just been a gateway to the story at the heart of QAnon: violent fantasies of political murder.

Chapter 7

The Wizard of Mattoon

Mattoon, Illinois, is a blue-collar factory and farming town on the mid-western prairie most renowned for its annual bagel festival. But when millions of dollars started flowing into the town in the 1990s, it came $100 at a time, wrapped in aluminum foil to avoid government agents.

Suddenly, wealth was everywhere. In the Mattoon post office, an overstuffed package burst open, spilling cash. Working-class residents deposited millions of dollars into their bank accounts. A sheriff's deputy bought a boat and a Harley-Davidson motorcycle. A new sawmill opened, along with a bakery and a diner. A fleet of new trucks appeared at a construction company that had seemed on the verge of collapse.

The mystery windfalls could all be traced back to Clyde Hood, an electrician with a background in running minor cons. Few people in Mattoon knew where his money was coming from, but he had a lot of it. He started opening businesses and handing out sizable, interest-free loans to his friends. He hired other Mattoonians to help with his mysterious income stream. Hood had once been convicted for helping to steal guns from a construction site, and only avoided prosecution for a scheme to sell fraudulent oil securities in Indiana by refusing to turn himself in. So, understandably, Hood's status as Mattoon's new benefactor came as a surprise to his neighbors. Living with his wife in a modest house, Hood didn't exactly look the part of a financial wizard.

"He listed his occupation at one point as a pool hall manager," recalled Carl Walworth, then a crime reporter for the *Mattoon Journal Gazette*. "You could see Clyde in a pool hall."

Whatever Hood was doing now, though, Mattoonians knew it had to be lucrative. Hood collected more than a dozen rare cars. He traveled to Europe, and stashed money in the Caribbean and the Middle East. It didn't matter if Hood looked like the sort of guy you'd find in the pool hall. To the more than ten thousand people across the United States who sent him a fortune later estimated at $50 million, he was a savior sent by God.

In 1994, Hood had begun traveling the country for meetings where he portrayed himself to people outside Mattoon as a banking wheeler-dealer of the highest order. In Hood's telling, he was one of only eight people in the world qualified to trade in "prime banknotes"—an exclusive financial system closed off to all but the most connected investors, where the wealthiest families in the world reaped enormous returns on risk-free investments. After making his fortune in prime banknotes, he had received a message from God. The Holy Spirit visited Hood and told him to "Keep the Lord's Warehouse full" by creating an investment pool called Omega Trust and Trading, selling shares at $100 each to "the little people." By funneling small investors' money into the prime banknote system, he could connect average Americans with the massive profits once reserved for tycoons and European aristocracy. Hood promised potential Omega investors 50-to-1 returns in nine months on each share of $100, which he would then reinvest three times. That meant each $100 share would, in just a few years, become $12.5 million.

Video of Hood making his sales pitch in a Portland motel circulated in church groups across the country, prompting them to send huge amounts of money to Mattoon. A Washington State chiropractor retired and put all his savings into Omega, certain that he would soon be a billionaire, while an ice cream shop owner sold her business and sent $50,000 to the fund. Hood hired more than a dozen people to enroll new investors and rented an office where they could count the money. One of Hood's associates even pulled in Omega's cleaning woman, convincing her to invest her life savings.

Obviously, there were no prime banknotes. Promising naive investors access to a "secret" banking system had become such a common scam in the 1990s that American authorities wondered whether con men like Hood were sharing their grifts with one another. The scam spread across the world, racking up a list of victims that included a major bank in the Czech Republic, a Chicago pension fund, and the government of the island of Nauru. The con also attracted a diverse set of charlatans, including a former pro baseball pitcher who bilked investors out of $7 million by promising sky-high returns from the secret banks. Instead, he blew the money on racehorses until the feds caught up with him. In 1994, a law professor studying prime banknotes estimated that a combined $500 million had already been stolen by criminals running the scheme. Few of Hood's colleagues in crime, though, were as successful or as clever as he was. Hood raked in tens of millions of dollars by targeting churches with his scam, tapping into their social networks to increase his take. He threw in plenty of conspiracy theories about the powers-that-be trying to stop him and keep down the small investor. Hood always promised to deliver the profits on a specific date a few months in the future, but he never came up with the money. Omega investors could call a hotline where Hood left prerecorded messages with his latest excuse, claiming, for example, that Earth's magnetism had delayed the financial transfer by interfering with Hood's satellites. Over the five years Hood ran the hotline, he updated the prerecorded message seventy-two times, always moving the date of the great payoff just a little bit into the future.

Rather than realize that they had been duped, though, most of the "Omegans" bought Hood's explanations. They complained in message boards that nefarious outside forces must be holding up their life-changing paydays. Hood claimed in one hotline message that "numerous individuals and entities"—the government, or rival bankers—didn't want his investors to receive the fabulous returns they were due. Omegans were instructed to wrap their cash contributions in foil before mailing them, to avoid government spies.

So much money flowed into Omega that prosecutors never knew with any certainty exactly how much Hood had made. Later, they estimated that Hood and Omega took in somewhere between $20 million and $50 million between 1994 and 2000.

"You would think that if somebody asked you to put a hundred-dollar bill in tin foil, that might be a bit of a red flag, but it really wasn't for a lot of people," Walworth said.

Stories like Omega or Q involve a huge number of people waiting for a world-changing moment that would never happen. When their predictions fail to come true, though, they commit to their beliefs even more, stunning people outside the movement who could see that they had been fooled. The question of why people believe conspiracy theories, even hurting their own interests in the process, has become a pressing one in a time where conspiracy theorists commit violence, destroy family relationships, and encourage one another to refuse vaccines. But when Syracuse University religion professor Michael Barkun became interested in conspiracy theories in the 1980s, there was practically no research in any academic discipline into why people became enthralled with them. As he worked on a book about a conspiracy-theory-crazed extremist Christian sect that had motivated white supremacist terrorists around the country, Barkun wanted to know more about conspiracy theories and what role they played in American politics.

Historian Richard Hofstadter's landmark 1964 essay, "The Paranoid Style in American Politics," which focused on decades of feverish anticommunism and conservative Barry Goldwater's doomed presidential campaign, created the modern American field of conspiracy theory study. Two decades after Hofstadter's essay came out, though, there wasn't much else for Barkun to go on. Some budding conspiracy theory scholars had begun to feel that one of Hofstadter's central claims—that conspiracy theories were an aberration in American politics, embraced only by the fringes—had stalled research in their nascent field. Contrary to what Hofstadter wrote, his critics said, conspiracy theories have been a powerful force in American politics and culture since before the country's founding, all the way back to the Salem Witch Trials.

American history is filled with conspiracy theory beliefs playing out in mainstream politics. In the country's first years, Thomas Jefferson's opponents accused him of colluding with Illuminati groups in Europe. In the 1830s, American Protestants reacted to waves of Catholic immigration by obsessing over claims that Catholic priests were sexually abusing Protestant girls in church schools, in a scheme organized by the pope and the Catholic head of the Austrian Empire. As the country was torn apart by slavery, abolitionist forces were motivated by conspiracy theories about "Slave Power," the idea that every death of an abolitionist could be attributed to a vast network of assassins run by proslavery states.

But defining exactly what a conspiracy theory is can be difficult, since even people with the most eccentric beliefs are unwilling to self-identify as conspiracy theorists. Joseph Uscinski, a University of Miami professor who has been at the forefront of research on QAnon, summed up conspiracy theories in 2014 with a colleague as "an explanation of historical, ongoing, or future events that cites as a main causal factor a small group of powerful persons, the conspirators, acting in secret for their own benefit against the common good." Another academic definition holds that a conspiracy theory is "a text that falsely accuses a group of individuals of orchestrating a plot that has harmed or will harm society."

Barkun has his own definition of a conspiracy theory. To a believer, Barkun writes, "Nothing happens by accident, nothing is as it seems, and everything is connected." At a time when QAnon believers see every random event—a flash of light off the Pacific Coast of the United States, or a ship running aground in the Suez Canal—as proof of a plot to shoot down Air Force One or a foiled scheme to smuggle children to Hillary Clinton, respectively, Barkun's definition fits.

The appeal of the belief that unseen, malevolent forces control the world isn't restricted by racial, gender, or class boundaries. Blaming personal failings on the misdeeds of an unseen cabal has an obvious emotional appeal, relieving a person of taking responsibility for their own problems. It's also a simple way to explain a complex world. Rather than accept that random, chaotic, deadly events can happen out of nowhere, the believer can simplify the world by blaming tragic events on a conspiracy.

QAnon is the latest American example of one of the most enduring kinds of conspiracy theory: a "superconspiracy," a conspiracy theory that explains dozens of lesser conspiracy theories by blaming all of the events on what Barkun calls a "distant but all-powerful evil force." In the 1990s, evangelical leaders and conspiracy theorists on talk radio claimed there was a sinister "New World Order" at play behind seemingly distinct events like the Waco siege, UFO sightings, and rising drug addiction in American cities. In the same way, QAnon believers now weave issues like Trump's 2020 defeat, the coronavirus pandemic, and child sexual abuse into one coherent narrative that puts all the blame on a shadowy cabal. The names of the villains have changed, but the human desire to believe in a single powerful force controlling the world remains.

Shaini Goodwin discovered Omega in 1998, when Clyde Hood was still promising to divert billions of dollars to his investors on God's orders. Goodwin sent Hood $200, good enough for two shares and a sizable fortune once Hood transferred Omega profits from a bank in the English Channel.

Without the money promised by Omega, Goodwin's future looked bleak. In her early fifties, Goodwin lived in a double-wide trailer in rural Washington State with her sick mother. She had a history of financial problems, including a past bankruptcy. When she bought into Omega, Goodwin had a $12,000 federal tax lien hanging over her head. She already dabbled in fringe beliefs, taking classes at Ramtha's School of Enlightenment—an alleged cult in Washington whose leader claims to channel the voice of a 35,000-year-old warrior named Ramtha.

On Omega forums, Goodwin adopted the moniker "Dove of Oneness" and began to imbue Omega-watching with a New Age spirituality. Styling herself as the "Deep Throat of the Northwest," she claimed that she had access to inside information that proved that the Omega payoff would soon take place. Goodwin amassed a following among dispirited Omegans. She also started to solicit donations from investors eager to hear more good news about Omega.

One day in August 2000, two years after Goodwin bought her shares in Omega, federal law enforcement officers arrested Hood, his wife, and seventeen associates. Hood eventually pleaded guilty, received a fourteen-year prison sentence, and agreed to testify against other defendants. But even after Hood admitted that Omega was a rip-off, calling it a "scam" while testifying against one of his underlings, Omegans continued to believe. Hood, they thought, was being pressured by prosecutors to say Omega was a con. They embraced British conspiracy theorist David Icke's claim that the world is controlled by reptilian aliens, blaming the lizard-people for delaying the Omega payoff. The Omegans' unflagging hopes created some sad scenes. Online, Omegan leaders insisted that Navy SEALs had been dispatched, possibly disguised as pizza deliverymen, to deliver the massive payoffs to investors on a particular date. Omega shareholders took time off work so they could wait at home for their millions of dollars, peeking out their windows when a pizza man passed by. The money never arrived. Others raised money for Hood's bail, convinced that he could turn Omega into a success if he could just get out of jail long enough for one more trade.

Scouring the internet for more proof that her Omega money would arrive soon, Goodwin came upon the writings of Harvey Barnard, an eccentric Louisiana engineer who believed he had written a law that would save American business. Barnard called his bill the "National Economic Stabilization and Recovery Act," or "NESARA." Barnard mailed one thousand copies of his draft legislation to congressional offices and awaited the swift passage of his bill. Because no one had ever heard of Harvey Barnard or NESARA, the draft was immediately ignored.

Long after Barnard's draft bill had landed in wastepaper baskets across the U.S. Capitol, Goodwin discovered his NESARA website. Barnard's original bill had no connection to Omega. Without his permission, Goodwin took it much further. NESARA wasn't just an amateur economic theory, Goodwin told her followers—it was a bill for restructuring the entire world. NESARA would eliminate credit card debt, mortgage payments, and the Federal Reserve. Omega was just one of fifty programs within NESARA, each of which would shower fabulous wealth on ordinary people. Notably, considering her own five-figure tax debts, Goodwin said NESARA would also abolish income taxes and the Internal Revenue Service.

Best of all, Goodwin told Omegans, Congress had already passed NESARA in 2000. In a story that echoes QAnon's vision of a "Storm" where heroic soldiers circumvent the democratic process in what could be seen less charitably as a coup, Goodwin claimed that special forces troopers ordered Bill Clinton to sign NESARA at gunpoint. Alas, the Supreme Court had put a temporary gag order on everyone involved to not discuss the bill's existence. Only Goodwin could reveal the truth.

As Goodwin kept up the updates from her trailer, NESARA started to mutate. Benevolent aliens were added to the mix. Goodwin won fans who had never been involved in the original Omega scam, ultimately attracting at least 15,000 people to her message. Supporters of the mythical law deluged newspapers with letters to the editor, demanding that Congress finally unveil NESARA. Believers wrote "NESARA NOW" on their utility bills, refusing to pay on the grounds that the bill absolved them of the debt. Postcards demanding NESARA's implementation flooded into the

Supreme Court. Baffled pedestrians in Washington, D.C., watched as bill-board trucks calling for NESARA circled the city.

While QAnon supporters would later interpret news events in the world as signals about the battle between benevolent "white hats" and malevo-lent "black hats" ahead of "the Storm," Goodwin saw everything as battles between good "white knights" and evil "dark agenda" agents, all centered on a fight to enact NESARA. The attacks of September 11, 2001, were organized by the U.S. government to prevent the Federal Reserve from en-acting NESARA from an office in the World Trade Center. Home lifestyle icon Martha Stewart was framed for insider trading because she supported NESARA. When a Malaysia Airlines flight disappeared in 2014, blogs sup-porting the conspiracy theory claimed that the vanished passengers volun-teered to be taken as hostages by the aliens overseeing NESARA. But like Hood before her and Q after her, Goodwin kept moving the date of the great moment that NESARA would be implemented, pushing it forward a few months each time. And like Q, she thrilled her audience with gruesome tales of their foes' demise, claiming at one point that "100,000 bankers" who opposed the legislation "have been eliminated."

Goodwin's fictional world even outlasted her death in 2010. After she died, the head of the NESARA website claimed that Goodwin had sacri-ficed herself to send a message to the aliens. But it wasn't all bad news. The webmaster also announced that Goodwin had prepared a few trades prom-ising "more than favorable returns" before her demise. All that was needed now was a little money from her fans.

These days, NESARA, now often called GESARA—the "national" has been replaced by "global"—has become a key part of QAnon lore. As early Q believers tried to puzzle out the clues, conspiracy theorists who already believed in NESARA claimed Q was talking about their law. NESARA offers something personal for QAnon believers waiting for the Storm: a world without debts or disease. QAnon followers write "NESARA/GESARA" on their signs and tell one another about the perfect world that awaits them.

Researchers have struggled to find what makes certain people more likely to support and believe in conspiracy theories. Some research suggests that people with Manichean worldviews who see the world as more black-and-white are more likely to support conspiracy theories. Other factors that indicate a tendency toward conspiracism include preferences for strict hierarchies, holding a dark view of human nature and higher distrust of other people, and viewing the world as a jungle where "the strong dominate the weak." Conspiracy theory believers often display obsessions with the sufferings of their own identity group—their religion, their race, their country—at the hands of sinister outside groups.

"Sometimes it's a group of plutocrats," Barkun said. "Sometimes it's Jews."

As a way of seeing the world, conspiracy theories offer their believers a chance to feel smarter than the average person, giving them a sense of agency or at least understanding over events that often seem totally out of control. "They give you a sense that you are one of the few people who's learned to see through the deception and the bullshit," said Peter Knight, a professor at the University of Manchester who studies conspiracy theories.

Conspiracy theory beliefs can promote other negative behaviors, too. Believers in conspiracy theories that AIDS was created by the government are less likely to use condoms during sex, one study found. Another group of researchers found that conspiracy theorists are much more likely than the average person to support political violence.

As strange as theories like QAnon can seem, though, conspiratorial thinking is in general widespread. A 2013 study found that 63 percent of Americans surveyed held at least one conspiratorial belief when asked to choose whether they believed in any of four conspiracy theories: whether Barack Obama was covering up significant information about his early life, the government knew in advance about the 9/11 attacks, or the 2004 or 2012 elections were marred by severe voter fraud. Another survey taken in 2011 found that 55 percent of Americans polled believed in at least one conspiracy theory when presented with seven options, ranging from the idea that Jews and oil companies caused the Iraq War to the claim that George Soros is deliberately destabilizing the American government. The most popular conspiracy theory in that poll, held by 25 percent of respondents, maintained that bankers caused the 2008 financial crisis deliberately to empower the Federal Reserve.

There's no one factor that makes someone believe in conspiracy theories. But after talking to QAnon believers for years, I've started to notice some commonalities that go beyond politics. They often seem angry about the state of the world and their place in it. Conversely, they get a special pleasure in the knowledge they think Q has shared with them, reveling in the secrets that set them apart from the average person. As one believer put it to me with a smile, they know the news before everyone else. In a confusing world, a conspiracy theory like QAnon gives people something to put their faith in.

"Many of them are perfectly normal," Barkun said of conspiracy theorists. "It would be nice to say, 'Well, they're all crazy people,' but they're not."

Despite the growing research into what causes people to believe in conspiracy theories, it can still be deeply unsettling to find it appearing in your home. In 2020, Amanda, a Portland homemaker, watched as QAnon took over her family. "It's been absolutely life changing," Amanda told me. "I've been a different person because of how it upended my foundational reality."

Amanda's uncle, her mother's brother, had long dabbled in conspiracy theories, encouraging his relatives to investigate the "Hollow Earth" pseudoscience that posits there's a lively separate world inside the planet. Amanda and her mother had laughed off his off-the-wall Facebook posts. Then, a few months into the pandemic, Amanda noticed that her mother was posting about the "real" king of England—a New Zealand man named

Joseph Gregory Hallett, whose farcical claim to the British throne has been embraced by QAnon believers. Amanda ignored the posts, only to see her mother write more about QAnon, and eventually block her daughter to stop her from criticizing Q on her Facebook page.

Soon other family members signed on to QAnon. A police officer her uncle was dating convinced the family to stock up on emergency supplies, claiming that the country would essentially be shut off for ten days as Trump reestablished control against the deep state. Amanda's grandfather posted a meme on Facebook claiming that Bill Gates was being tried in India for injuries caused by vaccines. But her grandfather didn't believe the meme, because he had read *another* post claiming that Gates had already been executed.

"My relationship with my family was just completely, completely upended," Amanda said.

Amanda became depressed for nearly a year, lying down for hours at a time, unable to comprehend how her family, and especially her mother, had turned on her for QAnon.

"One day she was a sane person and we laughed at her brother, and the next day she was all in," Amanda said.

Watching QAnon spread in her family, Amanda thought of a nature documentary she'd seen about a tropical fungus that takes over insects' minds and spreads by exploding out through their bodies.

"I think about the caterpillars and ants that can catch that fungus and makes them climb up to a high place, and then they explode and get it all over everybody else," Amanda said. "It's just like that. There's no more thinking to it."

NESARA and QAnon both fall into a category of political or religious movement called millenarianism: the belief that a utopian world is right around the corner. Millenarian movements get their name from early Christians, who thought the world would change with Jesus's return at the millennium. More recently, scholars classify millenarian movements as groups that believe the world will experience a final epochal change that brings in an unprecedented era of peace and prosperity. Often, the only people who will benefit from this new world are those who believed beforehand that it would happen. They can be religious or secular. Soviet communism, Nazism, and Islamic terrorist groups like al-Qaeda and ISIS have all been described as millenarian movements.

The United States' most famous millenarian movement ended, like so many others, in disappointment. Starting in 1831, preacher William Miller convinced thousands of people around New York that the world would end with Jesus coming back to Earth on March 21, 1844. Miller's followers, called the Millerites, threw themselves into proselytizing Miller's prediction and prepared for a new era. When March 21 came and went, Miller's followers were, for the most part, not dissuaded. It was only after Miller's second date for the Second Coming failed to materialize that Miller's movement fractured in a moment that came to be called the Great Disappointment.

QAnon can seem focused on the present, with followers litigating the meaning of 8chan posts or Trump's hand gestures. But its goal is a utopian one: the post-cabal world that follows the hyperviolent Storm, often with a NESARA-style economic utopia attached. Those hopes for their own personal betterment, with debts and diseases abolished, mean there's more on the line for believers than who controls the White House. They think this affects the most important parts of their lives: their children, their finances, their health. This is personal for them.

When conspiracy theories fail to come true, supporters are faced with a choice: admit they were wrong and deal with the humiliation, or commit to their beliefs even further.

"When you make that kind of psychic investment in something, the costs of saying 'I was wrong' are so high that it may seem cheaper to buy into some kind of rationalization, even if it seems absurd, than to say, 'I made a mistake,'" Barkun said.

Few Omegans proved willing to take that embarrassing step and admit they were wrong. Federal authorities ultimately recovered just $12.5 million of the money Hood was believed to have stolen through Omega, selling off his fleet of classic cars to recoup some of it. When they offered his estimated 10,000 victims the chance to receive the money, only 368 victims applied, receiving $1.69 million in restitution. Instead of asking for their money back, Omegans showed up outside the courtrooms where Hood or other Omega conspirators were on trial to show support for the people who had conned them.

The failure to distribute much of the seized money surprised Esteban F. Sanchez, the prosecutor who took down Hood and his associates. He had expected thousands of people to apply to get their money back. But most Omegans kept the faith, fearful that applying for money from the government restitution pool would mean losing out on millions when Hood's plans came to fruition. As the aggrieved Omegans saw it, Sanchez's effort to undo the damage caused by Hood's con was just another plot to rob them of their fortunes.

"This vast group out there still believes that this big truck of money is going to come in, despite all of our efforts to tell them it won't," Sanchez said.

Chapter 8

Those Who Know Can't Sleep

Kim Picazio was working late one night when a dozen Fort Lauderdale, Florida, police officers hustled into her office, guns drawn.

"Are you okay?" one of them said. "Are you Kim Picazio?"

Picazio, the officer said, faced a credible threat to her life. The FBI and the U.S. Marshals Service were involved. She had to go. As the officers led Picazio out of her office, she felt like her life as she had known it was over—QAnon wanted her dead.

Before that day, Picazio was a gregarious lawyer with a thriving family-law practice in southern Florida. But now, tens of thousands of people around the country who watched QAnon shows on YouTube thought of her as one of history's greatest villains. To them, she was the head of a cabal that kidnapped and trafficked children, then subjected them to Satanic rituals, all to extract a precious compound from their blood. Those YouTube viewers were told that they personally should take action to stop her—if necessary, with a bullet.

QAnon promoter Field McConnell, a former airline pilot turned 9/11 conspiracy theorist, urged his fans to arrest Picazio and send her to Guantanamo Bay. Waving around an edited picture of Picazio that showed her head cut off by a samurai sword, he read out her phone number and address to online viewers. "You're on my radar and you're going to die," McConnell said about Picazio in a video. "I hope that is clear enough."

"Can you imagine?" Picazio told me. "I have three children at home. I seriously didn't know what to do."

QAnon's focus on the concept of "Satanic ritual abuse" can seem absurd, but it is not unprecedented. The movement's fixations on child-trafficking and occult abuses are built on the ruins of an earlier hysteria: the "Satanic Panic" of the 1980s, when the fear that otherwise normal professionals around the country may be abusing children in Satanic rituals suddenly became an urgent issue. Both QAnon and the Satanic Panic demonstrate how adults who often have the best intentions can lose all sense of what is real when faced with grotesque stories about children being abused by devil-worshipping cults.

The case that would come to symbolize the Satanic Panic began in Manhattan Beach, California, in 1983. A woman named Judy Johnson became convinced that her two-year-old son was being sexually abused at a daycare called McMartin Preschool because, she claimed, his anus itched. Johnson's other evidence for her suspicions were just as thin. For example, her son had pretended to be a doctor with a thermometer, which she took to be symbolic of her son's teacher's penis. The child's doctor didn't see any evidence of abuse, but Johnson insisted he had been abused and soon reported the teacher, Ray Buckey, to the police as a child molester.

Police arrested Buckey and sent hundreds of families whose children had attended McMartin a letter requesting more information on potential molestation at the school. Parents were told to ask their children about whether they had seen any otherwise-innocuous events that police said could indicate "sodomy" or other sexual abuse had taken place, including Buckey leaving the room with a child during their nap time or taking a child's temperature. The letter proved a serious miscalculation. Rather than gathering evidence for the case, it inspired parents to see whatever comments their children made about the daycare as proof of molestation.

The police request that parents interview their own children about an emotionally charged topic like sexual abuse also backfired. The children, being children, made up outlandish stories that both investigators and their parents took seriously. The number of sexual abuse allegations against McMartin staffers exploded, pulling in not just Buckey but several other teachers at the school. Increasingly, however, the stories weren't only about sexual abuse. They were lurid accounts of children being buried alive, forced to drink blood, or flown in airplanes to distant locations for Satanic ceremonies. The children related accounts that were obviously untrue, featuring eyewitness stories of Buckey flying in the air, the appearance of a devilish "goatman," and electric drills jammed through children's armpits. Several stories featured animals, with kids claiming McMartin staffers had murdered animals and made the kids watch, or that the children themselves had been attacked by a lion.

Los Angeles's district attorney initially charged seven McMartin employees, including Buckey and his mother, who also worked at the daycare, with more than one hundred counts of child abuse.

The highly publicized McMartin case became the most visible trial of the Satanic Panic, but the mania wasn't limited to Manhattan Beach. In the early 1980s, ritual sexual abuse investigations appeared all over the country, each premised on the idea that covens of Satanists were torturing children. Police departments hired Satanism "experts" to train detectives on how to pursue devil worshippers. And like in the McMartin case, the detectives handling other investigations universally failed to find any physical evidence of this supposedly widespread phenomenon.

The Satanic Panic became a part of pop culture, in part because of credulous media reports. On the ABC newsmagazine show *20/20*, a reporter speculated that the Satanic rituals hadn't been reported earlier because the children were under the influence of mind control. Tabloid TV journalist Geraldo Rivera earned massive ratings with a TV special on the Satanism threat, warning that it was more likely than not that Satanists were in viewers' own communities. Faced with the prospect that the McMartin child witnesses were too scared to testify, *The A-Team* star Mr. T answered prosecutors' call for family-friendly celebrities who could attend the trial to cheer them up.

Both media coverage and law enforcement's treatment of the allegations ignored that the young children were incredibly suggestible, often to degrees that embarrassed prosecutors. In *We Believe the Children*, a history of the Satanic Panic, author Richard Beck describes an incident that blew up on the McMartin prosecutors. After a boy testifying at a hearing confidently identified several people he claimed to have seen at a Satanic ritual, Buckey's defense attorney showed the child a picture of another man and asked if he, too, had been at the ceremony. The boy answered without hesitation that the man had participated in the ritual. Buckey's attorney, triumphant, showed the picture to the rest of the courthouse. It was martial arts star Chuck Norris.

Historians and psychologists have pointed to several factors driving the Satanic Panic. One, it came as America was grappling with a history of ignoring genuine allegations of sexual abuse, making people more willing to believe claims no matter how improbable they seemed. It has also been described as a symptom of larger fears about social change, including the increasing number of working mothers reliant on daycare. "Recovered memory and the day care and ritual abuse hysteria drove the social repression of two ideas," Beck writes in his account of the Satanic Panic. "First, the nuclear family was dying. Second, people mostly did not want to save it."

The Satanic Panic was also powered by the rise of the religious right in America. Evangelical pastors promoted the idea that America was under attack by decadent forces from within, including Satanists. Speakers promoting the idea of ritual abuse gave lectures at churches, sometimes inspiring new clusters of Satanic abuse allegations in the communities where they spoke.

Still, despite the amateur investigators' best efforts, and after years of frenzied attempts to bring the Satanists to justice, the Satanic Panic began to totter under the absurdity of the allegations. Cases fell apart, convictions were overturned, and people who had supposedly been murdered during the rituals were found alive and unharmed.

The first McMartin trial finally ended in 1990 with Buckey's mother acquitted on all counts, and Buckey himself acquitted of most of the charges. At a second trial, the jury deadlocked on the charges against Buckey, with the majority favoring acquittal. Prosecutors opted not to try Buckey for a third time. At a cost to the government of $16 million, it remains the most expensive, longest criminal trial in United States history.

While Pizzagate was a fringe belief promoted by a few vocal conspiracy theorists and right-wing Twitter personalities, the Satanic abuse hysteria of the 1980s was championed by police departments, judges, prosecutors, and prominent members of the media. No one has been convicted for involvement in QAnon's fictional cabal, but during the Satanic Panic, dozens of people were sentenced to prison terms. Many of them received decadeslong sentences that were only overturned after they had already served time bearing the stigma of child molestation. Teachers accused in the McMartin case lost their homes, or temporarily saw their children taken into state custody. One former Miami daycare operator is still in prison on a Satanic Panic charge, serving a 165-year sentence.

The Satanic Panic lives on today in QAnon, down to specific imagery used in both cases. Planes became a key part of the Satanic Panic hysteria after several children in unrelated cases claimed that they were taken by plane to the rituals. Today, QAnon believers analyze publicly available flight trackers to find child-smuggling planes, or study flight logs that they claim prove Chief Justice John Roberts flew to an island owned by Jeffrey Epstein.

Just as parents in the McMartin case and other alleged Satanic ritual abuse incidents focused on tunnels, QAnon believers have their own special fixation on such secret pathways and networks, sketching out how they imagine the cabal traffics children, hidden from curious eyes aboveground. They sketch elaborate maps of the tunnels they believe connect cabal front-businesses, drawing lines between Comet Ping Pong and a bookstore where Barack Obama once spoke.

But the most dangerous parallel the Satanic Panic holds for QAnon comes from the amateur investigators, driven by their frustration with police indifference to attempt some detective work of their own. With little support from official authorities, QAnon believers have stepped up, building online and in-person networks willing to protect children when no one else will. If the police aren't going to do something about devil worshippers, they'll do it themselves.

Picazio's phantom life as the leader of a child-trafficking cabal began with a real disappearance. One day in February 2009, five-year-old Haleigh Cummings vanished from her father's trailer home in Satsuma, Florida, and was never seen again. Cummings's disappearance coincided with a boom in sensational television coverage of legal news, when millions of cable TV viewers could be titillated by a murder trial centered on a missing child or pregnant woman. The most successful ringmaster in cable news' lucrative true-crime circus was host Nancy Grace, who used her show on the HLN network to alternately berate and comfort the figures who suddenly found themselves at the center of the stories.

Cummings's disappearance had all the trappings of the kind of story that would be a hit on cable: volunteers conducting fruitless searches in the woods, feuding family members, and a long list of suspects with shady backgrounds for viewers to speculate about. As word of the missing child broke out of Florida media and into the national news cycle, the atmosphere in Satsuma became increasingly carnival-like. Geraldo Rivera, twenty years removed from his stint as the front man for the Satanic Panic, faced off with Cummings's father at his house and received an official trespassing warning.

As the media storm descended on Cummings's family in Satsuma, Picazio was building her family law practice four hours away in Fort Lauderdale. She took a pro bono position as the lawyer for Cummings's mother, Crystal Sheffield, who found herself embroiled in a media mess of her own after the press started looking into her past drug use and questioned her fitness as a parent.

As Sheffield's attorney, Picazio appeared on Grace's HLN show and other legal news programs. The media attention meant Picazio was contacted by a parade of psychics and armchair detectives, each with their own pet theory about the girl's fate. Amid the wave of off-the-wall tips, Picazio received an email from Timothy Charles Holmseth, a Minnesota blogger with his own ideas about what happened to Cummings. But when Holmseth sent her a list of interview questions, they were nothing like what an actual reporter would send. Instead, Holmseth's list included queries about "what I look like with my clothes off, the skin on my stomach, the positions he believes I enjoy having sexual intercourse" and even "the smell of consistency of my vaginal discharge," according to court documents later filed by Picazio.

"Then I knew this guy is not a real journalist," Picazio said. "I don't know what he is, but he must just be a weirdo."

Picazio ignored Holmseth, like she had so many cranks before him. But for Holmseth, Picazio's refusal to take his ravings seriously turned her into the villain at the center of the Cummings case. On his obscure blog, Holmseth began to write daily articles about Picazio, claiming that she was a sex trafficker covering up Cummings's murder or alleging that she was carrying on a string of affairs.

Holmseth seemed to have an inexhaustible amount of time to spend pursuing Picazio. Launching his attacks from his home, Holmseth devoted his life to the Cummings case. In his online appearances, he came off like a stereotype of an obsessive conspiracist blogger. He had glasses, a goatee, and an ability to talk for hours about every intricacy of his theory of the case.

Using the internet to draw connections between Picazio and those she knew and worked with, Holmseth began to target as many people as possible for whatever tie they had to Picazio. According to court documents, Holmseth harassed a woman whose children played soccer with Picazio's, sending a letter to that woman's employer claiming she was a criminal. He even mailed a letter to one of Picazio's children.

After months of harassment, Picazio would allege, Holmseth sent

Picazio a picture of her friend's teenage brother at a track meet, with "Registered Sex Offender" written across the image. If she didn't answer his questions about Cummings's disappearance, Holmseth told Picazio, he would write a story labeling the young man as a sex offender, poisoning the search engine results for his name and smearing him in his small town. Picazio broke down and called Holmseth, hopeful that a conversation might mean he would finally stop harassing her. She answered his bizarre questions about the Cummings case and thought that his harassment might finally be over.

"I was literally crying, calling that guy in the middle of the night to keep that horrible lie that could completely destroy someone's life forever from going out," Picazio said.

But even when Picazio capitulated, Holmseth didn't stop. Her business took a hit as potential clients came across Holmseth's articles. When Picazio hired a lawyer herself to write Holmseth a cease-and-desist letter, Holmseth wasn't deterred. Instead, he just started harassing her lawyer, and everyone at his firm, too. "It was so horrendous for someone to completely infiltrate every person and everything in your life," Picazio said. "You eventually want to isolate from everyone you know, professionally and personally, to protect them. And that's what I did."

Suing Holmseth for defamation would be pointless, Picazio knew, since he had few assets. Instead, she started to file complaints about Holmseth with police in the Minnesota town where Holmseth lived. In 2011, she won a protective order in Florida that required Holmseth to delete his attacks against her. Even if she had a protective order, it was useless if police officers wouldn't arrest Holmseth for violating it.

Holmseth violated the order and kept up the online assault. Picazio then had to spend nearly a year trying to convince law enforcement officials in both Florida and Minnesota to take Holmseth's attacks seriously. Tired of looking at Holmseth's daily attacks by herself, Picazio hired Alexandria Goddard, an Ohio true-crime blogger, to catalog Holmseth's smears so Picazio could later bring proof to police. Goddard started collecting Holmseth's attacks on Picazio to prove that he was breaking the law. She knew the evidence against him would have to be overwhelming before police would arrest Holmseth for internet harassment.

"A lot of police departments and prosecutors live by the old adage 'If you just turn off the computer, it's not there anymore,'" Goddard told me. "But that's not the case. Every person you know is online. They have the ability to be exposed to this garbage."

Finally, in December 2012, Holmseth was sentenced to one year of probation. As soon as Holmseth's probation ended, he started blogging about Picazio again. But this time, he sprinkled asterisks in her name, apparently thinking that he would somehow evade the restraining order if he didn't mention her full name. After years of legal battles with the slippery blogger, Picazio was ready to declare the asterisks a small victory and move on. If Holmseth wanted to blog about a child-trafficking lawyer named "K*m P*cazio" in blog posts that wouldn't show up in her Google results, she could settle for that.

Holmseth's obsession with Picazio lasted for nearly ten years, but he didn't appear to have convinced anyone else to join his crusade against her. Holmseth could rage about the lawyer on Twitter, but he had fewer than twenty followers. Then QAnon began, and Timothy Holmseth went from a crank with a blog to a heroic whistleblower fighting the cabal.

As QAnon grew in early 2018, Holmseth seemed to instinctively see it as an audience that might care quite a lot about his allegations of child-trafficking and abuse, especially since they could be tied, however tenuously, to a real missing-child case. Holmseth keyed into the budding conspiracy theory movement early, sprinkling each round of tweets and YouTube videos about Picazio with QAnon hashtags. Gullible Anons were easy marks for someone like Holmseth, who already had a well-formed, if nonsensical, theory about the Cummings disappearance to push. In return, Holmseth seemed to fall for QAnon's vision of the world. His ideas about a pedophile conspiracy grew far more elaborate. But most important, he offered a target for new QAnon believers seeking a place to put their rage: Kim Picazio.

Holmseth's Twitter following exploded, going in just a few months from a dozen followers to 20,000. Watching Holmseth's fan base grow, Goddard—herself a veteran of several years-long internet feuds—knew Picazio was in trouble.

"I'm not trying to scare the crap out of you or anything, but this is bad," Goddard told her.

Q never mentioned Picazio, and the vast majority of QAnon ignored Holmseth's claims about her. But using QAnon hashtags and his fevered blog posts, Holmseth managed to break off a portion of the QAnon fan base for his own ends, aiming them like a weapon at Picazio. After dressing up his lonely, decade-long grudge as a QAnon side quest, Holmseth started networking with other QAnon influencers. He claimed to be the head of the "Pentagon Pedophile Task Force," a top-secret government agency tasked by Trump with bringing down the cabal. He drew a *Q* on his car window, posing for pictures with it for his fans.

"He's going to be a danger to me," Picazio recalls thinking, as Holmseth's digital following grew. "This guy gets an army, I'm screwed."

It was too late. In 2019, Picazio tried again to enforce the restraining order against Holmseth. Holmseth's first arrest in 2012 went unnoticed on the conspiracy theorist internet, where there was no QAnon to twist him into a victim of deep-state persecution. But when police arrested Holmseth this time, Holmseth became a cause célèbre for QAnon believers.

Out on bail ahead of his August 2019 trial, Holmseth appeared on a YouTube show run by Field McConnell, a Wisconsin conspiracy theorist who had turned his channel into a sort of QAnon talk show. From his office in the small town of Plum City, McConnell hosted interviews with other QAnon promoters and thrilled his audience with the stories of children abducted by social workers working for the cabal. His show featured a rotating cast of characters with names like "Dr. Good Vibes" and "Agent Margaritaville," each of whom claimed to have some insight into the depravity of the deep state.

McConnell had 40,000 YouTube subscribers, a massive amount for conspiracy theory YouTube, and his videos were often watched more than 500,000 times each. When Holmseth appeared in McConnell's office for the first time in July 2019, Holmseth claimed that Donald and Melania Trump had ordered him to appear on the show. Holmseth became McConnell's new star, and Picazio was their shared victim.

McConnell, a bearded, elderly man with a fondness for wearing Hawaiian shirts, had lost his job flying planes for Northwest Airlines in 2007 after missing a required psychiatric exam. Using his knowledge of the airline industry, McConnell had created a second career as a 9/11 conspiracy theorist, claiming he had proof that shadowy forces had rigged planes to explode during terrorist attacks. McConnell pivoted to QAnon shortly after it began, using the popular new conspiracy theory to boost his own profile.

McConnell directed his audience's fury at Picazio, dubbing her "Ms. Piggy" and ordering fans to harass her. He urged his followers to take her into custody, reading out her address and phone number and speculating about exactly how she would be executed, debating if it would be by hanging or firing squad.

The death threats poured into Picazio's office, as McConnell and Holmseth asked their fans to send money so they could keep up the fight. But they weren't the only QAnon promoters Picazio worried about. Whenever a prominent figure in Trump's orbit like former national security adviser Michael Flynn refused to denounce QAnon or even suggested that the conspiracy theory was real, the QAnon believers targeting Picazio became emboldened, seeing it as more proof that they were right.

As the attacks ramped up, Picazio could only hope that Holmseth's trial, where he was expected to be found guilty, would stop the attacks from QAnon believers. But Holmseth had started to rile up his fans with a new conspiracy theory, alleging that Picazio wasn't just kidnapping children. She was drinking their blood.

———————

For QAnon believers like Holmseth, the imagined cabal's activities are in the pursuit of something more concrete than just worshipping the devil. They want a mysterious substance called adrenochrome. To the most radicalized QAnon believers, this elusive substance can only be found in the brains of children who have been sexually tortured in Satanic rituals and is highly sought after for its energizing qualities.

After it's been harvested from the children, the adrenochrome is distributed to the top Democrats, Hollywood celebrities, and bankers in the cabal and acts as a liquid fountain of youth that will keep them alive.

Adrenochrome is a real substance, created in the body when adrenaline is oxidized. In the 1960s, researchers speculated that it could be somehow linked to the appearance of schizophrenia. But adrenochrome's place in QAnon lore appears to truly derive from its unearned position in counterculture fiction as the ultimate psychedelic, a stand-in for a mythical illicit substance described in books like Anthony Burgess's *A Clockwork Orange*.

Hunter S. Thompson's description of adrenochrome in *Fear and Loathing in Las Vegas* as an ultra-rare drug that can only be harvested from a living person appears to have inspired the substance's place in QAnon fantasy. On YouTube, comments under clips from the *Fear and Loathing* movie are filled with knowing QAnon references.

In reality, adrenochrome is an uninteresting chemical substance. On drug experience forums, people who are inspired to try the drug complain about headaches, and say they generally had a boring experience. Terry Gilliam, who directed the *Fear and Loathing* movie, has said that Thompson explained to him that he had invented adrenochrome's powers.

The cabal wouldn't need to create a global harvesting network to get their hands on adrenochrome. Since it relies on the simple process of oxidizing adrenaline, anyone with an adrenaline-filled EpiPen meant to fight allergic reactions could expose the adrenaline to oxygen to create the drug.

In 2016, Pizzagate believers started to associate adrenochrome with the child sexual torture they believed took place at Comet Ping Pong. Pizzagate investigators on 4chan dredged up old videos about pedophiles and adrenochrome to explain why so many powerful Democrats would be interested in child abuse. And while no Q drop explicitly mentions adrenochrome, Pizzagate supporters brought adrenochrome into the QAnon mythos when the conspiracy theories merged.

Since then, the idea that global elites tap children for their adrenochrome like Vermonters tapping a tree for maple syrup has become so widespread on the far right, it often needs no explanation. In QAnon rallies, protesters hold up signs with the chemical formula for adrenochrome. Actor Jim Caviezel, best known for playing Jesus in Mel Gibson's *The Passion of the Christ*, said in a 2021 interview that he has been motivated to uncover the "adrenochroming of children." Some QAnon believers see the Pixar movie *Monsters, Inc.*, in which monsters scare children for their energy, as a sort of coded quasi-documentary meant to reveal the truth about adrenochrome.

QAnon's adrenochrome obsession also highlights the anti-Semitic beliefs at the movement's center. The idea that elites—and powerful Jewish people—are torturing children to use their substances in Satanic ceremonies is a direct echo of "blood libel," the idea that Jews use Christian children's blood for rituals, which dates to the Middle Ages

In 1144, the body of a twelve-year-old boy named William was discovered outside the English town of Norwich. While William's killer was never found, his death took on an enormous importance in the area after a monk wrote an investigation of William's death that claimed he had been killed by local Jews for his blood, which they needed for an annual ritual.

The monk's account of William's murder inspired claims that Jews were behind more child murders. The allegation that Jews were killing children for their blood spread across Europe, inspiring pogroms and violence against Jews even after a pope refuted them in the thirteenth century.

The blood libel persisted for centuries, with a German group working to counter anti-Semitism counting seventy-nine cases of blood libel allegations in central and eastern Europe in a ten-year period in the nineteenth century. The blood libel proved fatal as recently as 1946, when rumors that Polish Jews were conducting rituals with children's blood inspired a pogrom that killed more than forty Jews.

The similarities between QAnon's vision of adrenochrome harvesting and the blood libel myth aren't an accident. In 2014, conspiracy theorists on 4chan's /pol/ board were sharing an anti-Semitic video claiming that the "blood libel" was "ADRENOCHROME harvesting." The video spread and became a foundational source for conspiracy theorists, first in Pizzagate and then in QAnon. It's also helped fuel anti-Semitism within QAnon, where Jewish people like billionaire Democratic donor George Soros and members of the Rothschild banking family are seen as puppet-masters controlling the world.

For months, Picazio watched, terrified, as Holmseth and McConnell unleashed their segment of QAnon on her. In August 2019, she flew to Minnesota to testify against Holmseth at his trial. Picazio's husband had begged her not to go. She pondered whether putting Holmseth in jail was worth risking her life. Instead of staying away from the trial, Picazio decided to hire an armed guard to post outside her hotel room while she slept.

Monitoring online chatter in both communities ahead of the trial, Goddard and Picazio watched as Holmseth's supporters talked about somehow disrupting his trial. Both the FBI and the U.S. Marshals were involved in securing the courthouse ahead of the trial, according to Picazio. Dozens of Holmseth's supporters arrived at the Minnesota courthouse in buses, with people coming from as far as Europe. They saw the trial as a celebration, convinced that both Picazio and the prosecutor pursuing Holmseth would be executed. McConnell, who often discussed how Picazio would soon be killed, arrived at the trial in a hearse.

As McConnell's supporters waited outside the courthouse with QAnon signs and blown-up pictures of Jeffrey Epstein's face, however, it became clear that Holmseth wasn't going to show up at his own trial. He had fled.

Holmseth's supporters were confused at first. But that turned to elation. Holmseth had become a fugitive from the deep state. Now on the run and embraced by McConnell's media network, Holmseth would inspire QAnon crimes across the country and fuel a nationwide network of Q fugitives.

Picazio had spent years at the center of a QAnon hate-storm, as the movement grew from a few disconnected internet conspiracy theorists online into a menace. But QAnon was still expanding, adding more people willing to commit crimes in QAnon's name to its ranks. The old idea of occult child abuse, drawn from the Jewish blood libel and the Satanic Panic, could still attract people willing to do anything to stop what they saw as heinous crimes. Many of them, Picazio would soon learn, were happy to break the law themselves to protect children. Her own journey into the depths of QAnon was just beginning.

Chapter 9

The QAnon Kidnappers

Cynthia Abcug had a new pistol, a trained sniper acting as her bodyguard, and the address of the foster home where the cabal was holding her son. Abcug's fifteen-year-old daughter, Jessica, watched in their suburban Denver apartment as her mother and her new QAnon friends plotted an armed attack on the foster home. Jessica pointed out to her mother that any kind of "raid" would likely turn into a bloodbath. Abcug said her daughter shouldn't worry if the foster parents were hurt. After all, she said, they were Satanists.

Abcug's star had been rising in the heady world of conspiracy theory YouTube in recent months, and she finally had what she needed to turn her belief in Q into a new, potentially violent reality. But she had started to worry that the police were closing in on her. And for once, a QAnon believer's fevered suspicions about the government were correct.

Outside of QAnon, Abcug's life was falling apart. She had left behind financial and relationship troubles in Florida two years earlier and moved to Colorado to receive medical treatments for her critically ill seven-year-old son, Michael. As Abcug explained it, Michael had been dogged by unexplained illnesses since he was an infant. He couldn't swallow and lapsed into seizures if he went outside in bad weather. When a Colorado caseworker asked whether Abcug wanted an in-home nurse for her son, Abcug assured the caseworker that there was no point, since Michael would likely die soon of brain tumors anyway.

But that didn't make sense to any other adults who met Michael. He appeared by all accounts outside of his mother's to be a normal, healthy boy, albeit one who seemed unusually concerned about his mother's shifting moods. When he was an infant, Michael had been strangely lethargic, prompting one doctor to suspect he'd been exposed to marijuana. But after Abcug's exchange about brain tumors with the Colorado caseworker, staffers in the local Department of Human Services wrote in a report that they believed that Abcug was deliberately making her son ill to garner attention or sympathy for herself, a case of Munchausen's syndrome by proxy. In January 2019, child protective services workers took temporary custody of Michael and placed him in a foster home.

That's when Abcug turned to the QAnon YouTube circuit. Researching how to win back custody of her son, Abcug encountered Q groups online claiming that child services agencies acted as kidnappers for the cabal. She became convinced that the government had taken her son from her so he could be molested by Satanic deep-state operatives who were using the foster home as a funnel to steal children. She plugged her child custody battle on online shows hosted by conspiracy theorists like Field McConnell, where they feted her as a victim of cabal child-snatchers. McConnell asked viewers to send him money so he could help Abcug and warned her against hiring lawyers to help her with the case. Instead, McConnell would take her case directly to the Trump family.

"If it has enough sizzle—and yours certainly does, in my estimation—it'll get to Trump and Melania," McConnell said.

As QAnon believers rallied around Abcug, she became fully absorbed into its conspiracy theory world. She holed up in her apartment with her daughter, leaving only to meet with fellow Q supporters. Abcug attracted followers of her own, with Joseph Ramos, a Colorado medical student, becoming a sort of aide-de-camp to Abcug after seeing her on YouTube.

McConnell dispatched Ryan Wilson, a silver-haired QAnon activist from Arkansas with a hazy background whom Abcug introduced to her daughter as a "sniper," to serve as her live-in bodyguard. Abcug bought a gun and made plans to go to a shooting range.

Wilson, Abcug, and other QAnon supporters intended to carry out an armed raid of the foster home, according to her daughter, at some point before Halloween 2019. Before the alleged attack could happen, though, Abcug grew paranoid that the police were about to arrest her. There was only one choice, Wilson told her: they had to run.

Abcug was right to suspect the police were closing in. Unbeknownst to Abcug, her daughter, Jessica, worried about the raid's potential for violence, had tipped off a social worker. When officers finally arrived at Abcug's apartment with a warrant days later, though, she had vanished. As police searched the now-empty apartment, they found few clues to Abcug's whereabouts. Instead, they discovered piles of rubber QAnon bracelets with a message: "Storm is Upon Us."

Anons see the world as an abattoir, a place where innocent children are sexually tortured to keep Hollywood celebrities wrinkle-free. A world where this happens demands that bold, even criminal, action be taken. Yet the vast majority of Q's followers haven't committed violence on his behalf. Instead of inspiring mass violence in everyone who believes in Q, the conspiracy theory has influenced individual people to commit crimes in Q's name.

The world was introduced to QAnon violence in the summer of 2018, when a thirty-year-old Nevada car mechanic named Matthew Wright decided he was sick of waiting for the Storm. Facing post-traumatic stress disorder, a possible case of bipolar disorder, and $20,000 in unpaid medical bills, Wright had just one thing to look forward to: the June 2018 release of a Justice Department report on the Hillary Clinton email investigation.

Wright had lived on the margins of society since being discharged from the military for undisclosed medical reasons. Using his mechanic skills and equipment, he had turned his truck into an improvised armored vehicle straight out of *Mad Max*, stocked with an AR-15 rifle, hundreds of rounds of ammunition, and gun slots he could use to aim out through the defenses. Later, police described the vehicle as "armored like a Brinks truck."

In normal times, the release of a watchdog report 2,500 miles away likely wouldn't become a crucial moment in the life of a down-and-out Nevada mechanic. But Q had told his followers for months in advance that the report wouldn't be the dry investigation of Clinton's emails that it appeared set to be. Instead, the document would be filled with details about the cabal, the long-awaited revelations that would kick off the Storm.

A day before the report's scheduled release on June 14, 2018, though, Q distanced himself from his predictions, as if he was aware that his prophecy was about to implode. The mega-bombshell report QAnon believers wanted still existed, Q now said, and Trump had it. But Rod Rosenstein, the deputy attorney general whom Trump's base already despised for his role in the Russia investigation, had interfered and blocked its release. The public report might seem disappointing when it came out, Q's explanation now went, but believers just needed to be patient.

The Justice Department report turned out to be just as much of a letdown for QAnon believers as Q's backtracking suggested it would be. While it included enough material about the FBI investigation for Democrats and Republicans in Washington to argue over it, the report wasn't a knockout indictment of Clinton. It certainly didn't launch the Storm. That was too much for Wright, who used his amateur armored truck in protest to block a highway between Nevada and Arizona that stretched across the Hoover Dam.

As police officers from five different law enforcement agencies encircled him, a driver on the bridge saw a masked Wright aiming a rifle out of the truck. Inside the vehicle, Wright livestreamed himself holding up signs demanding the release of the "real" report, and angrily addressed Trump for disappointing him with "more bullshit."

"You said you were going to lock people up if you were elected!" he said.

After a forty-five-minute standoff with police on the bridge, Wright attempted to escape by driving his truck into the Arizona desert, only to trap himself in a canyon. After he surrendered, police found several handguns and rifles in the truck, along with an explosive detonator. In December 2020, Wright pleaded guilty to making a terrorist threat and was sentenced to more than seven years in prison.

Wright was just the beginning. In 2019, a man armed with a katana sword smashed up a Catholic church in Arizona, handing out "human trafficking investigator" business cards stamped with a *Q*. In Seattle, a believer who was convinced that his brother was secretly a "reptilian" humanoid lizard killed him with a samurai sword. In Washington, D.C., a man tried to burn down Comet Ping Pong by lighting curtains on fire while the restaurant was filled with children. But QAnon's real power to inspire violence wouldn't draw widespread attention until March 14, 2019, the night a Q follower murdered a mob boss.

Before his death, Frank Cali might have thought himself untouchable. "Franky Boy" was the head of the Gambinos, the second most powerful Mafia family in the country, and enjoyed close personal ties to Sicilian gangsters. He lived in a mansion in Todt Hill, a tony Staten Island neighborhood popular with mafiosi-made-good that had even been used as the fictional home to the Corleone family in *The Godfather*. Cali's life came to an abrupt end when Anthony Comello, an aimless twenty-four-year-old with no previous organized crime associations, slammed his truck into a Cadillac Escalade that Cali had parked outside his mansion. As Cali ran outside to confront the intruder, Comello pulled out a pistol and fired ten bullets into the Mafia don.

Cali's murder stunned mobsters and law enforcement officials alike. It was the first time a head of one of the Five Families had been murdered in more than thirty years. In the chaotic initial hours after Cali's murder, baffled Mafia lieutenants were caught on FBI wiretaps scrambling to figure out who Comello worked for, and what kind of war he might have started.

Comello gave the detectives interrogating him conflicting explanations for the murder. Someone who wanted Cali dead had blackmailed Comello into shooting the boss by threatening to reveal that Comello had contracted HIV after having sex with a stripper, he said. Then he claimed he wanted to date one of Cali's relatives, and the godfather had forbidden the match. Comello's real motivation only became clear during a court hearing a few days later. As Comello waited for the judge to enter the chamber, he smiled and held up one of his hands to reporters: he had written a *Q* in the center of his palm. Q had reached out from the internet and killed one of the most powerful criminals in the country.

As the court hearings dragged on and his family went into hiding to avoid Gambino reprisals, Comello remained devoted to QAnon. In one courtroom scene, he ranted to the judge about how his cell phone contained proof of child sex-trafficking and "Operation Mockingbird," referencing the Q belief that the CIA controls the media. Comello was later ruled unfit to stand trial and remains in custody.

QAnon is unmatched among modern American conspiracy theories in its ability to inspire violence. As of September 2021, 101 QAnon followers had been inspired to commit crime by their beliefs, a list that includes 61 defendants from the Capitol riot, according to data compiled by University of Maryland researchers. No other conspiracy theory, from 9/11 trutherism to birtherism, gets even close to inspiring that level of violence.

Marc-André Argentino, a PhD candidate at Montreal's Concordia University studying extremism, told me QAnon stands out among conspiracy theories in its ability to inspire violence. Argentino attributes that in part to the ubiquity QAnon achieved on social media, giving it a permanent online presence that makes it feel more pervasive in a way that earlier conspiracy theories didn't. As a result, it has more of an influence on its followers' minds.

"No one killed anyone because they wanted to find out how JFK died," Argentino said.

———————

The FBI joined the hunt for Abcug. Her son's foster family stepped up the security at their home, fearful that the vanished mother and her supposed team of armed QAnon believers could attack at any moment. But for the many believers following Field McConnell's YouTube channel, Abcug's disappearance became just a new soap opera twist. In a video posted a few days after Abcug fled Colorado, McConnell assured his viewers that Wilson was with her somewhere out in America, carrying out a violent mission. He was, according to McConnell, "in one of my cars with a gun that I own doing something that would please everybody on our team, especially President Trump."

A day later, Abcug, joined by Wilson and Ramos, arrived at McConnell's house in Plum City, Wisconsin, a small village on the state's border with Minnesota. The trio had been driving for nearly one thousand miles without stopping, constantly looking out the rear window for police. Now they planned to lie low with McConnell.

Thanks to QAnon, McConnell had grown from a YouTube conspiracy theorist into the hub of a loosely knit criminal network. In 2019, McConnell started a Q group called the Children's Crusade. McConnell's new position of authority gave him the platform to galvanize believers who were otherwise fed up with simply relying on comforting QAnon slogans like "trust the plan" and "enjoy the show" to take real action by confronting the deep state with military force. The Children's Crusade also offered McConnell a chance to ramp up the spy-game drama that enthralled his audience.

The Children's Crusade's tendrils spread all the way to Europe, as evidenced by a 2019 launch party in Wales for supporters of McConnell's budding network. Ramos recalled later that during his stay with McConnell, he would overhear his long phone calls with operatives in the United Kingdom, calling them by what Ramos considered "hokey codenames." Despite its ambitions to take on the global power structure, though, the Children's

Crusade seemed focused mostly on child custody cases. In Facebook groups manned by supporters of McConnell and allied conspiracy theorists, confused mothers desperate to win back custody of their children were encouraged to abandon the regular legal system in favor of chasing publicity through QAnon media outlets.

For mothers like Abcug, the version of QAnon promoted by the Children's Crusade offered a more comforting reality than the real world. These parents hadn't lost custody of their children because of mental illness, abuse, or drug addiction—they were victims of the deep state whose children had been kidnapped. And like every other branch of the government, it turned out that social workers, too, were working for the pedophile-cannibals.

A week into her flight from the law, Abcug was still deep in the Children's Crusade's clutches. After eight days of hiding out at McConnell's house, Ramos and Abcug were shopping in a nearby Plum City store when McConnell called. The FBI were at his house, he said. They had to run.

Abcug and Ramos fled Plum City, throwing themselves once again on the mercy of the QAnon underground.

When the FBI wanted to find Abcug, they went to a woman who knew more about QAnon than anyone. In October 2019, an FBI agent called Kim Picazio for information on the network that was still directing death threats to her and her family.

"We're looking for a lady named Cyndie Abcug," the FBI agent said, Picazio recalled later. "She's on the run."

The agent wanted to know if Picazio could help track the Children's Crusade. Picazio said she could do more than that. By the time the FBI called her, she had transformed her law firm into a makeshift intelligence agency tracking QAnon leaders online, amassing what amounted to dossiers on leading QAnon personalities like McConnell.

"I know everything about these people," Picazio told the agent.

Picazio had struggled for years to get the FBI to look at QAnon seriously, to see them as more than a group loosely affiliated with lone-wolf incidents like Matthew Wright's Hoover Dam standoff. The FBI's 2019 memo listing QAnon as a potential source of domestic terror had noted that believers could be inspired "to commit criminal, sometimes violent activity." But the FBI still seemed uninterested in pursuing QAnon criminals who operated in coordinated ways.

For example, Holmseth had kept up his attacks on Picazio while on the run, using the free Wi-Fi in McDonald's parking lots to post videos accusing her of working for the cabal. Police in Minnesota didn't seem to consider arresting Holmseth for breaking the restraining order a priority. But as Picazio suffered through another wave of death threats, she realized something: McConnell, Holmseth, and the Children's Crusade appeared to be engaging in plenty of other activities that could interest the FBI.

Gathering her law firm's staff, Picazio told them it was time to fight back against QAnon in terms the FBI understood. "You're on money fraud, you're on threats," Picazio told her secretaries and legal associates, assigning them topics one by one. "You're on the sovereign citizens, you're on the practicing law without a license."

Field McConnell, for example, was selling his followers near-worthless Zimbabwean "Zim" currency, on the theory that a NESARA-style global financial reset would soon equalize world currencies and make Zim holders incredibly wealthy. A man impersonating former Trump secretary of defense Jim Mattis called into McConnell's show, enthusing that his Zim holdings had exploded in value after the reset reached his account. If McConnell's listeners would follow his lead and buy Zim from McConnell, they would soon be rich, too.

"It was a very profitable scam," Goddard, who monitored McConnell's thousands of devoted viewers interact with him in his frequent broadcasts, said. "These little old ladies in there loved him. I'm waiting for them to throw their bloomers at him through the internet."

McConnell also asked his fans to fund the McConnell Veterans'

Ranch, an imagined utopian community where he claimed veterans with post-traumatic stress disorder and children rescued from the cabal could recuperate together. McConnell's chat rooms filled with resumes from supporters hoping to work at the ranch, which never came to fruition.

To get a better view of McConnell's activities, Picazio's employees sent Facebook requests to residents of Plum City, McConnell's home base. They recruited a diner owner to report to them anyone suspicious in the small town. One of Picazio's staffers even made an account on a dating site with a fake location in Plum City and matched with a local firefighter. After getting to know him online, Picazio's employee revealed her true intentions in a phone call: she didn't want a date, she wanted a spy. He agreed and became another link in the web tracking developments at McConnell's headquarters. The group found success—discovering, for example, that McConnell's allies were even harboring a fringe congressional candidate, helping her evade an arrest warrant on shoplifting charges in Minnesota by putting her up in a Wisconsin motel.

By the time the FBI asked Picazio for help, she already had "eyes and ears" in Plum City. Picazio fed this intelligence to the FBI, explaining how McConnell made his money and who he worked with.

"Leave it to a bunch of women at a divorce law firm," Picazio said.

Back on the run, Abcug and Ramos bounced around the Children's Crusade underground network. They stayed in another small Wisconsin town with a McConnell supporter who called himself "Dr. Good Vibes," then drove to the mansion of a well-heeled Children's Crusade supporter in Northern Virginia who was convinced Abcug could escape the country on a diplomatic passport.

As the weeks passed, Abcug began to believe the Children's Crusade found her more useful as a symbol in their fight against the cabal than as someone they could genuinely help. For all of McConnell's promises, she was further away from regaining custody than ever, with her family court case stalled, this new felony kidnapping case hanging over head, and her son still in a foster home halfway across the country.

After one month on the run, Abcug had had enough by late October 2019. If McConnell couldn't get her son back, maybe a McConnell ally and wannabe lawyer named Chris Hallett could.

Rather than hire attorneys to win their children back, the women who sought help from the Children's Crusade ended up relying on Hallett, often to their detriment. Despite having no formal legal training, Hallett had become convinced that Trump had empowered him to essentially overturn the entire American legal system with his own ideas in a movement he dubbed "E-Clause," after the Constitution's emoluments clause. His bumbling maneuvers were soundly rejected in every courtroom where he tried them, with a federal judge describing his arguments as "patently frivolous." Even after those rebukes, though, Hallett still made thousands of dollars from distressed mothers seeking his help.

"I'm really intrigued by this Mr. Hallett and his company E-Clause," Abcug said, Ramos recalled later.

Abcug and Ramos moved south from Virginia on their way to meet Hallett, driving slowly to avoid being pulled over and paying for cheap motel rooms in cash provided by members of the Children's Crusade, alongside other contributions totaling roughly $7,500 to help Abcug remain a fugitive.

The Children's Crusade could reach them anywhere, with the pair brushing up against emissaries from the group along the way. Wilson reappeared, delivering messages from the leadership. According to Ramos, they also met with the Children's Crusade's own John F. Kennedy Jr. impersonator, a man who goes by the alias Juan O. Savin. McConnell's followers had become convinced that Savin, rather than more prominent JFK Jr. double Vincent Fusca, was the real heir to the Kennedy legacy.

Abcug and Ramos met Hallett in Ocala, the central Florida city where he ran E-Clause out of his house. E-Clause had spread across the country by the time Abcug reached Ocala, recruiting new mothers as clients and hiring another legal dabbler in Idaho named Kirk Pendergrass to echo Hallett's claims.

Much of Hallett's legal doctrine came from sovereign citizenship, an antigovernment movement also popular with other extremist groups. All sovereign citizens believe the same basic thing: whether by choice, birth, or grammatical trickery, they have somehow become "sovereign" and separate from the laws of the United States. A sovereign citizen facing a tax evasion charge, for example, might claim that a gold-fringed flag in a courtroom means the judge is operating under maritime law, and thus unable to enforce laws on land. This approach means that sovereign citizens can get into hopeless, sometimes comical situations during police stops or court hearings. Compilations with names like "Sovereign citizens getting owned" have racked up millions of views on YouTube.

In one representative video, a sovereign citizen pulled over for reckless driving refuses to admit to a police officer that he was driving. Instead, he insists that he was merely "traveling"—the type of meaningless legal distinction sovereign citizens think make them immune to consequences. Unfortunately for this sovereign citizen, the ruse doesn't work and the officer arrests him.

But sovereign citizens' refusal to abide by even basic laws can turn violent, too. Sovereign citizens have killed police officers during traffic stops, or when sheriff's deputies try to enforce a court ruling.

After a few days in Ocala, Abcug started to feel Hallett was failing her. Word reached Ramos and Abcug that the FBI had visited the Virginia mansion where they had stayed just before driving to Florida. It was time to move again—this time, to the protection of a Trump administration appointee.

In early November 2019, Abcug and Ramos drove to Arkansas, the home state of Children's Crusade board member Sarah Dunklin. While the earlier stages of their flight had centered on fringe figures like McConnell and Hallett, Dunklin was well-connected in her state's Republican politics.

At the time, Dunklin led the Republican Party in Desha County,

Arkansas, and had been appointed to a U.S. Department of Agriculture committee by agriculture secretary Sonny Perdue. Dunklin's father was a candidate for the state senate.

Dunklin told the fugitive QAnon duo to hide out in Dumas, a small town so desolate it was the setting for the 2012 Matthew McConaughey rural-crime thriller *Mud*. Ramos and Abcug lived for weeks in a dismal motel by the Arkansas River. It wasn't a great place to hide out—half of the rooms at the motel had been blown up in an oxygen-bottle fire years earlier. But it turned out Dunklin and the rest of the Children's Crusade didn't seem to be in a hurry to get Abcug back to her old life.

Their best idea seemed to be to send Ramos to a flea market to buy fake passports and flee the country, an idea he said he rejected when he recalled the story later. In a note to Ramos and Abcug explaining how to avoid attracting attention to themselves in Dumas, Dunklin told them to stay away from stores, toss their cell phones, and finally, to stop talking to strangers about Abcug's children. "Time to get expenses down and LAY LOW," Dunklin wrote. "Don't move off river!"

Abcug languished in Dumas, but still evaded arrest. McConnell wasn't so lucky. In November 2019, he was arrested in Wisconsin, pending extradition to Florida for violating a restraining order Picazio had obtained against him. Ahead of his transfer from the Wisconsin jail, his supporters fumed that their leader's capture was illegitimate. One filmed the jail where McConnell was held, noting that it was on a riverbank—proof, in the twisted logic of McConnell's supporters, that he was being treated as riverboat "cargo" and should therefore be released.

A day before New Year's Eve 2019, Abcug's fugitive life came to an end in Kalispell, Montana. FBI agents surrounded Ramos's car with their guns drawn. Abcug surrendered and was charged with a felony, conspiracy to commit a kidnapping, over the alleged plot to abduct her son from the foster home. Considering whether to grant Abcug bail, a judge noted that QAnon believers were "assisting her in trying to elude capture by law enforcement." As of this writing, Abcug was awaiting trial.

QAnon abandoned Abcug even before she could be extradited back to Colorado. Abcug, like so many people accused of committing crimes in Q's name before, had become an embarrassment to the movement. In an email to an associate after news of Abcug's arrest broke, Savin, the JFK Jr. impersonator, groaned that Abcug would make QAnon look like "hillbilly militias" and "internet patriot kooks."

"The Q operation cannot endorse or appear to assist this type of idiocy," he wrote.

Abcug's arrest was initially described in the press as the desperate actions of yet another QAnon lone wolf. But after I covered her initial arrest in an article for the Daily Beast, Goddard approached me with dozens of hours of footage of Children's Crusade figures demonstrating that Abcug wasn't acting alone. The Children's Crusade was recruiting more desperate people to their brand of QAnon, and they weren't done.

Neely Petrie-Blanchard, a thirty-three-year-old QAnon devotee who had lost custody of her children to their grandmothers years before QAnon began, perfectly fit the profile of someone who would fall under the sway of the Children's Crusade and E-Clause. She had struggled for years with opioid addiction and mental health problems and spent a year in jail after trying to kidnap one of her daughters from school.

"Don't fuck with me or my kids, I will shoot you in the head," she had once told her mother, in a heated custody fight. "I will cut you in little pieces and put you where you will never be found."

Hallett insisted he could get her children back, promising for years that he had concocted a legal scheme where a U.S. marshal would win her custody of her children. Hallett, who had been involved in custody battles over his own children, promised he had a sort of magic formula that would finally resolve Petrie-Blanchard's drawn-out one. She even started to suspect that Hallett was Q himself. Petrie-Blanchard became devoted to Hallett's cause, collecting thousands of dollars in donations for him on social media, putting an "ECLAUSE" license plate on her car, and dressing her daughter in an E-Clause shirt. Hallett became her mentor in the upside-down world of QAnon, saying their relationship was "more of a father-daughter thing."

In March 2020, a few weeks into the pandemic, Petrie-Blanchard kidnapped her twin daughters from her mother's house in Kentucky. Days later, sheriff's deputies found Petrie-Blanchard and her daughters hiding out in a neighboring county with another E-Clause member and a group of sovereign citizens. As deputies entered the house to recover the girls and arrest their mother, the people in the house feigned being sick with the coronavirus. After Petrie-Blanchard's arrest, one of Hallett's associates bailed her out of jail.

I first wrote about the Children's Crusade criminal network for the Daily Beast in 2020. A few months later, I got a call from Meko Haze, an independent journalist in Kansas who frequently reported on McConnell and the Children's Crusade. I expected to hear more of the kind of news that Haze often dug up—another arrest, maybe a new mother abducting her child.

"Neely killed Chris," he said.

Out on bail on her kidnapping charge, Petrie-Blanchard had returned to work on her child custody case and told Hallett she wanted to see him in person to discuss it. She drove to meet him in Ocala. To Hallett, it must have seemed like just another visit from one of the distraught mothers he had whipped up into a frenzy. But secretly, Petrie-Blanchard's long-simmering frustrations with the legal system were now turned on Hallett. She had come to believe he was as much a part of the cabal Q talked about as Hillary Clinton or George Soros. As she saw it, Hallett was deliberately sabotaging his legal maneuvers on her behalf to keep her from her family.

The evening of her arrival at Hallett's office, Petrie-Blanchard asked him for some coffee, then followed him into the kitchen. With Hallett's back to her, Petrie-Blanchard pulled a gun, according to witness reports from Hallett's girlfriend and her teenage daughter.

"You're hurting my children, you bastard," Petrie-Blanchard said. Then, according to witnesses and police reports, she pulled the trigger, firing a round into his shoulder. Hallett stumbled into the living room, his face split with pain. As Hallett's girlfriend and her daughter fled, they heard Petrie-Blanchard fire more bullets into Hallett's head. Detectives arriving on the scene found the house empty save for Hallett, dead from "numerous" gunshot wounds. Police caught up with Petrie-Blanchard in Georgia. After her arrest for Hallett's murder, Petrie-Blanchard asked police whether the military or the CIA were investigating E-Clause, and claimed the group was being used by family courts to steal children.

Kirk Pendergrass, E-Clause's surviving leader in Idaho, opted for a fresh conspiracy theory to explain Hallett's death. He claimed that Petrie-Blanchard was working for the cabal.

"You know how the deep state doesn't like to be exposed," Pendergrass told his viewers.

Jack Maro, Petrie-Blanchard's lawyer, plans to use an insanity defense at her trial.

"He just really led her down the primrose path," Maro told me.

In September 2021, Kim Picazio came face-to-face with McConnell in a courtroom. The QAnon leader had been chastened, at least for now, and taken a plea deal for violating Picazio's protective order that would sentence him to a year of probation and a prohibition on contacting either Picazio or Holmseth, who remains at large. As part of the sentencing, Picazio was allowed to address her tormentor.

"When you're telling them that I'm a child trafficker, that I eat children, that I did horrible things in the world, they want to come and kill me," Picazio told McConnell, reciting his fantasies about Marines or his supporters riddling the woman he called "Ms. Piggy" with bullets. Picazio savored a moment of sanity in a world that had, for her, gone mad years before. At least this time, the legal system said you could not encourage waves of QAnon believers to murder someone and get away with it.

"You said the Marines were going to come and shoot me seven times in the head, that when I showed up at the courthouse they'd come out from the trees and get me," Picazio said to McConnell. "I don't see any Marines here, sir. What I see is a judge who's just sentenced you, because you need to learn to follow the rules."

After an explosive few years, the Children's Crusade appeared to be ebbing. Abcug was awaiting trial in her kidnapping case, while Petrie-Blanchard faced her murder charge. The social media companies' crackdown on QAnon had made it harder for people like Holmseth to organize their online mobs, or for E-Clause to find new recruits. In her courtroom statement, Picazio brought up the QAnon murder that struck closer to McConnell: the recent slaying of Chris Hallett, his friend and legal adviser. There was an obvious irony to Hallett's death: he had used QAnon to take advantage of vulnerable and often unstable people, feeding their delusions for his own purposes. Now that deranged violence had come to Hallett's front door.

"One of your sovereign-citizen legal counsel isn't even here with us anymore," Picazio said. "One of your followers murdered him."

McConnell's conviction represented a rare legal win against QAnon. Even after years of violence and harassment from QAnon believers, though, federal law enforcement still appears to be taking a mixed approach to QAnon.

In an April 2021 congressional hearing held in the aftermath of the Capitol riot, FBI director Chris Wray told Congress that the bureau was looking "very seriously" at QAnon's connections to violence. But Wray said there was still no broader FBI investigation into the movement.

"We're not investigating the theory in its own right," Wray said.

Chapter 10

When Dad Takes the Red Pill

There comes a moment in every new Q follower's life when the person closest to them realizes that they aren't joking. The Facebook binges and the sudden adoration for Donald Trump have been waved off until now. The stray remarks about missing children and experimental vaccines have been chalked up to eccentricities. But eventually there's no more denying it: your wife, or your son, or your father now believes in QAnon, and they want you to join them.

For the person outside QAnon, there's a scramble to the internet that mirrors the Q believer's own frantic online searching weeks or months earlier. Adrenochrome? Underground bases? *What*-Anon?

For David, a blue-collar union tradesman in his fifties, that moment came one month into the pandemic when his son Nathan walked into their family home in suburban Chicago with an announcement. In his late twenties and looking uncharacteristically grave, Nathan said he wanted to prepare his parents for some big news before they saw it on TV.

"Hey, I just want you guys to know that there are a bunch of Hollywood people that are going to be arrested," Nathan said.

Nathan listed the names of celebrities who would soon be arrested for pedophilia: Tom Hanks, Steven Spielberg, Oprah Winfrey. David thought his son was kidding.

"Well, I hope it's not Tom Selleck," David said. "Because I like Tom Selleck."

Nathan wasn't joking. He laid out how the arrests would take place, like he was letting his parents in on a secret mission. David started taking notes. The phrases and code words all seemed to center on an idea David had never heard before: a global cabal runs the world, and Trump is about to take it down. A journey that began on Nathan's laptop weeks earlier was finally manifesting itself into the offline world, right in David's living room. His son believed in QAnon. Their family would never be the same.

David emailed me about his son in early 2021 after reading some of my articles about QAnon. We started talking regularly, with David giving me updates as Nathan slipped in and out of his belief in Q. Confounded by the new digital soldier living in their son's childhood bedroom, David and his wife, Lucy, became QAnon experts themselves. David was an articulate guide to the unique despair of seeing Q take root in your family. He ran his son's life back over and over in his head, looking for some clue about what led Nathan to this place. David was open with me about his disappointment and anger with Nathan, and sometimes even darkly amused by the twists that had allowed an anonymous internet poster named Q, someone no one in his family knew, to bring him to the brink of never speaking to his son again.

David, Lucy, and Nathan were lost deep in a novel kind of personal unraveling: family alienation through QAnon. Ever since the fateful day Nathan started talking about mass arrests in Hollywood, their family had been thrown into a wilderness with no obvious way out.

"I don't think that people who don't have a loved one involved with this have any idea how bad this is," David said.

QAnon's most eye-catching consequences can involve murders, mobs storming the U.S. Capitol, or millions of people primed to accept a fascist takeover. But its most frequent tragedy is far less visible. It's made up of innumerable stories of human connections destroyed, a story that plays out every day across the country in kitchens, office break rooms, and tense car rides.

From the outside, Nathan appeared to be living much the same life he had before he discovered QAnon. But for those closest to him, the Nathan who existed before Q was gone. In his place was an angry, frustrated young man with a monomaniacal interest in fantasizing about the Storm. QAnon made Nathan's life smaller and sadder, and strained his relationships with everyone around him.

The arrests Nathan predicted that day never came, but that family meeting was just the start of his attempts to red-pill, or convert, his parents. He argued with them constantly, and used any opportunity to steer them back to the conspiracy theory. In a way, David had to admit he was impressed by QAnon's ability to explain the entire world. Leaked texts showed actor Armie Hammer fantasizing about cannibal sex acts? More proof that Q was right about the Hollywood sickos. Elon Musk launches a rocket into space? A chance for Nathan to mention that the moon landing was faked.

Nathan's few remaining friends started to drift away. David had a vivid image of what Nathan's future looked like if he didn't give up on QAnon: living in a cardboard box under a bridge, abandoned by everyone who once loved him.

I've talked to dozens of people like David, whose relationships with someone close to them were destroyed when that person got into QAnon and became obsessed with recruiting everyone around him. There was the mother who had to find a way to explain to her ten-year-old son that he couldn't see his uncle anymore, because he had become obsessed with QAnon. A woman whose husband picked up a cocaine habit so he could stay up decoding late-night Q drops, and carried on affairs with fellow believers he met online to get an understanding he couldn't find in his marriage to a Q skeptic. I heard from more than one person who was surprised to find that their spouse, now a QAnon believer, suddenly didn't want to vaccinate their children.

The personal destruction wrought by QAnon has put people outside of it in positions they never imagined. There are parents afraid to speak to their children, and children who realize the person they trusted most in the world has lost their connection with reality. QAnon can seem like a distant problem, something confined to Trump rallies and the darkest corners of the internet—until it transforms someone you know, falling on them like an exotic, incurable virus. For David, his son's QAnon indoctrination pointed at something missing in Nathan's life, but he didn't know what it could have been.

David's own reaction to Trump had been much different. He had been an apolitical, white, blue-collar worker in the Midwest, exactly the kind of voter to whom Trump was supposed to hold a special appeal. But the election of a man he called a "two-bit con man" had pushed David in the other direction. He became a dedicated MSNBC viewer. He tracked the myriad legal cases against Trump associates, hoping that one would finally flip on Trump and break whatever spell had been cast on Q believers like Nathan.

On January 6, 2021, David watched on MSNBC as rioters breached the U.S. Capitol. A friend doing the same called him with a question: Was Nathan rioting in Washington, too? David was grateful that his son was at home, but he admitted that it seemed like exactly the kind of thing Nathan would do.

"Thank God we don't have any guns," he told me.

Nathan had always been drawn to strange ideas. As a teenager, he was fascinated by Bigfoot and aliens. But Nathan's interest in conspiracy theories didn't take off in earnest until the pandemic began, when Nathan moved back in with his parents and his social circle shrank down to the walls of his home. Without roommates around, he had been spending a lot of time on his laptop. Nathan gave up any pretense of living in the real world after coming out as a QAnon supporter. He spent his days locked up in his room at his parents' house, smoking marijuana and reading the Q boards. He emerged only to get food and pressure his parents to watch QAnon videos. Their arguments became repetitive, always starting with Nathan making some bold claim, like that John F. Kennedy would return to life to run as Trump's vice president.

For David, Nathan's transformation from his somewhat off-kilter son into the Q-entranced stranger living in his house raised questions about what kind of father he had been. He admitted that he hadn't been the perfect dad, but until Nathan got into QAnon he had thought they had a normal father-son relationship—maybe a little stiff, but nothing that should prompt this.

David clung to the few apolitical topics he shared with Nathan, including a family fantasy baseball league. But Nathan soon lost interest in baseball, saying it wasn't "real" enough to him when compared to QAnon.

"I can't understand it," David told me. "For a rational person to fall for this stuff, how do you sympathize with them? How do you put yourself in those shoes?"

After nearly a year of increasing tensions with Nathan about QAnon, David's wife suggested they go to a therapist. But when David and Nathan sat down for the counseling session, they realized the therapist had never heard of QAnon. David spent the first session trying to explain Q to the therapist, fearing he was coming off just as unhinged as his son. The counselor eventually decided that Nathan's QAnon delusions would lift if he would stop smoking so much marijuana.

For David and his family, as for so many others caught up in the conspiracy theory, QAnon had become a story about institutions failing. Mental health specialists were caught nearly entirely off guard by its spread, and unable to offer any useful advice for reaching family members caught in Q's grip. But they weren't alone.

The American government had missed QAnon's spread. Even if the government had wanted to step in, it wasn't clear that there was anything legal to do about it. The social media companies profited from the engagement QAnon stirred up, right up until it threatened to no longer become profitable. Now that entire mess, a package of failures from anyone who should have stopped QAnon before it ensnared so many people, landed on David and Nathan.

David tried to find resources online for pulling someone out of QAnon but found little he could use. The plague of people losing family members to QAnon has inspired a small industry that promises to deradicalize QAnon members. There are books and news articles offering tips for "blue-pilling" loved ones out of QAnon and other conspiracy theories, nearly all of them premised on maintaining a civil relationship with the QAnon believer and avoiding confrontation or trying to debunk their beliefs. In time, the theory goes, the QAnon supporter will come out of the conspiracy theory on their own, and reach out for help in leaving QAnon.

That passive strategy for dealing with QAnon radicalization may be the best approach. It's also nearly impossible. It asks the family members of QAnon believers to shoulder an enormous burden, acting as a psychologist, epidemiologist, historian, debater, and social worker—all while having the mammoth amounts of patience required to put up with feverish ravings and verbal abuse.

"When you're confronted by him virtually every night with this stream of nonsense, you can't keep quiet," David said of his son.

At best, David thought his son might someday break out of QAnon on his own, or lose interest and move on to some other strange obsession. But David didn't see that happening anytime soon. QAnon had become the one constant in his son's otherwise aimless life. In a strange way, Nathan finally had a purpose.

"He's never been this committed to anything," David said.

Jake, a twenty-seven-year-old in California, had always been close to his mother, Brenda. She was a Green Party hippie who burned sage and ate raw food. She loved putting wheatgrass shots in her smoothies. Growing up as a gay teenager, Jake saw his mother as his protector.

"She was always the hero of my story," he said.

But Brenda took a scary turn when the pandemic started. A few weeks into the spring of 2020, she had a nervous breakdown. She told Jake that waves from 5G cell towers were going to give her the coronavirus.

"What the heck is going on with my mom?" Jake recalled thinking.

The most common QAnon story involves a conservative who already likes Trump becoming convinced, through QAnon, that Trump is a messiah figure. But by 2020, QAnon had evolved far enough into its "Pastel QAnon" form to appeal to a left-wing, New Age hippie who loved health food and esoteric spirituality.

Unbeknownst to Jake, his mother had been getting into QAnon for months. Her introduction came through a company she worked for selling essential oils. It was structured as a multilevel marketing business, a format that has been compared to a pyramid scheme. The woman who recruited Brenda—her "upline," in multilevel marketing parlance—started posting on Facebook about NESARA and the financial relief it would bring.

For Brenda, one thing about NESARA stuck out: the promise that renters would come to own the homes they rented after NESARA's utopian world came to pass. Brenda had rented the same apartment for more than a decade. Now, with NESARA, she thought she could finally own it outright for free. As she researched NESARA, she discovered QAnon in its "Save the Children" form.

Under that guise, QAnon had been transformed into a more palatable format. For people like Brenda who fell for Save the Children on Facebook, it wasn't about decoding breadcrumbs and military tribunals at Guantanamo Bay. It was, initially, just about a vague sense of protecting children. Brenda and her progressive friends on Facebook all started posting about "Save the Children," but soon they were trading explicitly pro-QAnon messages.

"It was perfectly crafted to capture her and her friend group," Jake said.

Brenda grew incoherent, warning her son about conspiracies behind every news event. She turned against the concept of vaccines and refused to get vaccinated for Covid-19. Jake scoured every article he could find about dealing with a QAnon family member. But each tip required him to invest a huge amount of time into patiently trying to lure her out of QAnon. Dealing with his Q mom became a second job that left him exhausted.

He couldn't explain what he was going through to his friends, who would laugh when they saw news stories about whacked-out QAnon believers storming the Capitol or worshipping JFK Jr. But for Jake, QAnon wasn't a news article he could click away from. It had become his life. He felt incredibly lonely.

At night, Jake read his mother's Twitter posts to track her descent into QAnon. Brenda claimed that the January 6 rioters were working for Antifa. When a massive winter storm knocked out electricity across Texas, she posted conspiracy theories claiming that the snow was artificial, meaning that the snow was being created by a weather control machine to punish a red state. Eventually Twitter banned Brenda, forcing her into more obscure online communities like the messaging app Telegram and conservative social media network Parler. Jake found it harder to follow her there, but by then, he had all but given up trying.

Jake read stories about people who had lost parents to the pandemic and thought he could relate. He felt like he was grieving the loss of a parent, too. But he worried that the public underestimated QAnon's threat, thinking that their families were safe from QAnon's influence if they weren't Republicans.

"This is far beyond the Republican community," Jake said. "This is so far beyond what you think of as the far right."

Just as new people drawn to QAnon are welcomed into its online communities, the personal damage left in QAnon's wake has created parallel online communities for people suffering from its spread. Ex-QAnon "apostates" and grieving family members swap stories and advice on forums like Reddit's "QAnon Casualties" board. The rare success stories are vastly outnumbered, though, by posts about the frustrations of trying to persuade someone to leave QAnon behind.

Every time I wrote an article about QAnon, people would email me asking for a solution to a loved one lost to QAnon. I didn't have any answers, so I asked experts who had ideas of their own, hoping to come up with some way to help these distraught families. What I found out from talking to people involved in reducing QAnon's harm is hard, but unavoidable: there's no guaranteed way to dissuade a QAnon believer.

"The reality is that we don't really know what really works or if anything does work to get someone out of QAnon," Dr. Joseph M. Pierre, a University of California, Los Angeles, psychiatrist who has studied QAnon, told me.

For one thing, QAnon apostates almost never leave the movement because of treatment from a therapist or psychiatrist, according to Pierre. Instead, people who walk away from QAnon often describe experiencing a personal "disillusionment" with the cause that had nothing to do with the efforts of loved ones or mental health professionals. It can be as simple as personal fights with other believers, losing faith in a once-beloved QAnon leader, or stumbling upon a debunking video that somehow pierces their reality-denying defenses.

One thing experts who have studied QAnon exit methods almost all agree on is that the most obvious and temporarily satisfying option—a full-frontal debunking assault—is also the worst. Reacting to a QAnon believer's claims with anger, ridicule, and insults about tin-foil hats will only cause them to shut down or sever the relationship. Many QAnon believers are drawn to the conspiracy theory because they feel marginalized or disrespected, according to Dannagal Young, a professor of communication and political science at the University of Delaware who researches what drives people to believe in misinformation. Mocking QAnon to them only demonstrates further that they're not valued in their real-life community. Because their beliefs in QAnon aren't driven at their heart by a desire to truly understand the world, trying to dissuade a believer with facts might not work.

"All that's going to do is confirm their worldview that they're an outsider and people aren't to be trusted," Young said.

Instead, the people left grieving in QAnon's wake are generally encouraged to keep the relationship going and avoid mentioning Q. While the believer may need to come to their own revelation that the movement is fake on their own, having personal connections that survived their QAnon experience will make that easier. That advice may be good in theory, but it is often maddening to implement, given how persistent and aggressive QAnon believers can be. Young says that trying to bring someone out of QAnon is "so, so hard" and urges people considering it to first conduct a cost-benefit analysis on whether they want to maintain their relationship with the Q follower.

A high school friend on Facebook or a crazy uncle you only see once a year at Christmas might not be worth the aggravation. But working for the remote possibility of restoring a spouse or parent to the real world might make waging what Young calls "a long game" more reasonable. Rather than directly confronting a QAnon believer, Young and other deradicalization researchers suggest a less direct approach that relies on just getting them away, mentally and physically, from QAnon. Take them for a walk or a dinner, or anything else that gets them offline. Young suggests reminding them of positive memories from the past to help them see themselves as existing beyond QAnon.

"You're working to dilute what has become a superconcentrated identity based on QAnon," Young said. "The way you are gently diluting it is by adding other memories, constructs, experiences, and emotions to their minds in ways that will sort of diversify how they think of themselves."

Maryland psychiatrist Sean Heffernan started researching QAnon after he noticed Q bumper stickers while driving around an affluent suburb of Annapolis, Maryland, the home of the U.S. Naval Academy. The media image of QAnon often presented believers as uneducated bumpkins, or Trump die-hards. But he was noticing Q and "WWG1WGA" bumper stickers on cars in wealthy areas, soccer moms passing him on the highway.

Finding QAnon's proliferation in his community "bizarre," Heffernan researched how to bring people out of QAnon. He came to believe that many people were drawn into QAnon because of a lack of social connections in their real world, leaving them hunting for community online instead. To come out of it, they would need to see that social connection they were looking for outside of QAnon.

Like other experts, Heffernan agrees that the best option is being emotionally available for a QAnon supporter when they reach that epiphany on their own.

"I don't think that it's something that you can pull somebody out of," Heffernan told me. "I think they have to be ready to leave it."

David knew all too well how hard it could be to maintain a relationship with a QAnon believer. He called me again in July 2021. Now Nathan had latched on to a new QAnon rumor that claimed the Chinese army was storming across the Canadian border into Maine. There were videos of strange lights in the darkness. There would be a climactic battle, then the Trump restoration. The Storm finally seemed to be at hand.

It had now been more than a year since Nathan first told his parents about his interest in QAnon, and David had seen plenty more predictions fail to come true before this one. When Biden won the election, David was ecstatic, feeling sure that Nathan's interest in QAnon would deflate once Trump left the White House. In the six months after the inauguration, though, his son's interest in QAnon had risen and fallen with the news cycle, but had never gone away entirely. Now it was back at a high point, with Nathan convinced that Trump would retake the presidency any day now.

For David, the initial shock of Nathan's QAnon beliefs and his frantic attempts to fix them had been replaced with resignation. Nathan reminded him of Linus in the comic strip *Peanuts*, a child waiting alone every year for an appearance from the mythical Great Pumpkin, who never arrives.

"I keep going back to Linus in the pumpkin patch," David said. "That's my son. Except he's angry about it."

Later that summer, David called me again. Nathan still believed in QAnon. They had just finished arguing about how Nathan was convinced that the Biden people saw in the White House was a body double, and the real Biden was either dead or imprisoned. Nathan warned his parents to stock up on water bottles and a generator ahead of a societal shutdown—something Nathan dismissively said David no doubt missed on "*your* news."

"It didn't die with Trump like I thought it would," David told me. "The critical thinking that doesn't take place is astonishing."

By August, Nathan's QAnon enthusiasm seemed to have settled down a little. Now he was getting into the all-beef diet, a diet favored by conservative college professor and author Jordan Peterson, who had become a sort of father figure for lost young men.

David was learning how to live with QAnon in the family, walking around it delicately in every conversation. He had developed a set of internal rules for avoiding an eruption from his son.

"You just talk about general, life things," he explained. "You don't go into the controversial stuff."

By November 2021, as David and his family wrapped up their second year of living with QAnon, he messaged me again with a hopeful message. Nathan had a girlfriend, which gave him less time to spend online. David was hopeful that Nathan might finally be returning to the real world.

He sent me an update a week later: never mind. Nathan had started talking about QAnon again, this time convinced by something he read online that the earth is flat.

Chapter 11

The Q Caucus

Republican congressman Adam Kinzinger brought his gun to work on January 6, 2021, and warned his wife not to leave their Washington apartment. As a rare, elected Republican critic of Donald Trump, Kinzinger knew better than most in his party what kind of people Trump's rise had unleashed in the conservative grassroots. Now those same forces, including Proud Boys, militias, and thousands of furious Americans united only by the shared lie that the election had been stolen from them, were marching on Congress.

Watching television coverage of the protests from his congressional office that morning, Kinzinger was struck by the number of Q shirts and signs he saw. The sizable presence of QAnon followers made Kinzinger worry even more about the potential for violence later that day, when Congress would vote on certifying Joe Biden's presidential win. Kinzinger hoped he wouldn't meet any of the QAnon followers in person.

"I had the sense that I did not want to run into this crowd, because I had been a bit of the GOP face calling out this bullshit," Kinzinger recalled later.

He might have been a rising star in a different kind of Republican Party. A forty-two-year-old former Air Force pilot with a taste for political combat, Kinzinger first won his Illinois seat in the 2010 Republican wave election. But Kinzinger's stand against QAnon and other Trump-era grotesqueries had turned him into a pariah among conservative activists and, increasingly, with his Republican colleagues in the House.

Kinzinger saw QAnon as the culmination of a conspiracy theory derangement that had been bubbling on the right since at least the Obama administration. He remembered the panic in 2015 over "Jade Helm," a series of military exercises in southern states. In an early sign of the internet-based conspiracy culture that would spawn QAnon, rumormongers cast Jade Helm's official purpose as a ruse. In fact, they said, Barack Obama wanted to use the exercises as cover to launch an armed federal takeover of Texas and imprison conservatives in makeshift Walmart prisons. Texas's governor, worried that the conspiracy theorists were onto something, ordered the state guard to monitor the exercises to make sure the military didn't get out of line.

Kinzinger first started researching QAnon in 2020, when he saw tweets ending in the cryptic message "WWG1WGA." He was soon shocked to see how far it had spread among conservatives. Kinzinger worried that QAnon's message about an "underground cabal" controlling the world had a special ability to provoke people who believed in it. Conspiracy theorists who think the moon landing was fake didn't tend to pick up guns to fight for their beliefs, Kinzinger noted. But someone convinced the world's most powerful people were sexually abusing children in Satanic rituals just might.

That August, Kinzinger started what would become a lonely fight against QAnon's proliferation within his party. After pro-QAnon candidate Marjorie Taylor Greene won a Republican primary runoff that all but guaranteed she would soon join him in the House, Kinzinger declared that there was "no place in Congress" for QAnon. He cosponsored a resolution denouncing QAnon and recorded a video of himself debunking QAnon believers' claims.

In the video, Kinzinger urged QAnon believers to consider stepping out of the movement, and asked politicians to disavow it. Knowing that QAnon promoters could seize on anything to add to their theory, Kinzinger pointed out the framed art behind him and felt the need to stress that it wasn't "my secret message to the Illuminati."

"If you believe these theories, I'd actually encourage you to do your own research, and do it with an open mind," Kinzinger said.

Those efforts didn't do much to stop QAnon's spread. A Trump campaign spokesman even attacked Kinzinger, not QAnon, tweeting that the congressman should focus on Democratic conspiracy theories instead. The campaign was sending a message to Republican officials ahead of the election. Stay quiet about QAnon. Don't offend them.

For Kinzinger, the model for confronting his party's fringes came from late Republican senator John McCain. During his 2008 presidential run, a woman at a campaign town hall told McCain she couldn't trust Obama because "he's an Arab." Rather than ignoring her remark, McCain grabbed the microphone and corrected her. Obama, he said, was a "decent family man."

Republicans could have a McCain moment of their own with QAnon, Kinzinger thought, if only they could summon a small bit of bravery. Kinzinger envisioned Republican politicians recording a video talking QAnon believers down, like the one he did on his own. They would debunk QAnon and urge its supporters to return to reality. The message wouldn't be about judgment, he thought. There would be reconciliation. The video would say, as Kinzinger put it, that "QAnon is BS."

"We're not mad at you for believing it, because no one had told you otherwise, but here's the truth," Kinzinger said.

He knew his fellow Republicans would never send a message like that. They lived in a world where incumbents were threatened with primary challengers if they stepped out of line, and Fox News hosts held more power than senators. If you wanted to stay in office, QAnon and other problems on the party's right flank were best ignored.

The mob outside the Capitol on January 6 wasn't in the mood for that kind of gentle correction, either. More than a few were convinced that the election had been stolen by bloodsucking pedophiles, and God and

Trump had anointed them to bring those people to justice. The time for debunks and fact checks was long past.

The rioters wanted to impose their sense of the world on the lawmakers inside Congress, not the other way around. And as Kinzinger had learned a few days earlier, plenty of his colleagues already agreed with them about the election.

In a House Republican conference call leading up to the vote, Minority Leader Kevin McCarthy, the body's highest-ranking Republican, announced how he wanted his members to handle the vote to certify Biden's win. Objecting to the certification of Biden's electoral votes was doomed to fail since Democrats controlled both branches of Congress, and it wasn't clear that it would hold any legal power even if Republicans succeeded. But voting against Biden's certification might save the careers of Republican politicians eager to avoid blowback from voters who had been riled up by Trump and QAnon.

On the call, McCarthy said that he would object to the results himself. Kinzinger was stunned. Then more members said they would object, too. The idea of trying to reverse Biden's win with some parliamentary sleight of hand had at first been supported only by the caucus's most extreme members. Now Kinzinger saw that dozens of his fellow Republicans, including their leader, were signing on to the lie.

Kinzinger warned McCarthy that his decision to back the stolen-election fiction would only increase the potential for violence on January 6.

"Look, you're convincing people the election was stolen," Kinzinger recalled telling McCarthy. "You know damn well it wasn't."

To Kinzinger, the Republican leader's calculation was obvious: McCarthy knew the election wasn't stolen, but he felt that incumbent Republicans would be destroyed by primary challengers if they admitted Trump lost the election legitimately. QAnon and its conspiracy theory thinking had infiltrated the party. Republicans were content to step aside and hope they wouldn't be Q's next victim.

"They know it's wrong, but you can convince yourself of anything if you know you need to do it to survive," Kinzinger said.

Kinzinger's unease about where the devil's bargain that Republicans had struck with extremist forces like QAnon would take the country was validated in the early afternoon of January 6. Unable to sort out what was going on outside as the first attacks began, Kinzinger left his office to get a better sense of what was happening. He passed a Capitol Police officer with a warning—the rioters from the party of Blue Lives Matter had started attacking police with bear spray.

Kinzinger looked for updates on the riot on his phone, only to see that his Twitter mentions were filling up with legions of QAnon trolls. The messages included threats and a picture of a hangman's noose. They read like they were coming from the rioters themselves.

I hope you're in your office, one message read. *We're going to find you.*

Republican leaders faced a choice when QAnon attached itself like a parasite to their party. Republicans could have attacked it early, when it was still in its nascent phase on social media. A coordinated push from Republican politicians could have come after QAnon supporters hijacked the Trump rally in Florida in 2018, or after QAnon followers started murdering people. They might have said that QAnon was a sad farce, as Kinzinger imagined they might, and denied that there was any Q team working with Trump to bring on a right-wing utopia.

Fighting QAnon directly would have meant alienating QAnon voters and temporarily dividing the party. But it might also have hindered QAnon's spread. Over and over, I talked to grieving families of QAnon believers who told me that the person they had lost to Q saw their beliefs solidified by Republican silence over the conspiracy theory. If there was no secret QAnon war to join, the believers said, why didn't the people in power just say so?

Instead, Republican officials ignored QAnon, hoping it would go away before it became an embarrassment. They chose to look the other way as QAnon made itself at home in the GOP, desperate to avoid taking even a small political loss.

Once it became clear that QAnon believers were welcome in the Republican Party, it was only natural that they would start running for office themselves.

I had been covering QAnon for almost a year in December 2018 when I started to see the first signs that, incredibly, QAnon believers were gaining a foothold in politics. By then, QAnon supporters regularly flooded into Trump rallies, and a QAnon promoter had posed for a picture with Trump in the Oval Office. But the idea of a QAnon believer wielding real governmental power was still hard to imagine.

That changed with Pamela Patterson, a city council member in the small California town of San Juan Capistrano who became the first visible QAnon believer in an elected position. After losing her reelection bid in 2018, Patterson devoted her goodbye speech at a town council meeting to her love for Q. She read out a Q clue during the meeting and closed with a flatly pro-QAnon message.

"God bless America," she said. "God bless Q."

Right in the mundane setting of municipal government, there was someone who had overdosed on red pills. I couldn't believe it. But QAnon's invasion of electoral politics was only getting started. In the spring of 2019, the first QAnon candidates started to run for Congress.

At first, they were exactly who you would expect to become the public face of QAnon: fringe oddballs with no hope of winning office.

The first QAnon congressional bid in the 2020 election came from Matthew Lusk, a political amateur in Florida. Lusk included a Q section on his list of campaign issues, urging Congress to take Q seriously as a source of "prophetic" information. If elected, Lusk assured me he wouldn't use QAnon breadcrumbs to legislate—unless, of course, Q revealed some proof that he could use in a congressional investigation.

Lusk was soon joined in the wannabe Q caucus by Danielle Stella, a QAnon believer from Minnesota. Like Lusk, Stella never really stood a chance in her bid for the seat held by Democratic representative Ilhan Omar. As she announced her bid, Stella was facing multiple charges for shoplifting from Target. Stella's primary campaign fizzled out when she became a fugitive from those charges, fleeing across the state border to hide in a Wisconsin motel with help from supporters of QAnon leader Field McConnell.

If the only Anons on the ballot were of the caliber of Lusk or Stella, Q seemed destined to remain, in electoral terms, at the far edges of the party. These candidates could barely get on the ballot, much less win a primary.

But then the QAnon candidates started winning. Jo Rae Perkins, an outspoken QAnon devotee in Oregon, won the Republican primary for a U.S. Senate seat, meaning she would be the rare QAnon believer to make it to the general election.

That presented a problem for Republican leaders in Washington, D.C. Perkins's win elevated her from the countless other eccentrics of all types who run for office every cycle, only to vanish from public view after losing their primaries. Their views can't be blamed on the party they hope to represent, but a nominee is different. Perkins was still unlikely to win any statewide seat in deep-blue Oregon, but her devotion to QAnon was hard to ignore now that she was the party's pick for federal office.

Making matters worse for Republican bigwigs, their new Senate candidate appeared to be one of the most vocal, unembarrassed QAnon believers in the country. After nearly 180,000 Republicans voted for Perkins in the primary, she recorded a victory speech that played like a fan video about QAnon.

"I stand with Q and the team," Perkins said in the video. "Thank you Anons and thank you patriots. And together, we can save our republic."

Looking to tamp down backlash from Perkins's embrace of Q, her campaign put out a statement insisting that the candidate didn't believe "everything from QAnon." But then Perkins distanced herself from her own campaign, telling a reporter she was "literally physically in tears" at the idea that her campaign disavowed Q. Perkins said that she was still devoted to the movement.

"Some people think that I follow Q like I follow Jesus," Perkins said.

Perkins lost the general election that November by nearly twenty points, but she still received nearly 1 million votes. For Republican voters, supporting QAnon was not disqualifying.

She wasn't the only Q candidate running. Alex Kaplan, a researcher at liberal media watchdog group Media Matters for America, started to notice in the months before the election how QAnon candidates were proliferating on the ballots. He tracked how many QAnon supporters were running for Congress, updating his list every time he saw a picture of a candidate posing in a Q shirt, or posting "Trust the Plan" on Twitter. On Election Day, Kaplan's list of QAnon supporters who had run for Congress that cycle stood at ninety-eight people.

Not every candidate was a die-hard QAnon believer like Perkins, though. As Kaplan studied QAnon's growing candidate slate, he drew a line between true believers like Lusk or Perkins and Republican aspirants who saw signaling to QAnon believers as merely a way to improve their electoral chances.

Several candidates seemed interested in QAnon merely as a way to stand out from their primary competition. By 2020, QAnon followers had built up an entire social media apparatus that could be harnessed by campaigns. QAnon was now a constituency with organizing backbone and political contributions that candidates could essentially court for an endorsement, like a union or the Chamber of Commerce.

Some wannabe politicians appeared on the Patriots' Soapbox, the nonstop QAnon livestream on YouTube that had helped launch the conspiracy theory. But a Q-curious candidate didn't even have to go that far. They might post "#WWG1WGA" or "#TrustThePlan," a message that would be well received by the faithful while going unnoticed by voters outside of the movement.

Kaplan suspected that candidates who made those overtures to QAnon were hoping to exploit its online organizing powers.

"There was an infrastructure here that they could take advantage of," Kaplan said.

The split between the candidates hoping to exploit QAnon and the dedicated supporters was typified by the two QAnon candidates who would make it to Congress in 2020: Lauren Boebert in Colorado and Marjorie Taylor Greene in Georgia.

For Boebert, QAnon seems to have been just another way to get votes. Boebert was versed in the kinds of culture-war issues that could propel someone to social media stardom. She ran Shooters Grill, a restaurant where the main draw was that the waitresses were armed. Boebert's willingness to court controversy in search of political attention extended to QAnon. In an appearance on QAnon figure Ann Vandersteel's show, Boebert appeared to awkwardly endorse QAnon, if only to avoid offending Vandersteel and her fans.

"Do you know about the Q movement?" Vandersteel asked Boebert. "Are you familiar with what that is?"

"I am familiar with that," Boebert said. "That's more my mom's thing, she's a little fringe. I just try to keep things on track and positive. I'm very familiar with it, though."

Vandersteel frowned at Boebert's suggestion that QAnon was a kooky idea reserved only for the elderly and people on the "fringe." In an apparent attempt to lighten the mood, Boebert quickly changed course, saying that QAnon "could be really great for our country."

"Everything I've heard of Q—I hope this is real," she said. "Because it only means that America is getting stronger and better." Boebert's campaign later denied that she supported QAnon.

Boebert's interest in QAnon was nothing compared to Greene, who had been on board with the conspiracy theory nearly from the beginning. Unlike Boebert, Greene was a dedicated QAnon supporter, which she proved by leaving a lengthy digital trail of support for QAnon.

Greene signed on with QAnon in early 2018, long before there was any political advantage to it. Greene's social media posts reveal someone who was deeply engaged in the world of QAnon. In June 2018, she posted on Facebook praising an "awesome post by Q today," adding references to "WWG1WGA" and "Q+," the code QAnon followers use for Trump. Greene was even active in QAnon debates over the authenticity of individual Q posts, insisting in a May 2018 tweet that Q's posts were legitimate in a tweet that read, *Trust the plan.*

Greene also embraced the grab bag of individual conspiracy theories that make up QAnon. She was a 9/11 truther, claiming that a "so-called plane" crashed into the Pentagon, in an apparent reference to the idea that the 9/11 attack on the Pentagon was somehow faked by the government. She claimed that the Charlottesville, Virginia, white supremacist attack in 2017 was also an "inside job," and taped herself taunting David Hogg, a gun control activist and survivor of the 2018 mass shooting at Marjory Stoneman Douglas High School in Parkland, Florida.

Greene acted out the racism and anti-Semitism at the heart of QAnon. She said progressive Democrats like Muslim members of Congress should "really go back to the Middle East if they support Sharia," the Islamic law system, and said black voters are "held slaves to the Democratic Party." In a 2018 Facebook post, she suggested that wildfires in California were caused by space lasers controlled by a group that included the Rothschilds—a Jewish family that has long been a trope of anti-Semitic conspiracy theories.

In August 2020, Greene defeated a more traditional Republican in a primary runoff. Because she was now the Republican nominee in a heavily conservative district, Greene was all but guaranteed a seat in Congress. Greene's runoff win represented a challenge for top Republicans who had avoided acknowledging QAnon up to that point. A hard-core QAnon believer was now running to represent their party in Congress.

At first, Greene's win prompted a bipartisan disavowal of QAnon. All but seventeen Republicans joined Democrats in the House in voting for the resolution condemning QAnon that Kinzinger had cosponsored.

Beyond that symbolic resolution, though, Republicans either ignored Greene's win or supported her. A spokesman for the House Republicans' campaign arm, which handles funding for Republican candidates, defended her. Trump dubbed her a "future Republican star."

No one better typified Republican leaders' attempts to ignore QAnon than McCarthy, whose position as the House minority leader made him one of most important Republicans in the country. McCarthy initially took a hard line against QAnon after Greene's primary runoff win, forcing top Republicans to finally acknowledge QAnon.

"There's no place for QAnon in the Republican Party," McCarthy said.

Three months later, though, McCarthy suffered a bout of selective amnesia. He couldn't remember what QAnon was. Talking to reporters shortly before Democrats and just eleven House Republicans voted to strip Greene of her committee assignments over her past comments, McCarthy acted like QAnon had never been a problem for Republicans. Referring to the conspiracy theory as "Q-On," McCarthy said again that Greene had denounced the conspiracy theory. It was time to move on.

"Denouncing Q-On—I don't know if I say it right, I don't even know what it is," McCarthy said.

Ron Watkins, the former 8kun administrator best known for possibly being the mastermind behind Q, announced in October 2021 that he wanted a new title: the gentleman from Arizona. Until a few months into 2021, Watkins had lived in Japan. But as his star on the right rose, he moved to Arizona and started maneuvering to run for Congress. Watkins had become a right-wing media star separate from the Q persona after positioning himself as an amateur expert on voter fraud. A cowboy-hat-wearing Watkins appeared on pro-Trump cable channel One America News, where he was cited as a "cyber analyst." Trump retweeted him, boosting the profile of one of QAnon's biggest promoters in the process. Trump lawyer Rudy Giuliani had even listed Watkins in a planning document as an ally who could be trusted to push the Trump administration's stolen-election message.

Now Watkins wanted to be a congressman. He wasn't exactly brimming with charisma, and his past as the administrator of a forum known for hosting mass-shooter manifestos offered promising opposition research targets for his better-funded primary opponents. But his run had a certain logic to it. QAnon supporters were already in Congress. Why not cut out the middleman and send the person who's allegedly Q himself to Washington? Shortly after Watkins announced his bid, I called him to discuss his political ambitions. In a conversation with Watkins and his campaign manager, a man named Tony, Watkins insisted that he wasn't Q. Tony added that Watkins wasn't running as a QAnon candidate.

For Watkins, running for office meant maintaining just the right amount of distance from QAnon. He couldn't escape Q entirely—no one, including me, would have been interested in his campaign if he wasn't suspected to be behind Q. But he could hardly win an election or even a Republican primary on an all-Q platform. That meant nodding to his QAnon fandom, but not openly embracing it.

That strategy was complicated by Watkins's campaign itinerary, which included a trip in a few weeks to a poker-themed QAnon conference in Las Vegas called the "Patriot Double Down." The signs that it was QAnon affiliated were everywhere, including the number 17 on a promotional poster. I asked Watkins about the sign.

"The number seventeen is just an auspicious number," Watkins said.

That was too much for Tony.

"Ron, Ron, oh God, oh God," Tony said in dismay.

Watkins quickly ended the call when I asked him about QAnon's role in the January 6 riot. Watkins 2022 was off to an unsteady start.

Unlike Boebert and Greene, Watkins will likely never reach Congress. He struggled to raise money or stand out from more traditional candidates. A Republican operative in Arizona told me Watkins had "no chance" of winning his primary, much less the general election. But Watkins isn't the only

QAnon celebrity grasping for some semblance of power, sometimes successfully. Tracy "Beanz" Diaz, the QAnon YouTube promoter who played a key role popularizing the conspiracy theory, won a seat on the executive committee for the South Carolina Republican Party. QAnon leader and John F. Kennedy Jr. impersonator Juan O. Savin has organized a multistate coalition of candidates for secretary of state positions who would hold crucial power over elections if they win. One of them, a state representative in Arizona who has promoted QAnon, earned an endorsement from Trump.

Beyond individual QAnon personalities running for office, QAnon's popularity in the Republican Party has grown as party elites refuse to confront it. Even people who don't see themselves as QAnon followers have come to see QAnon as a respectable political position. Sarah Longwell, a Republican strategist who opposes Trump, has studied QAnon's sense of acceptance within the party. In 2021, some news reports had claimed, often with little evidence, that QAnon was in shambles after Biden's inauguration and Q's disappearance. Yet while conducting focus groups of Republican voters after Biden's inauguration, Longwell found that QAnon was more popular in the party than ever, even among average Republicans who didn't consider themselves to be QAnon believers.

The Trump years had introduced conspiracy thinking to the party's mainstream, to the point that QAnon was just considered another political affiliation or policy preference. A Republican voter could be focused on lower taxes, or abortion, or QAnon. Within the party, QAnon had become just another faction.

"They're swimming in a cultural soup where Q is now much more mainstream," Longwell said of the Republicans she interviewed.

The rise of conspiratorial thinking among the Republican grassroots went beyond QAnon. It wasn't necessarily that everyone was donning Q shirts or picketing their local pizza parlor. In her focus groups, Longwell found that Republicans she interviewed were increasingly living in what she called a "post-truth nihilism." They saw reality as a multiple-choice question, where you could select the facts you most preferred. They didn't bother to investigate whether what they received from Facebook or conservative social media outlets was true. For them, there wasn't a single truth. Instead, you could choose whatever was most comfortable to believe.

"They have lost a sense of what is true generally," she said.

With the Republican Party slipping deeper into conspiratorial thinking, Kinzinger announced nine months after the riot that he wouldn't run for reelection. Kinzinger's time fighting QAnon didn't pay him any political dividends. Reviled by his party's voters and fellow congressmen for serving as one of only two Republicans on the House select committee investigating January 6, Kinzinger's political future going forward looked bleak.

As Kinzinger headed for the exit, the conspiracy theories he fought against were still dominant in the party. Trump remained dominant in the party and attacked any Republican politician who suggested he lost legitimately. The flood of QAnon candidates hadn't stopped, either. When Media Matters researcher Alex Kaplan counted the number of QAnon candidates at the start of 2022, he found fifty-two candidates with QAnon ties running in the midterms.

Closing out his final months in Congress, Kinzinger wasn't optimistic that his party had been swayed by the events of January 6. If anything, QAnon believers and other conspiracy theorists seemed to have more power in the party than ever.

"I can't imagine what happens if the Republican Party becomes taken over by actual QAnon believers," Kinzinger said.

There's evidence that Q has already made inroads in the Republican Party's highest echelons. A few days after Trump's election defeat, Ginni Thomas—the wife of Supreme Court justice Clarence Thomas and a powerful activist in her own right—texted Trump chief of staff Mark Meadows with some good news. It might look like Trump had lost, she said, but she had just discovered that the election could have been a ruse to arrest top Democrats all along. Quoting from a QAnon website, Thomas shared the plan: Biden and his co-conspirators would soon be headed for Guantanamo Bay to face military tribunals.

Chapter 12

Baby Q

Kasey Mayer watched in the first months of 2020 as her older sister Kiley's Instagram posts went from sunsets and brunches to QAnon and Trump. By the summer, Kiley was living with Q—or at least with a man who said he was Q. "I'm worried she's in serious danger," Kasey Mayer wrote me in an email.

After I started writing about QAnon, I started to receive a lot of these messages about getting friends or relatives out of the movement. People wanted to know how to solve whatever problem QAnon had created in their lives—a son who had become unreachable because of his obsession with adrenochrome and pedophiles, or a nightclub owner whose partner was ready to reopen their club and flout mask laws because some YouTuber had convinced him that the coronavirus was fake. The emails were filled with anguish, and a desire to reconnect with the person they knew before QAnon grabbed hold of them. But I had never received an email like this before.

Kiley had been working as a sales contractor for AT&T when, she claimed, she found proof that the telecom giant was letting intelligence agencies spy on customers' phone calls. She became convinced the deep state knew about her discovery and was going to punish her for it. Strangers she saw on the street were stalking her. Kiley started to describe herself online as a "targeted individual," a term used by a thriving internet community of paranoiacs who believe they're being pursued by shadowy forces.

Kasey had a simpler explanation, telling me her sister had become "mentally unstable." A friend who knew about Kiley's interest in conspiracy theories showed her a video by an upstart QAnon promoter named Austin Steinbart, a tall, unnervingly confident twenty-nine-year-old with slicked-back hair. Steinbart was different from every other conspiracy theorist pushing Q online. He didn't just promote QAnon; he claimed to be Q. According to Steinbart, his future self, some twenty or thirty years in the future, was using a time-traveling computer to post messages on 8chan that now appeared as the Q posts.

"Put that in your pipe and smoke it, haters," Steinbart said in one of his first videos. "I'm not just associated with Q, I *am* Q. Me, personally. This is my operation. The guy posting on the boards and running point on this operation is actually me in the future."

Back in our timeline, the fans of the younger, present-day version of Steinbart dubbed him "Baby Q" to distinguish him from his future self. In the summer of 2020, Steinbart started to gather his followers together in a suburban Phoenix house. Informally, Steinbart's followers called this makeshift headquarters "The Ranch." They also gave it a more martial name that made it sound like a key part of a military operation, rather than the Airbnb rental it was: Forward Operating Base Geronimo.

Kiley Mayer and other Steinbart followers often cite one March 2020 video in particular as the moment they realized he was Q. It's called "Black Ops 101," but it's better known as the one where he boasts about burning a man to death.

Wearing a backward baseball cap and sitting in front of the Anonymous hacker logo, Steinbart looks more like a YouTuber about to dole out video game tips than the globe-trotting spy he claims to be. He sketches out the world according to Steinbart, where the *Titanic* was deliberately sunk to kill critics of the Federal Reserve and the Swedish DJ Avicii died not by suicide, but from murder because he was about to expose the cabal. Now,

Steinbart proclaims on camera, he is here to put the world right as an agent of the Defense Intelligence Agency.

Steinbart explained to his then-nonexistent audience that he had been recruited into the DIA when he was seventeen years old—an important age for QAnon believers, given the associations between Q and the number 17. After a few years of covert operations that involved hacking John Mc-Cain's cell phone, smuggling drugs, and even setting a man on fire, Steinbart learned what his training had been leading up to: the revelation that he was Baby Q. Thanks to time-traveling messages from his future self, he'd had the foresight to invest early in bitcoin and was now "rich as hell," with billions of dollars in cryptocurrencies that he could use to fund Trump's new branch of the military devoted to outer space, the United States Space Force.

"We are not going to be gangbanging or drug dealing anymore to fund our black ops," Steinbart said. "I'm actually just going to pay for it myself. Isn't that fun?"

In the spring of 2020, Kiley moved into the Ranch.

"She picked up her entire life, drove out here, and is living in a compound," Kasey told me.

Steinbart's time-travel story was bizarre, even by the standards of a movement where adrenochrome and sex dungeons are taken as givens. Kasey watched Steinbart's videos, where he declared that he would soon run the Space Force or denounced one of his followers for a perceived betrayal. She felt like Kiley had joined a twenty-first-century, internet-enabled version of Charles Manson's Manson Family—and now her sister was one of the Manson girls. Still, Steinbart had attracted the most visible devotion of any QAnon promoter yet. While figures like Neon Revolt had more reach and higher follower counts on social media, they hadn't yet built QAnon communities in the real world like Steinbart had.

People trying to grapple with the meaning of QAnon often call it a cult. There are obvious similarities, from the fact that these ideas could grow in a new follower's mind to become the most important thing in their lives, to the way that leaders within the movement encourage members to cut off skeptical family members.

Psychiatrist Robert Jay Lifton, one of the country's leading cult researchers, has three criteria he uses for any group to be considered a cult: a "charismatic leader," methods of "thought reform" aimed at changing how followers think in ways that keep them in the cult, and the "considerable exploitation" of followers.

QAnon meets the third criteria easily, with believers duped into alienating those close to them and spending money on quack medical cures or QAnon merchandise. QAnon also has tools of "thought reform," with the frequent use of what Lifton calls "thought-terminating clichés" meant to stop QAnon believers from questioning the movement. Lifton explains thought-terminating clichés as "highly reductive, definite-sounding phrases, easily memorized and easily expressed" that can be repeated to prevent deeper thought. In QAnon, believers tell one another to "trust the plan" when everything in the world suggests there is no plan. When a Q prophecy fails to come true, they reassure themselves with the phrase "disinformation is necessary"—meaning that whatever QAnon prediction failed was really just a ruse posted by Q to confuse his enemies.

QAnon also has a central figure, but the anonymous Q fits awkwardly among the canon of dangerous, charismatic cult leaders. Q might be one person, or many, and his identity has never been confirmed. Most Q followers direct their adoration toward Trump, not Q. They see Trump as the world-changing messiah figure, with Q as just his messenger, albeit one who knows the future before it happens.

While most cult leaders exploit their followers for money and sex, it still wasn't clear what Q was getting out of fueling QAnon, cult expert Rick Ross told me. Whatever Q got out of creating QAnon—some political advantage or a sick amusement from stirring up strife—his goal wasn't typical of a leader. "The idea that a cult leader would be anonymous and not appear and have no ability to be seen and adored—that goes contrary to what most cult leaders are like," Ross said.

Steinbart seemed intent on resolving the semantic debate over whether QAnon is a cult by turning his QAnon group into a cult in the classic 1970s sense, complete with a compound, guns, bitter internal feuds, and showdowns with federal law enforcement. To Ross, my description of "The Ranch" was suggestive of a budding cult.

"One of the most obvious red flags that a group is a destructive cult is its desire to socially isolate its members," he said.

Cult or not, Kasey didn't want her sister involved with Steinbart's group. Kasey knew that Kiley was an adult and free to join whatever strange organization she wanted to. But it gnawed at her, watching Kiley opt to live in a fantasy world.

"I don't want my sister to be part of something like this," Kasey said. "What can I do to help?"

QAnon is riven by factions and personalities who often hate one another more than any outsider could. Conspiracy theorists grow furious when I write about them personally, assuring their fans that I work for my paymasters in the pedophile deep state. But when the calls are off the record and the text messages encrypted, they are happy to draw my attention to a rival's old criminal conviction or fraudulent side business. If I was going to help Kasey, I needed to know more about how Steinbart's group operated. And so I called Dustin Nemos, a QAnon leader and Steinbart nemesis. To Nemos, Steinbart was a con man and the people who believed he was Q were easy marks falling for a false prophet. Nemos had turned QAnon into a moneymaker himself, raking in what he claimed were millions of dollars by selling merchandise and nutritional supplements to an audience that saw him as a Q expert. He was also a close observer of his rivals in the movement and a dedicated gossip. I knew that if anyone in QAnon was willing to talk about Steinbart it would be Nemos.

In other words, Nemos was eager to help. "I love to destroy my enemies," he said.

Steinbart's claim that he was Q infuriated Nemos and nearly every other QAnon leader—Steinbart was clearly trying to take over the whole eco-system. His rivals either had to challenge his status as the Q pretender, or accept a lesser position in Baby Q's orbit. They christened him Austin "SteinLARP," insinuating that his claims about being Q were a ruse or a fantasy game, like "live-action role playing." Steinbart pushed right back at them, warning that dire, potentially fatal consequences lay ahead if they continued to deny his legitimacy. "I'm nowhere near as nice as Q-Plus," Steinbart said in one video, referring to Trump. "And I'm under no obliga-tion to be nice to any of you."

Like me, Nemos found Steinbart's operation to be an enigma. Steinbart emerged from nowhere to become a powerful new voice in QAnon, and it wasn't clear how he had done it. No one knew where he was getting the money for his compound or his professional social media production. But Nemos was curious, like everyone else I talked to in Q-world, about what exactly Steinbart was planning.

"I would not be surprised if he did try to create a cult," Nemos said. "Who knows? That guy's probably dangerous. He's nuts, he's insane."

Steinbart and his followers represent the outer limits of commitment to QAnon, giving up their old lives to work for his vision. All Q support-ers embrace a worldview that defies everything they have been taught in the conventional world. But except for those who have committed actual crimes in Q's name, they haven't done much about it. Meanwhile, in Phoe-nix's triple-digit heat, there was a guy who was creating the closest thing QAnon had to a new way of living. Steinbart had a chief of staff and a bud-ding digital media empire. A rotating crew of roughly ten people lived at the Ranch, with several other followers living elsewhere in the area and many more online. Steinbart's supporters had risked plenty themselves, investing their own money into his quest. Now he was trying to take over QAnon right at the height of its pandemic surge, when new recruits flooding into QAnon were looking for direction.

Kasey had asked me to help get her sister out of QAnon. But selfishly, I had to admit that her request also offered me an invaluable chance to see how belief in Q worked up close. Steinbart's organization went beyond the trash talk and idle chatter of other QAnon groups. They were living an entire QAnon lifestyle. Now I had to go to Phoenix to see Steinbart's world for myself.

Austin Steinbart grew up in a well-off, churchgoing family in Round Rock, Texas, just outside of Austin. A friend from high school, who asked me not to use her name because of the threat of harassment from Steinbart's followers, remembered him as a popular student enamored with his own ability to manipulate his classmates and girlfriends.

"He was smart, but he definitely cared more about outsmarting people than he did grades," she said.

Steinbart attended Arizona State University, where he met his wife—a woman who would later want nothing to do with her husband's newfound Baby Q persona. A few years in, he dropped out and became an IT technician, fixing tech issues at hotels or conference centers. Steinbart later claimed he left the school to pursue his covert operations.

Steinbart made his first foray into Q in the shadow of another QAnon entrepreneur. Their relationship would explode in classic QAnon fashion, with Steinbart accused of being an agent provocateur intent on undermining good-thinking patriots.

In May 2018, an Arizona QAnon believer named Lewis Arthur discovered an empty homeless camp near Tucson. Arthur became convinced that this long-abandoned pile of trash was in fact a way station for cabal child sex-traffickers. Q believers from across the world flocked to his cause. Arthur, on the verge of becoming a sort of QAnon warlord, organized his new supporters and began running patrols into the desert with his supporters, looking for the deep-state agents.

Steinbart volunteered for Arthur's patrols soon after they began. While returning to base one afternoon, Steinbart's teammates accused him of pressuring them to shoot off their guns to heighten the drama for Facebook—or, less charitably, to make QAnon believers look like gun-crazed lunatics chasing ghosts in the Arizona heat.

Suspicions in the armed camp, already rife with paranoia about federal provocateurs and informants, fixed on Steinbart. By suggesting that they fire their guns off, Steinbart's erstwhile comrades said, he was trying to create a public relations disaster for the camp. Arthur and his troops had spent weeks searching fruitlessly for the cabal's agents. Now they had one among themselves.

"He keeps talking about trying to find ways to heighten this," Arthur grumbled to himself on a Facebook livestream.

Arthur and a knot of sour-faced vigilantes in military gear confronted Steinbart about his attempts to convince the cabal-hunters to shoot their guns. Outnumbered, both by Arthur's men and the legions of furious Arthur fans flooding the Facebook video chat with angry emojis, Steinbart slinked off.

Steinbart vanished from QAnon groups after the camp debacle. Then, in March 2020, two years after Arthur effectively banished him from Arizona's Q circles, Steinbart took to his obscure YouTube channel with an announcement: he was Q. Refusing to seriously explain what had drawn him back to QAnon, Steinbart cast his return as another mission from his handlers in military intelligence.

QAnon created a community where Steinbart could remake himself, pretending to be a desert vigilante one year and Baby Q the next. But Steinbart stood out from the other QAnon boosters by talking endlessly about the crimes he had committed in Q's name, claiming he had smuggled drugs across the southern border and threatening in a video to kill the queen of Denmark if she didn't cede Greenland to the United States. For his fans, Steinbart's gleeful flouting of the law merely demonstrated that he was in fact Q, and therefore shielded from legal consequences.

To prove any doubters wrong, Steinbart decided to go on a mini crime spree. He started with some old footage he had surreptitiously recorded at a doctor's office.

In January 2020, two months before he debuted as Q, Steinbart's mother sent him to a California branch of the Amen Clinics, a world-renowned psychiatric center founded by Dr. Daniel Amen. It's not clear why Steinbart's mother sent him to the clinic, though the timing—coming right before he started to publicly proclaim he was Q and told people he was exchanging messages with himself in the future—doesn't seem like a coincidence. For his part, Steinbart claims his mother sent him to the clinic because she was worried about his attention-deficit disorder.

Taking a test on a computer at the clinic, Steinbart realized he could also view the files of former patients, many of them professional football players who had been treated for chronic traumatic encephalopathy, or CTE, at the same facility. Steinbart rifled through the digital files, including those belonging to former football star turned commentator Terry Bradshaw. Steinbart filmed the former Pittsburgh Steelers quarterback's brain scans and doctor's notes closely enough that a viewer could read them.

Steinbart released the footage in one of his first QAnon videos, offering it as proof that he operated above the law, while not mentioning that he had been a patient himself. If MI6 gave James Bond a license to kill, Austin Steinbart wanted to prove that QAnon gave him, somewhat less exaltedly, a license to film celebrities' brain scans, enjoying what he called an "obvious immunity from prosecution."

"Brain's a little holey, Roy, not gonna lie," Steinbart said as he pointed at what appeared to be brain damage on another player's MRI results.

When an employee at Amen Clinics asked him to take down the video, Steinbart tried to conscript the clinic into his fantasy world. Steinbart said their only choice was to put out a press release claiming the brain scans had been hacked by a DIA agent as part of a "military intelligence operation." When the clinic complained to his parents instead, Steinbart warned them in an email that they faced "NUCLEAR ARMAGEDDON."

"You tell me whether or not I'd be in huge trouble for hacking these famous people's medical records if I wasn't Q," Steinbart said in his video about the medical data.

Steinbart seemed to be locked into pursuing QAnon fame at all costs, no matter how self-destructive it could be to his own life. If the original Q had gained with his outrageous assertions, Steinbart was set on proving that he was Q by brazenly committing crimes and getting away with them.

The personal risks of that strategy became clear six days after Steinbart published the video, when the FBI knocked on his door.

Steinbart, who was at this point living in a house with his wife and had not yet moved to the Ranch, answered with a Desert Eagle pistol in hand, according to the FBI agents. Putting the gun away, Steinbart apologized, explaining that he had to deal with "a lot of psychos." His mood brightened more when he learned his new visitors were from the FBI, and explained that he was an agent for the government, too.

Steinbart's interview quickly turned into a defense attorney's nightmare of self-incrimination, according to an account provided in court later by FBI agents seeking his arrest. Steinbart said he had smuggled marijuana across the Mexican border, and confirmed that he had accessed the clinic's files, saying it was "actually not hard." Asked about the brain-scan video, Steinbart said he did "outrageous" things to prove he was a spy, on orders from his future self, transmitted through an implant in his brain. Steinbart assured the agents he only committed the crimes to "show people I won't get in trouble" because he was already the head of the Space Force.

The FBI visit didn't dissuade Steinbart. Two days later, he picked a new fight and urged his supporters to harass a cloud storage company called Datto, which had taken down files Steinbart had put on the site for breaking copyright laws. When Datto's CEO asked Steinbart to call off his fans, who had cost the company more than $10,000 by tying up their customer service lines, Steinbart told the executive he was impeding "Operation QAnon" and would soon be dealt with.

"*I will send some PSYCHOS to come see you in person,*" Steinbart texted him.

Ten days later, FBI agents arrested Steinbart on an extortion charge for the Datto threats. Despite prosecutors' warnings that Steinbart had "significant unaddressed mental health issues," a judge released him from jail, putting him on house arrest with an ankle monitor.

Steinbart's backstory as a superspy working for the military started to unravel after the indictment, when prosecutors were unable to find proof that he worked for his supposed employer, the DIA. But his name in QAnon had never been bigger. Thanks to the handful of videos he had posted before his arrest, he attracted more than 20,000 YouTube subscribers, plus roughly a dozen followers who showed up at his court hearings waving a Q flag.

After one hearing, Steinbart was met outside by Jacob Chansley—the "Q Shaman" whose painted face and horned helmet would become infamous a few months later when he joined other rioters breaking into the U.S. Capitol. Chansley, already wearing the backwoods mystic by way of the *World of Warcraft* look destined for newspaper front pages and parodies, treated Steinbart like an elder statesman of QAnon. For his part, Steinbart—dressed in a suit for court and no face paint of his own—winced when Chansley gestured with his spear to emphasize his points about metaphysical truths and realms beyond our imagining.

"We have the high ground, and we're taking down them low-ass motherfuckers," Chansley assured Steinbart, turning to bellow at the federal courthouse behind him. "Where we go one, we go all, motherfuckers!"

Michael Khoury was deep in a chemotherapy brain fog when he discovered QAnon. And for the first time in a while, the world started to make sense.

Khoury, a mortgage salesman in Michigan, contracted lymphoma in 2018. As he lay in bed, recovering from his cancer treatments and suffering from an unrelated disease that left holes in his skin and required him to bandage his body like a mummy, Khoury started watching videos of Donald Trump. Here, Khoury thought, was a guy who was willing to fight.

"I got that fire to do the same," he told me.

Khoury began to feel the chemotherapy working on his mind. He quit his job when he started to forget things. But after the government ruled him ineligible for Social Security disability payments, Khoury, furious, burrowed deeper into pro-Trump conspiracy theories. Surfing the internet, housebound and newly unemployed, he found the Q drops.

Khoury was thrilled by Q's revelations. He already felt marginalized because of his Social Security rejection, stunned to find out that the government apparently didn't care whether he lived or died. Q's story of a villainous cabal fit Khoury's life perfectly. It was no accident that life had been so unfair to him. The cabal had made the world that way, twisting it so the little guy always got crushed. Down and out, angry, and with nearly limitless time to spend on the internet, Khoury made for the perfect QAnon recruit.

Khoury appreciated what he learned from QAnon, but he struggled to see any larger purpose to it until he saw Steinbart's videos. That's what Khoury realized what QAnon was all about: helping Austin Steinbart achieve his destiny as Q by bringing down the cabal.

"Suddenly, here's this guy telling us, 'It's me!'" Khoury said.

Q was real, and Khoury could meet him. He could even move in with him. Shortly after Khoury's cancer went into remission, Steinbart, under house arrest and wearing an ankle monitor ahead of trial, started collecting his followers at the Ranch. The plan: launch the Space Force, bring down the cabal, and help Steinbart achieve his destiny as Baby Q. Khoury left his fiancée behind in Michigan to live with Steinbart and his supporters.

Steinbart brought on a chief of staff named Sabrina, who talked frequently to her comrades about how eager she was to swear Steinbart in as the head of the Space Force. There was a woman known publicly only as "Ms. Qniverse," and a man who had lost his wife because of his fascination with UFOs. Along with the live-in roommates, there were hangers-on who filtered through—a New York Republican running a doomed write-in campaign against Representative Alexandria Ocasio-Cortez stayed for a few weeks and proclaimed that Steinbart was the second coming of Christ. The group even had a doctor, Tammy Towers Parry, who traveled to Trump's 2020 speech at Mount Rushmore to wave her Q flag.

Kiley shared a room with Taylor Stiller, a New Age twenty-four-year-old who had been researching conspiracy theories since the 2016 election. The other members of Steinbart's group dubbed them the "Crystal Sisters." Stiller's journey to QAnon was typical among Steinbart's followers. She had been researching conspiracy theories online for years, so when QAnon appeared it wasn't a huge step for her to believe that, too. Stiller cast her QAnon beliefs in mystical terms. Q's story, she said, proved that "dark forces" were keeping humanity in a "consciousness prison." Stiller drew a clear line between her life before and after she discovered conspiracy theories.

"I never really came back," she said.

Phase One of Steinbart's master plan to become the public face of QAnon relied on making a lot of YouTube videos. Steinbart and his acolytes launched a series of YouTube channels about QAnon, with names like "Qame Theory" and "What on Earth? Ask Q." Each channel was meant to target a specific demographic: millennials, or Fox News–loving boomers, for example. Much of the programming played on the idea of the "quantum internet," the technology Steinbart claimed his future self used to send messages back in time. A gluten-free cooking show was planned.

Khoury and two others created a QAnon talk show, where they hashed out Steinbart's latest pronouncements and railed against the "Q Pharisees"— the Steinbartian term for QAnon leaders who doubted Steinbart was Q. Kiley and Stiller launched "Quantum Consciousness," a show aimed at millennials and New Age spiritualists where they toasted new QAnon developments with White Claw hard seltzers. One episode centered on how the quantum internet could be used to time travel, and even see into the brains of historical figures like Julius Caesar or John F. Kennedy.

"We're just supposed to put out content," Kiley said in one video, describing Steinbart's plan.

Steinbart's group appeared inexplicably well funded. They managed to rent a sprawling house and a studio for producing their YouTube videos in a Phoenix office tower, even though their only visible source of revenue came from little-watched videos about QAnon.

Much of that money, it emerged later, came from his followers, who had been assured they would receive high-ranking positions in the Space Force once Steinbart took over. Khoury estimated that he put at least $40,000 of his own money into Steinbart's media operations and the Ranch, a figure Steinbart didn't dispute.

Khoury's devotion to Steinbart could be difficult to understand. He had explanations for his beliefs, but they didn't make any sense to me—it was like he was speaking on a wavelength that only QAnon believers could understand. Once, when I asked him about why he believed Steinbart's obviously untrue stories about himself, he said it was because Steinbart "knew that there was something weird about my DNA." Khoury had recently discovered, via a DNA test, that his mother and father were distantly related to one another.

Thanks to the money from Khoury and other believers, Steinbart's operations took on an off-kilter professionalism never before seen in QAnon communities. Visitors at the Ranch and volunteers for the newly founded "Steinbart Media Group" were required to sign nondisclosure agreements (NDAs) swearing them to secrecy about what went on inside the house. His staff received corporate-sounding titles—Khoury became the assistant director of communication—in anticipation of the positions they would take in the Space Force.

Kasey watched as her sister, now living just a few blocks from where they had grown up outside of Phoenix, tried to put a girl-power branding on QAnon. In phone calls, Kiley urged her sister to come to the Ranch and meet Steinbart and her other roommates, encouraging her to keep an open mind about QAnon. When I talked to Kasey in July 2020, a month after she had first asked me for help, she was losing hope that her sister would ever leave Steinbart's group. QAnon believers had recently pushed into the mainstream the idea that the furniture website Wayfair was smuggling children inside its furniture, and Steinbart's crew, falsely, was taking credit for it.

"She's more into it than even before," she said.

Kasey fumed after former Trump national security adviser Michael Flynn and members of his family posted a video on the Fourth of July taking the "QAnon oath." Inspired by Flynn's video, Steinbart, Kiley Mayer, and six of Steinbart's supporters had filmed themselves solemnly taking the oath in front of a green screen, before collapsing into laughter and high-fives. To Kasey, videos like that seemed meant to show what a great time Steinbart's followers were having at the Ranch. It creeped her out.

In our call, Kasey raged at Trumpworld figures like Flynn for playing along with QAnon, and at Steinbart for posting the video of her sister and her dead-eyed friends taking the QAnon oath.

Steinbart's disciples started posting online about adrenochrome, trying to convince their Facebook friends that Hollywood celebrities tortured children for their youthful essences. Mutual friends who saw Kiley's increasingly QAnon-focused posts asked Kasey if her sister had lost her mind.

I never heard from Kasey again. After our call in July, she stopped responding to my calls and text messages. But in videos posted by Steinbart's group, Kiley addressed her sister's recent death. That's how I learned what had happened to her: Kasey died of a heart attack at twenty-seven years old.

With Kasey gone, I lost my closest connection to Steinbart's group, right as he drew in more followers and became a more vocal figure in QAnon. But internally, Steinbart's compound had already started to collapse.

The Ranch crew projected a cheerful image online, coming off like a season of *The Real World* with a time-traveler for a roommate. Judging by comments under their social media posts, it worked. Steinbart's videos garnered tens of thousands of views, filled with responses from QAnon believers convinced he was Q. Steinbart's online followers became a roving internet army attacking other QAnon promoters who disputed his attempts to take over the entire movement.

Steinbart's operation had succeeded for months at suspending his followers' disbelief. It seemed like there was nothing those closest to Steinbart wouldn't accept. They didn't seem to mind that there was no evidence that he worked for the DIA or that he had billions of dollars. At times, it seemed like Steinbart had set up a force field outside the Ranch that no sense of the real world could penetrate. Instead, Steinbart's group was undone by something he couldn't lie away: personal drama.

The fun-loving portrayal of life at the Ranch belied the fact that Steinbart faced a mountain of legal problems that could send him to prison for years. Steinbart's bail conditions prohibited him from drinking alcohol or using drugs, rules he freely flouted in the company of his followers. Tellingly, the NDAs that visitors were required to sign prohibited them from discussing any such drinking or smoking "habits" they witnessed at the Ranch. But Steinbart's drug and alcohol use became a vulnerability as some of his followers started to become suspicious about his claims.

A follower named Mike became disaffected and left after developing doubts about Steinbart and the rest of the residents' motivation. Instead of working to carry out "Operation QAnon," Mike noticed, residents at the Ranch just drank all night and slept the day away. Meanwhile, Mike spent all his time trying to get publicity for Steinbart and started to feel like he had fooled himself into becoming an unpaid volunteer for Steinbart's own ego.

Mike wondered about Steinbart's wealth, too. Steinbart said that he had stashed away billions in cryptocurrency, thanks to tips from his time-traveler future self. But while Steinbart claimed that he had enough money to fund the entire Space Force, he asked his followers to pay whenever he wanted a six-pack of beer.

"He never paid for a single thing there," Mike said in a video posted online, urging other Steinbart followers to abandon their leader.

Mike and other disgruntled members of the group took their allegations on a media tour in more mainstream QAnon circles, infuriating Steinbart. The Ranch purge began. Steinbart excommunicated several ex-members, accusing them of working for the FBI to entrap him and holding trysts in the Ranch's basement. He began to suspect that his once-loyal aides had installed hidden cameras around the house to catch him breaking his bail conditions.

"They put a hidden camera in my house and took a picture of me drinking a beer," Steinbart complained.

The number of hosts on Khoury's show dwindled to two. Drinking from a mug whose label announced that he was drinking the tears of Q Pharisees, Khoury lamented that one of his now-vanished friends had secretly been working for the deep-state infiltrator.

"I think they've been infiltrators from the start," Khoury said of the ex-members.

Steinbart's wife, who had never moved to the Ranch, told him she wanted a divorce. Steinbart broke the news in a video to his fans. Steinbart claimed his marriage had ended because his wife feared what the deep state might do to their family if he kept up his QAnon campaign.

"She doesn't care if I have all the power in the world," Steinbart, who seemed at times to be talking as much to himself as he was to his YouTube audience, said.

Somehow, whether from one of Steinbart's defectors or some other means, court officials discovered that Steinbart had been violating his bail restrictions. He was arrested again on September 1, 2020, and admitted to drinking alcohol and smoking marijuana. When police searched his house, they found a "Whizzinator," a prosthetic penis meant to cheat drug tests. Because Steinbart had been caught breaking rules while on his pretrial release, a judge ruled him held until trial.

Steinbart's imprisonment shattered Steinbart Media Group. Their movement had been based on a clear plan: proving that Steinbart was Q, accessing his billions of dollars in cryptocurrency wealth, making the Space

Force, and destroying the cabal. But now Steinbart was in jail indefinitely, with the prospect of months or years in prison to come. With their charismatic leader now in only sporadic contact via a jailhouse telephone, some of Steinbart's remaining followers began to wonder what they were doing with their lives.

The infighting consuming the Ranch didn't stop with its leader's incarceration. Steinbart had become convinced that Khoury's fiancée was also working with the FBI. Khoury learned that he had been ousted from a recording he received of Steinbart calling from the jail.

Khoury was stunned. He had sunk the majority of his savings into the Steinbart Media Group, and now he was being banished without even speaking to his hero. In an open letter published under a QAnon letterhead, Khoury said he was in a "financial bind" because of how much he had spent on Steinbart. "I left behind my fiancée and family under the agreement that everything I provided financially would be reimbursed," Khoury wrote. "This was reiterated many times to me and my fiancée when my finances began to dwindle."

Steinbart had taken Khoury for a ride and nearly destroyed his relationship with his fiancée. At his lowest point, QAnon had promised Khoury the world—a high-ranking position in the Space Force, a sense of purpose, and a community. Now Steinbart was pushing Khoury out, and leaving his one-time devotee at least $40,000 poorer. But in his letter, Khoury asked for only one thing: a single phone call to his imprisoned leader to prove his loyalty.

Steinbart was out of jail by the summer of 2021, after pleading guilty in April 2021 to the extortion charge and being sentenced to eight months time-served. But his path back to QAnon greatness had vanished. The Ranch collective dissolved in his absence. The post-riot social media crackdown on QAnon followers obliterated his YouTube and Twitter accounts. And while Steinbart claimed he had won new adherents in jail, many of his genuine followers had returned to their pre-Steinbart lives.

Steinbart's fellow inmates were initially baffled by his claims that he was the leader of QAnon. They had never heard of it, and they didn't care about Steinbart or his futuristic alter ego. After the Capitol riot, however, Chansley—the Q Shaman—was briefly incarcerated in the same jail before being transferred to Washington. Chansley's notoriety from the riot helped. Suddenly everyone knew what QAnon was, giving Steinbart what he called a new level of respect from his fellow prisoners.

"They called me the *jefe* of the Q Cartel," Steinbart told me.

After Steinbart's release, he decided that Khoury's fiancée wasn't an FBI agent after all. Khoury could finally return and work again for Steinbart. Khoury invited me to Phoenix to see Steinbart give a speech at the premiere of an election fraud documentary. Other QAnon believers treated Steinbart's flock like "lepers," Khoury complained, but they didn't know what was really going on since Steinbart's release. I should come see it for myself.

I couldn't turn down the chance. Steinbart's QAnon experiment had burned itself out, but it was still one of the strangest ways that QAnon had played out in the real world. And I wanted to find out what had happened to Kiley Mayer.

Steinbart had somehow snagged a speaking spot at the premiere of *The Deep Rig*, a conspiracy-theory-heavy film about election fraud in the 2020 presidential race starring former Overstock.com CEO Patrick Byrne. The onetime online furniture retail magnate first insinuated himself into the political news cycle in 2019, when he claimed he had a sexual relationship with accused Russian spy Maria Butina. In the final days of the Trump administration, Byrne finagled his way into the White House and urged Trump to have the military seize election ballots.

Steinbart helped secure a church on the outskirts of Phoenix for Byrne's premiere, and his remaining followers passed out flyers to drum up interest. The premiere coincided with the end of Arizona Republicans' controversial inspection of millions of votes—an attempt to find any scrap of evidence to dispute the fact that Biden had won the state—and Byrne's premiere doubled as a party for the audit team. It had drawn some boldface names on the right, including Michael Flynn's brother and some state lawmakers.

Steinbart struggled to get invited to conferences for mainline QAnon believers, who still saw him as, at best, a crank. But he had no problem getting a booth at the premiere, where his roughly dozen remaining supporters advertised a club service called "Q Meetups"—Steinbart's latest attempt to take his version of QAnon nationwide.

I met Steinbart in the church lobby and saw that he had traded his backward baseball cap and polo shirt for a Young Republican–approved navy blazer and wingtips. Kiley was with him. I had never talked to her before, with her sister dying before I could get her phone number. Rarely leaving Steinbart's side ahead of the premiere, Kiley seemed like his second in command, or perhaps something more. While Kasey had hoped Kiley would leave Steinbart's orbit, she had in fact only risen higher in the group. Before the movie started, Kiley told me that she and Steinbart were now a couple.

Months earlier, Steinbart had been eating prison food and trying to redpill other inmates. Now he was hobnobbing at a film premiere backstage with Republican Party officials and giving speeches. And while his speech at the premiere turned out to be unremarkable—he told me later that the event's organizers told him not to mention QAnon—the fact that he was even able to make it onstage at all was unbelievable.

Steinbart's QAnon compound had failed, but in a way, he had found something even better. Thanks to Republican leaders' willingness to accommodate QAnon and treat it as a legitimate faction of the party, Steinbart, an obvious grifter and charlatan who specialized in sucking vulnerable people dry to support his own delusions, would be treated like a credible political figure. He had even managed to insinuate himself into the team handling the Arizona ballot recount, becoming one of the audit's staffers shortly after his release from jail.

After the movie, Steinbart and Kiley took me backstage for an interview. Sitting alone with them, I had a fleeting thought that no one else in the world knew where I was. I had put myself in the hands of a recently convicted felon who claimed he killed people, and often spoke of the violence he had witnessed and inflicted. But he was all charm this time.

Steinbart seemed like a conservative operative on the make. He talked about his so-far unsuccessful effort to recruit a candidate for one of Arizona's U.S. Senate seats in 2022, and the need for a QAnon rebrand—its image was too affiliated with conservativism. QAnon, Steinbart thought, should be for everyone. And he thought that, in retrospect, trying to create a QAnon compound wasn't the right move after all.

"I didn't do myself any favors doing the ranch thing," he said.

Kiley was still entrenched in QAnon, too, and not just because she was now Steinbart's girlfriend. She told me lengthy stories about her own brushes with the deep state as a "targeted individual." Steinbart said he still listened to episodes of her old YouTube show about his QAnon adventures.

"Two pretty girls talking about me?" he said. "How could I not love that?"

I asked Steinbart what he made of claims that he was leading a cult, pointing to the fact that Khoury seemed to still be in his thrall despite being exiled from the group and out of $40,000. Steinbart said he had only expelled Khoury from the group so his follower would get his own life in order, concerned that Khoury's fiancée was on the verge of breaking up with him. And of course, Steinbart did think at the time that she was an FBI mole.

"When you get called a cult leader—would you be like, 'Hey, you've got some issues with the people who are closest to you and your wife and that's important and you need to make sure you make that priority and don't just put it to the wayside'?" Steinbart said. "That's what cult leaders do, right?"

The Phoenix event was Steinbart's coming-out party into a mainstream brand of Republicanism. But as Steinbart, Kiley, and I rejoined his supporters in the lobby after the interview, it was clear the once-festive mood had changed.

Khoury, frowning, approached Steinbart, holding out his phone so his leader could read it.

Steinbart's QAnon detractors had been watching the event on a $45-per-person livestream and were outraged that Steinbart was allowed to give a speech. His QAnon critics slammed Byrne, accusing him of either being duped into promoting Steinbart's claims that he was Q or an FBI plant. Cowed, Byrne's organization denounced Steinbart on Telegram, the encrypted social media app that became popular with QAnon supporters banned from more mainstream apps.

"Austin Steinbart was somehow put into the lineup last minute by an unknown party," Byrne's post read. "He certainly has no part in The Deep Rig movie."

The tide was rapidly turning on Steinbart's moment of triumph. His followers were twitchy, looking around the lobby like they could be bounced by security at any moment.

"Patrick Byrne's people are getting jumpy now," Steinbart said as he read the statement on Khoury's phone. "They're scared, right? They don't want to be associated with Q. But Austin Steinbart was the one who got them their venue."

"That's what's so funny," Kiley said. "People don't realize we don't mind the controversy."

"I thought I handled myself like a gentleman," Steinbart said.

Before I left, I asked Kiley about her sister, and her hope that Kiley would leave QAnon. Kiley said her father was coming around on Steinbart, and had attended the premiere—only leaving early because he was so upset by the idea that the election had been stolen.

"They're very supportive of everything," she said of her parents. "And I would hope if my sister was alive, she would be in that same camp."

Chapter 13

Q Goes Abroad

Australian prime minister Scott Morrison took the parliamentary podium in October 2018 for what was supposed to be a moment of national healing. After years of investigations into sexual abuse cover-ups, Morrison had come to the heart of Australia's government to deliver an apology to victims. At the most somber moment of Morrison's speech, as he listed the types of organizations where abusers had preyed on children, he slipped in a shout-out to QAnon. From scout troops to churches, Morrison said, Australian children had been victims of "ritual sex abuse."

That phrase stuck out. Until then, the inquiry into sexual abuse cases in the country had never featured the phrase "ritual sexual abuse." But the idea of children being sexually abused during rituals, ones that sometimes involved hooded black robes, daggers, and pentagrams, does play a significant role in QAnon. Those theories about dark sexual rituals landed a mention in Morrison's speech because Q had someone on the inside. Morrison had been friends for thirty years with a man named Tim Stewart. But when Stewart wasn't hanging out with the prime minister, he led a double life as one of his country's most devoted QAnon backers.

Under the pseudonymous Twitter handle "Burned Spy," a reference to the schlocky USA Network covert action show *Burn Notice*, Stewart urged Australians to get on board with Q. Stewart even hobnobbed with QAnon celebrities, posing for a picture with pro-QAnon actor Isaac Kappy when

Kappy traveled to Australia. That interest in Q had alarmed some of his family members, who reported him to a hotline for national security threats.

Stewart had more than 20,000 followers on Twitter, but his friendship with the prime minister promised to be a much larger platform for QAnon. In messages to a fellow believer, Stewart wrote that Morrison was in the midst of an "awakening," inching closer to becoming a QAnon believer himself. Ahead of the sex abuse speech, Stewart tried to convince his friend to include the phrase in his remarks. Just hours before the speech, Stewart messaged a QAnon ally that the prime minister "is going to do it!"

Morrison's use of the phrase thrilled QAnon believers in both Australia and the United States, who saw the nod from the prime minister as proof that their beliefs were legitimate. A major QAnon account declared that Morrison's mention of "ritual sexual abuse" meant that he was a "fellow rider in The Storm."

As it turned out, though, the only storm Morrison's speech would set off was one of bad publicity for himself. Reporters seized on Morrison's friendship with a Q Twitter power user, while Stewart's sister blasted her brother's indoctrination into QAnon in a TV interview. Morrison, who refused to disavow his friendship with Stewart, could only insist that he didn't believe in QAnon himself. Whether Morrison knew what he was doing or not, the mention of "ritual sexual abuse" was a victory for QAnon's budding movement. One of the most powerful people in the world had given a public nod to QAnon in one of the most-watched moments of his administration.

The Great Awakening had gone worldwide.

QAnon might seem like a hard sell outside the United States. "Where we go one, we go all," its most popular slogan, comes from a thirty-year-old sailing movie that's barely remembered in its home country, much less abroad. QAnon's followers have a die-hard devotion to an American reality TV host, Donald Trump, who first made his name in the brashly American worlds of Manhattan real estate and New York City tabloids. Even most Americans can't keep track of Q's cast of characters, so how can a German be expected to care where John Podesta eats pizza?

QAnon's details are incredibly specific to the United States, but its appeal is universal. Even outside America, QAnon has found plenty of pathways into new believers' minds. QAnon reaches vulnerable people who feel dislocated in the modern world, assuring them that their lives have a greater meaning and that the people they dislike are inherently evil. It preys on anti-Semitic tropes that have taken root across the world. There's nothing more natural than an urge to protect children. The ubiquity of American social media companies means that QAnon's success on those platforms could be replicated on a global scale. And in every country, there are unscrupulous people willing to use QAnon to take advantage of others, especially if it means accumulating money or influence for themselves. QAnon has been able to spread abroad using some of the same methods it used to spread in the United States: social media, the coronavirus pandemic, and an inherent vagueness that can be twisted into appealing forms to attract new recruits.

Across the world, local factions have taken QAnon and adapted it to their own circumstances. Trump is still venerated in foreign QAnon variations, but in those versions he's often working alongside that country's own right-wing politicians. Meanwhile, that country's left-wing leaders are added to the list of pedophile-cannibals to be destroyed.

As divided as QAnon believers in different countries can be by differences in language or QAnon interpretation, they all see themselves as different parts of Q's worldwide struggle to help Trump destroy the cabal. This global QAnon mission has helped connect right-wing movements from different countries, becoming a sort of lingua franca of paranoia and violent fantasy.

In Japan, QAnon grew so big that it split into two factions: "J-Anon" and the "QArmyJapanFlynn," a group with a special devotion to former Trump national security adviser Michael Flynn. When Trump visited Finland in 2018, local QAnon believers held up a sign with a *Q* celebrating his visit.

Social media analytics company Graphika has located QAnon Facebook groups on five continents. Brazil, led by the Trumpian populist president Jair Bolsonaro, has a booming QAnon community online.

QAnon moved out of the United States almost as soon as it began, traveling on the same social media pathways that enabled it to jump between users in America. It seems to have first appeared abroad in Canada. In QAnon's early days, Q posted often about "Uranium One," an American pseudo-scandal revolving around a Russian company's attempt to buy uranium rights in the United States and Hillary Clinton's supposed perfidious role in the deal. Uranium One also implicated liberal Canadian prime minister Justin Trudeau, drawing anti-Trudeau Canadians researching their foe into QAnon social media networks. Soon conservative Facebook groups in Canada started to fill with mentions of Q.

Marc-André Argentino, the Canadian QAnon researcher who has analyzed the growth of QAnon internationally, says QAnon's importation into Canada reflects a larger online exchange between right-wing politics in both countries. Canadian media personality Gavin McInnes founded the far-right Proud Boys men's group, which saw several of its leaders charged in the Capitol riot, while the United States gave Canada the seed that grew into a new branch of QAnon.

"I don't know who lost most, but it's not a great deal for either side," Argentino told me.

Since so much QAnon baking was already written in English, its material could be easily repurposed for jumps to Anglophone countries like the United Kingdom and Australia. After QAnon took root in Canada, French-speaking Canadians in Quebec translated Q posts and explanations into French, priming the conspiracy theory to spread to France and Belgium.

While QAnon reached its peak in the United States during the pandemic, Covid-19 also powered QAnon's spread abroad. Interest in Q had been bubbling in the United Kingdom almost since the movement started in the United States, with one wealthy devotee even raising a Q flag over his castle. But the movement in the United Kingdom was mostly a side-show until the pandemic. Angered by lockdown restrictions and united by the spread of the "Save the Children" movement, hundreds of Q believers marched in front of Buckingham Palace at a protest in 2020. At one point during the march, protesters turned to the palace and shouted "pedophile" in unison.

The coronavirus also powered an explosion of QAnon in Germany. As in the United Kingdom, some fringe German activists had started to pick up the QAnon faith before the pandemic began. Once lockdowns started in Germany, however, QAnon achieved a new relevance for people looking for explanations in a world thrown off balance. Analysts tracking QAnon think Germany has roughly 200,000 QAnon devotees active in online groups, making it the largest non-English QAnon community.

QAnon's proliferation in Germany demonstrates the conspiracy theory's uncanny ability to adapt to local conditions, like some invasive plant species of the mind. Because QAnon clues are so vague that they can mean anything, QAnon can become relevant to whatever activists in a country want. Miro Dittrich, a German researcher who tracks the far right in his country, watched in the first weeks of the pandemic as the marginal QAnon accounts he followed exploded in followers. One Telegram account he followed quadrupled in size in just a month, going from 20,000 followers to 80,000 followers, echoing similar lockdown-driven booms experienced by American QAnon promoters. Many of the German users seized on QAnon's anti-Semitic themes, filling the newly popular groups with posts and memes attacking Jews.

"QAnon has this special ability that could be easily adaptable for your specific regional context, because of the big tent that it has," Dittrich told me.

In Germany, QAnon was embraced by adherents of the Reichsbürger, or "Reich's Citizen," a movement akin to American antigovernment sovereign citizens. Just like sovereign citizens in the United States, Reichsbürger members refuse to recognize laws they disagree with, avoid paying taxes, stockpile weapons, and engage in occasional violent clashes with the police.

And, like American sovereign citizens, many of them have gotten deeply into QAnon.

Reichsbürger members claim that the German government set up after World War II is a fiction, and that Germany is still under occupation by Allied forces. The real German government, they believe, is the German Reich that existed until 1945. They describe themselves as "citizens of the Reich" and give their allegiance to various crackpots who lead supposed Reich "governments in exile."

For Reichsbürger adherents, QAnon offers a vision for a final utopian moment that would end the Allied occupation. In the United States, the Storm is about liberating humanity from the Satanic cabal. But the Storm in Germany became about freeing Germans from a decades-long foreign imposition and installing the "true" German Reich government.

Like QAnon supporters elsewhere, German believers began to interpret pandemic events to fit their own narratives. When NATO canceled a series of large military exercises because of the virus, Reichsbürger supporters enamored with QAnon claimed that Trump originally planned the war games as a cover for a military invasion that would free Germany from its occupation government. In their telling, the Allied occupation forces secretly in control of Germany created the virus to foil Trump's rescue effort.

One German faction even has their own Q, a mysterious Telegram user named "Commander Jensen" who makes cryptic Q-like posts. Other leaders of German QAnon factions started issuing their own execution warrants, calling for the deaths of prominent liberal Germans. But Dittrich says QAnon's biggest impact in Germany and other parts of Europe is as a funnel for American conspiracy theories and culture-war issues outside of QAnon, uniting far-right movements across the Atlantic.

Earlier right-wing movements in America struggled to gain international followers. They were too focused on internecine American issues to spark a broader movement. The white supremacist alt-right may have grabbed headlines in America during the 2016 election, before it imploded during the 2017 white supremacist rally in Charlottesville, but it failed to create the kind of global influence of QAnon. Stories promoted by American white supremacists trickled days or weeks later into online far-right groups in Germany and generally failed to gain traction.

But QAnon isn't about only the United States. It's a global story. The Q clues are so vague and have enough empty spaces that anyone can feel like their own favorite political movement is part of Q's army. Posts alleging the American election in 2020 was stolen were translated within hours into German in that country's QAnon groups. From there, the stories echoed out beyond QAnon into the broader right-wing German internet. Thanks to the networks set up by QAnon believers, right-wing German activists were suddenly closely following the twists and turns of supposed ballot thefts and rigged voting machines in American battleground states. The connections between QAnon communities in the United States and other countries have become pipelines for pushing out the United States' polarized politics to the rest of the world. "QAnon is a sort of hub for these talking points," Dittrich said. QAnon has proven to be so successful at spreading abroad that some countries even have their own Q-like heroes.

In the summer of 2021, Romana Didulo, a Filipino immigrant to Canada in her mid-fifties, made a startling announcement: Donald Trump and the Q team had appointed her to be the new queen of Canada. Trudeau was out, and Canada was now a monarchy. QAnon wasn't Didulo's first dip into extremism. For years, she tried and failed to interest people in a marginal political party she called "Canada1st." By embracing QAnon, though, Didulo finally found a way into a stream she could capitalize on. In May 2021, Didulo started making videos about QAnon.

She declared that the "white hats and the U.S. Military" appointed her to be QAnon's representative in Canada. The city where she lived, Victoria, British Columbia, was now Canada's capital. Prominent American QAnon promoters supported Didulo's claim to queenship, helping her amass more than 70,000 followers on Telegram. In communiques signed with "Q" and "WWG1WGA," Didulo indoctrinated her new Canadian followers into her fantasy world beyond orthodox QAnon, claiming that, among other things, Queen Elizabeth II had been executed for crimes against humanity. While the idea of a strange woman no one had ever heard of before becoming Canada's sovereign was bizarre, her new supporters pointed to the auspicious fact that Didulo's name is an anagram for "I Am Our Donald." Didulo's followers fly the purple flag of Didulo's kingdom outside their homes, displaying a golden maple leaf bisected by a sword. But Didulo's interests go beyond Renaissance Faire role play. As the pandemic dragged on, Didulo encouraged her followers to challenge coronavirus measures like masking orders and vaccine requirements.

Eventually, Didulo's messages to her flock turned darker. Didulo started talking about bringing in former U.S. special forces soldiers she called "duck hunters" to carry out violence on her orders against supporters of anti-Covid measures. Canadians who wanted to sign up for "duck hunts" posted pictures of their rifle collections on Telegram.

In November 2021, Didulo issued her most dangerous proclamation yet. She declared that it was time to go "duck-hunting" against anyone who gave the coronavirus vaccine to minors.

"Shoot to kill anyone who tries to inject Children under the age of 19 years old with Coronavirus19 vaccines/bioweapons or any other Vaccines," Didulo's note read. "This order is effective immediately."

Didulo's threats to unleash her tens of thousands of supporters on duck hunts finally earned a response from Canadian law enforcement in December 2021. A Didulo supporter was arrested after he posted in a Didulo chat room about his plans to "duck hunt" at his child's school over a vaccination campaign. Didulo herself was detained that same month and held for a mental health exam. After her release, Didulo started traveling across Canada with her followers to promote her opposition to vaccines.

It's not clear whether Didulo's budding kingdom will survive her brush with the law. But Didulo's sudden, bizarre rise in Canada demonstrates QAnon's lingering power, even divorced from its origins in the United States and the original Q figure. Q's messages created an audience for any conspiracy theory leader deluded or power-hungry enough to cater to them.

With her dreams of an icy QAnon kingdom and bloody special forces duck hunts, Didulo went far beyond the original QAnon texts.

Consciously or not, though, Didulo realized that QAnon created a community of people desperate to follow orders, even from a self-crowned queen. After Q went silent, QAnon believers look to anyone aggressive or crazed enough to seize the mantle of leadership, a quandary that will persist no matter what happens to Didulo.

QAnon has even inspired child kidnappings in Europe, just as it did in the United States. In April 2021, a group of QAnon believers in France kidnapped a five-year-old girl whose grandmother had custody of her. To win back custody of her daughter, the girl's mother had fallen into QAnon, just as QAnon mothers in the United States had. She started posting about coronavirus conspiracy theories on Facebook, claiming she was going through an "awakening."

One day, two QAnon believers posing as social workers appeared at the grandmother's house. To save the girl from what they saw as the predations of a child-abusing cabal, the two men abducted her. After a weeks-long search, police located the girl and her mother in an abandoned factory in Switzerland.

The investigation of the kidnapping, however, revealed that France has a militant QAnon network far more organized than anything seen in the United States. It soon became clear that French QAnon's ambitions went far beyond a family court dispute. Searching one of the alleged kidnapper's houses, investigators discovered chemicals that could be used to make explosives.

As agents for France's version of the FBI pursued the two men involved in the abduction, they discovered that the abduction plot was allegedly the brainchild of Rémy Daillet-Weidemann, a failed politician who allegedly spent 3,000 euros funding the kidnapping. Daillet recruited a band of supporters online by promoting QAnon, then allegedly organized them into a highly structured shadow QAnon army called "The Overthrow." Daillet's group allegedly intended to overthrow the French government—or, as members put it in QAnon terms, stop the "Satanist, pedocriminal elite." As of this writing, Daillet faced criminal charges over the kidnapping plot and an alleged terrorist plan to attack vaccination sites.

The rise of QAnon criminal groups in Canada and France demonstrates that QAnon's ability, unusual among conspiracy theories, to inspire law-breaking isn't limited to the United States. Because of its vagueness and appeal during the pandemic era, QAnon has traveled quickly outside its original American context, spawning new branches of the conspiracy theory. It's become a rallying cry for far-right activists working in their own countries, and a way to unite them with fellow travelers abroad. Even if changing political forces in the United States diminish its power in the original home of QAnon, the movement will remain a destabilizing force around the world for years to come.

While QAnon has helped export the most toxic elements of American politics to the rest of the world, it has also twisted American politics by distorting the meaning of events outside the country. The Myanmar military's coup in February 2021, for example, was universally denounced across the world as an attempt to end that country's nascent democracy. But many QAnon believers hoped something similar would happen in the United States.

The Myanmar military alleged that democratically elected president Aung San Suu Kyi had stolen her election, a potent charge for QAnon believers smarting from what they claimed was a stolen American election just three months earlier. Rather than recognize the Myanmar coup for what it was, they came to believe it was just the first domino falling ahead of the Storm, another moment of righteous military officers taking back their country from election fraudsters.

For Q, a successful military coup was something to envy. At a May 2021 QAnon convention in Dallas, one attendee asked Michael Flynn why a Myanmar-style coup couldn't happen in the United States.

"Why can't what happened in Myanmar happen here?" the man asked.

As a former member of the military who rose to become a three-star general, Flynn had sworn an oath to defend the Constitution. But as the QAnon crowd cheered, Flynn seemed to endorse the idea of replicating the Myanmar coup in the United States.

"No reason," Flynn said. "I mean, it should happen here. No reason."

Conclusion:
Patriots in Control

In May 2021, hundreds of QAnon believers traveled to Dallas to celebrate their movement's survival. Trump was out of office and Q had gone silent, but QAnon was still here. In fact, it seemed to be doing better than ever. QAnon was doing so well that its members could spend thousands of dollars in a luxury hotel ballroom on Q tchotchkes sold at auction by Michael Flynn.

With a giant inflatable Trump balloon looming behind him, Flynn held up a QAnon quilt for sale. He auctioned off a T-shirt with his name on it for $575. A baseball bat signed by Flynn sold for $7,000. A holographic image featuring Flynn and pro-Trump lawyer Sidney Powell with the QAnon slogan written across it sold for $3,500. But the biggest draws were a series of digitally edited posters that reimagined Flynn, Powell, and other QAnon luminaries as tricorne-hat-wearing Revolutionary War heroes. A poster of Flynn toting a flintlock musket sold for $7,000.

Watching from the edge of the ballroom, I couldn't believe how much these souvenirs were going for. Spending thousands of dollars on a photoshopped picture of Michael Flynn as an extra in *The Patriot* seemed irrational. Then again, I realized, it was far from the craziest thing QAnon believers have done. The auction was part of the "Patriot Roundup," a Memorial Day weekend celebration of all things QAnon featuring the conspiracy theory's leaders, C-list Trumpworld celebrities, and even a member of Congress. The conference meant three days of talk about the malevolent influence of the cabal, the stolen election, and how QAnon believers could stop relying on Q and seize the levers of government themselves.

I had come to Dallas and paid $500 for a general admission ticket because I wanted to see what QAnon was like in the post-Trump, post-Q era. Joe Biden's inauguration was supposed to kill QAnon. When Biden put his hand on the Bible and the military failed to swoop in to arrest him and put him on trial, QAnon believers should have realized that Q's much-discussed plan wasn't coming to fruition. The 100,000 sealed indictments waiting to send their enemies to Guantanamo Bay weren't real. Trump would no longer be the god-emperor-in-waiting. As the inauguration wrapped up without any mass executions, online QAnon communities filled with anguish, a sense of betrayal, and, for some, an intense desire to throw up. I watched the reaction live in a QAnon chat room on Telegram, as believers' elation over the impending arrests they expected at the inauguration turned to disappointment and physical revulsion.

"I'm going to puke," said one QAnon believer.

"Sick to my stomach," said another.

QAnon didn't stop. Since Biden took office, its hard-core members have become more committed, and its organizing infrastructure has grown. To them, Biden's win wasn't proof that Q was lying to them—it just meant that the deep state was more powerful than even Q realized. The Storm hadn't been canceled; it had just been postponed. Q's posts had taught them everything they needed to know about the world. Now they needed to put those beliefs into action offline. The earlier QAnon events I went to in 2018 and 2019 had been loosely planned marches and rallies in the streets of Washington. But in 2021, QAnon was serious enough to host its own packed events, with tickets going for hundreds and even thousands of dollars per person.

The Patriot Roundup's organizers booked an Old West–themed wedding hall in Dallas that looked like a *Scooby Doo* ghost town, complete with fake storefronts and a saloon. The setting made for a subtext that was impossible to ignore. Older white Republicans had gathered for a weekend to bemoan the death of an imagined America, all in a cartoon version of the country's past. The event's blatant QAnon affiliations didn't stop prominent Republican officials from attending. Texas Republican congressman Louie Gohmert spoke, as did Texas GOP chairman Allen West, a potential future governor of the state. West had recently changed the state party's slogan to "We Are the Storm," a phrase weighted with Q imagery, though he insisted it wasn't about QAnon.

I bought a ticket under my own name to the conference knowing there was a good chance I wouldn't be allowed inside. The conference organizer, a man who went by the alias "QAnon John," sent mandatory refunds to other journalists who bought tickets. When I gave my name at the door, though, a volunteer handed me the pass everyone else had received: a placard bearing the familiar words "Where we go one, we go all."

QAnon believers were even angrier than usual after Biden's victory. I once had an underdeveloped sense of the personal risks I took at right-wing rallies and protests, but seeing reporters attacked outside the Capitol on January 6 made me more concerned about my own safety. For Dallas, I grew out my beard and put on glasses and a baseball cap. If I was recognized, I figured someone would try to confront me about what I had written about QAnon.

The task of keeping people like me out fell to an aspiring QAnon security company called the 1st Amendment Praetorian, named after the Roman soldiers famous for carrying out coups and murdering the emperors they were supposed to protect. The founder of these modern-day Praetorians, a former Green Beret, worked as a bodyguard for QAnon leaders when he wasn't writing feverish intelligence memos about a liberal plot to coordinate with the Chinese government to bring down America. The group provided security for VIPs at a pro-Trump rally the day before the January 6 riot and was later subpoenaed by the House's January 6 committee. Still, the Praetorians in Dallas were far from the tactical operators they aspired to be. After giving my name at the door, I had no trouble walking past QAnon's paramilitary wing and into the conspiracy theory's heart.

The conference's speakers covered a range of topics, from the evils of vaccines to the importance of battling Satanic "Luciferians" in your everyday life. Shirts that said "Save the Kids" on the front and "What Are the Tunnels?" on the back were especially popular with the attendees. But there was one overarching message: QAnon followers were no longer content to follow Q. Now that he had gone silent, they were stepping up to carry his message into the real world on their own.

For all QAnon's talk about revolution, it had imposed a complacency on its believers. There had been no need to get involved in politics, because Trump and the Q Team had everything handled behind the scenes. QAnon slogans told supporters that they were "watching a movie" and to "get the popcorn." They should "trust the plan" and accept that there were "patriots in control." But the new breed of QAnon leaders made clear at the conference that they wanted more action.

"We are the Storm," said Jason Frank, the believer Kayleigh McEnany once interviewed at a Trump rally, now elevated to the movement's thought-leader class.

Jason Sullivan, a right-wing social media expert who once worked for Trump adviser Roger Stone, used similar language about QAnon believers taking a more active role.

"I'm going to let you in on a little secret: you are the plan!" Sullivan said, then started pointing at people in the audience. "You, and you!"

The best way to get involved, they said, was by running for local office. Flynn told the audience that "local action has a national impact," a slogan he had started repeating at every opportunity as he pushed for more QAnon believers to enter politics themselves.

After Trump's defeat, Q went virtually silent. In his place, QAnon believers latched on to a series of substitute Qs—prominent right-wing figures they believed held secret knowledge in the same way Q once had. They could choose from Flynn, Lin Wood, and countless other pseudo-experts gathering their own tribes of QAnon followers. I saw the mechanics of being a stand-in Q in action when onetime Trump campaign lawyer Sidney Powell came to the stage. Powell smiled as the crowd begged her for insight about when Biden's election fraud would be revealed.

Q's disappearance cut off his supporters' assurances that everything would turn out all right. Now they had questions for Powell. When Trump inevitably retook the White House later that year, would he get an extra year added onto his term for the time he lost to Biden? Would Powell accept when a restored Trump nominated her to be chief justice of the Supreme Court? Powell knew how to keep the believers enthralled. Something big but unspecific was coming, she said, and it would be "biblical." The audience gasped.

"She knows things that we don't!" the talk radio host interviewing Powell said with delight.

It was like a Q breadcrumb came to life. Powell had taken up Q's mantle, even wearing a leather biker vest with a giant *Q* on the back. (Q still had one advantage over his successors: his anonymity meant he couldn't be served with a lawsuit. While Powell spoke to the QAnon believers in Dallas, a voting-machine company she had claimed stole the election was suing her for $1 billion.)

The strangest moments of the conference came during breaks between speakers, when the organizers played pro-Q videos from an anonymous creator. "City State Corporations." "Maritime Law." "Satanic Dark Cabal." A picture of Joe Biden bound for Guantanamo Bay.

"The only way is the military," the video stated, over video of spec-ops soldiers, fanning out in a field with their rifles drawn. The crowd of hundreds stood up and applauded. They loved the video's message: only a fascist takeover of the government could save America.

On the second day of the conference, things started getting weird. A middle-aged man in a black 1st Amendment Praetorian shirt sat in front of me. He pulled up another person's Twitter account on his phone and kept looking back at me, like he was comparing the account's profile picture to my face. Two other members of the 1st Amendment Praetorian sat down behind me. I tried to walk away. But by the faux-saloon, another Praetorian with an imposing dog on a leash approached me. He had questions. Why wasn't I paying enough attention to the speakers? Why wasn't I clapping? He let me go, but as I walked through the conference, I got the sense that I was being followed.

Only later could I piece together what had happened. A local reporter had sneaked into the event under an assumed name and was posting taunting messages about his ruse on Twitter. That put the Praetorians on the lookout for anyone who didn't look happy to be sitting through their second straight day of QAnon speeches. I fit that profile perfectly.

As I sat back down in the audience, I had the unpleasant feeling that a lot of people were looking at me. I tried to focus on a panel discussion with Flynn. The former general was talking about how angry he was that reporters had come to the event. It seemed like he was talking about me. I began to think my disguise hadn't been that effective.

Suddenly a Dallas police officer tapped me on the shoulder. Would I come with her, please?

QAnon John had found me. Despite selling me a ticket, QAnon John told the police I was trespassing after I was discovered by the Praetorians, whose titular commitment to the First Amendment apparently didn't extend to the press. The idea of a reporter being booted by the police from their event made for excellent Q social media content. I was trailed by roughly a dozen QAnon personalities, each with their phone out to record the scene. As hundreds of people turned to boo me, I gave them a wave goodbye.

"You should be ashamed of yourself!" an elderly woman told me as I exited the Old West town.

My walk of shame was also an opportunity for QAnon believers with personal grievances with me to have a word. Conspiracy theorist Jordan

Sather had threatened to sue me in the past when I criticized him for telling his fans to consume chlorine dioxide, a substance the Food and Drug Administration warns will function on the body just like drinking bleach. As I told the police I was there legally, Sather cut in.

"I don't know how legal some of your reporting is, actually," he complained from behind a police officer. "It's pretty defamatory."

"There's a reason why we don't want you here," QAnon John said. "It's because you don't know how to report accurately."

"The Daily Douche!" Sather said.

My unwelcome entourage pursued me to my rental car. One of them, a tanned, shirtless middle-aged man holding a microphone, got up in my face.

"Trying to get in, huh?" he said. "Not good, Will!"

As I drove away, I reflected on the path in life that had led me to being bounced by this shirtless man and a motley crew of other QAnon oddballs. Was I the equivalent of a journalistic carnival barker, exaggerating the political influence of the weirdest people so I would have an excuse to write about them? The sputtering, shirtless man alone was unlikely to achieve any political power. But for the past few years, the story of my life had been that there were a surprising number of people like him. Despite themselves, they always seemed to be gaining more influence.

Minutes after I left the conference, a man in the audience asked Flynn when the United States could have a coup like they had in, as he pronounced it, "Minimar." That prompted Flynn to issue his apparent call for a Myanmar-style coup in the United States. The crowd cheered him on. (Flynn would claim later that he was opposing the idea of a coup in America and accused the media of twisting his words.)

Flynn's remarks were the classic QAnon moment: both ridiculous and deadly serious. And as my ouster from the conference made clear, QAnon believers didn't want anyone on the outside to know what they were planning.

Q's last post came on December 8, 2020, and consisted of only one line: a link to the song "We're Not Going to Take It" by the hair-metal band Twisted Sister. That turned the song into a must-play track at QAnon events, but that final post also prompted a question: What would happen to QAnon without Q?

As it turned out, Q's disappearance wasn't all that disruptive to the movement he'd made. Even before Q stopped posting, QAnon believers started to lay the groundwork for him to vanish. Having a single leader posed too many problems. If he was discovered to be a weirdo sitting in a basement somewhere, they'd be embarrassed. Worse, if Q came out and revealed that he had run the entire movement to troll gullible Trump supporters, QAnon would be discredited entirely.

Instead, as the years passed and the Storm failed to arrive, QAnon leaders and followers started to distance themselves from the original narrative about Q's identity. Perhaps Q wasn't really a high-level intelligence official, the thinking went. Maybe his predictions didn't come true. But what was important was what he taught us about how the world works. They ditched the embarrassing QAnon story line about the Storm and predictions that never materialized, but kept all the talk about the cabal, deep-state corruption, and mole children. They created QAnon without Q.

Still, Q's disappearance left a leadership vacuum. There was no longer a pope to issue an ex cathedra ruling to keep the Church of Q in line, as Q had when he attempted to cut Alex Jones and the JFK Jr. believers out of the movement. Now anyone could say whatever they wanted without fear of Q's repudiation.

QAnon had always consisted of different, sometimes rival factions. But without Q, those branches became more eclectic, and the movement splintered. While some believers reacted to their disappointment with Q's failed predictions by abandoning the group, others burrowed deeper into hate. Those new variations on QAnon were even uglier than the ones that had come before. A Telegram account under the name "GhostEzra," posing as a former Trump administration official, introduced Q believers to virulently anti-Semitic memes. GhostEzra became one of the most influential QAnon accounts on Telegram, recruiting QAnon believers into a more viciously anti-Semitic version of the core conspiracy theory.

Six months after the QAnon conference in Dallas, the city and QAnon were in the news again. Hundreds of members of a breakaway QAnon sect obsessed with the Kennedy family had come to Dealey Plaza, the site of the Kennedy assassination. Their leader, an Oregon man named Michael Brian Protzman, had promised them that both John F. Kennedy Sr. and Jr., plus a host of other "dead" celebrities who had faked their deaths to avoid the cabal, would return in a parade. As Protzman's followers lined Dealey Plaza in a rainstorm, it slowly became clear that Robin Williams and Kobe Bryant weren't coming back, at least not that day. But Protzman's followers stayed in Dallas for months, worrying cult members' families who claimed their bank accounts were being drained.

Q's disappearance also created a space for feuding among the wannabe Q replacements. In November 2021, Wood, now feuding with Flynn, released a secret recording he had made of a phone call with the ex-general. On the tape, Flynn denounced QAnon as a "disinformation campaign" created by the CIA, calling it a "nonsense" psychological operation preying on conservatives. Even in a movement that attracts hucksters like flies to honey, Flynn's cynicism was remarkable. QAnon's greatest hero had no compunctions about making money from believers, selling them shirts, or auctioning off Q garbage with his signature on it. But privately, he thought it was all lies.

Even as new branches of QAnon appeared, many of the conspiracy theory's believers were going undercover on Q's orders. In September 2020, Q asked supporters to start disguising their support for the movement, urging them to "deploy camouflage" and "drop all references" to Q and QAnon to avoid being banned from social media. Shortly before the election, Q went further, claiming there "is no QAnon." Instead he created a new formula for QAnon believers, writing: "There is Q. There are Anons. There is no QAnon."

Clearly, "QAnon" as a brand had become too damaged. Q ruled that it was better for those Anons to push his ideas without the seventeenth letter of the alphabet attached. Those believers responded to Q's call to go underground by insisting that there had never been a QAnon movement. These were patriots, of course, and yes, they did believe in an adrenochrome-guzzling cabal—but what's QAnon? Asked by reporters about his support for Q, Flynn feigned ignorance, saying he didn't know what QAnon was. Even QAnon John changed his alias.

Those attempts to underplay their QAnon affiliations, along with the group's banishment from social media, can make it hard to gauge how strong the conspiracy theory remains without Q. But supporters have built online apparatuses of their own, using less-regulated social media networks like Telegram as well as YouTube and Twitter knockoffs that cater to conservatives, to rebuild what they lost when they were banned from the major platforms.

It's difficult to know how QAnon, a personality cult built around Donald Trump, would react to another Trump presidential bid. As Trump recedes from his omnipresent position in public life, banned from social media and forced to issue press releases to get out the taunts and boasts that he previously would just tweet, there is naturally less for QAnon believers to be excited about. But a Trump run in 2024 could easily reignite QAnon's passions, giving them an opportunity to both bring their leader back to office and prove that Q's predictions about revanchist Trumpism weren't wrong after all. It's not hard to imagine Trump, who was unable to denounce QAnon in 2020, reinvigorating the movement with just a few admiring remarks about its believers.

In the meantime, QAnon believers are eagerly gathering local-level positions. The precinct strategy mentioned at the Dallas QAnon convention has been a hit with believers and other far-right activists, especially after former Trump adviser Steve Bannon encouraged Republicans to follow it. By seizing these previously little-known local positions, QAnon supporters and their fellow travelers will have a new level of influence over how elections are carried out. One county-level Republican leader in Arizona told ProPublica she had been flooded with QAnon believers running for precinct commission spots.

QAnon has also entered local politics. Following Flynn's advice, Anons are running for school board seats, where they can influence school coronavirus policies and lesson plans. In Las Vegas, a pro-Q candidate elected to the school board declared that human traffickers exploit mask laws to smuggle children. QAnon's larger message that Democrats are out to prey on and traffic children has sunk in on the right, even among people who don't consider themselves believers. Increasingly, parents angry about sexual passages in books in school libraries don't just complain about them—they call the police and try to file criminal child pornography charges.

Worst of all, the idea of a deep-state cabal that operates with impunity has become ingrained in the Republican Party's mindset. Senate Republicans fought Biden's nomination of Supreme Court justice Ketanji Brown Jackson by accusing her of being pro-pedophile—a ludicrous charge that's impossible to imagine being deployed pre-QAnon. Even conservative voters who laugh at believers' excesses have bought into the idea that the 2020 election was stolen by a cabal whose crimes are always just on the verge of being exposed. A year after the Capitol riot, an NPR poll found that two-thirds of Republicans still believe Biden stole the election from Trump. If Republicans think elections aren't legitimate, then it's more likely that they'll support any measure to take power. American democracy will enter a death spiral.

In January 2022, right-wing activists attending a rally starring QAnon speakers near the Mexican border in Texas targeted a butterfly sanctuary. The sanctuary's staff had opposed the construction of both government and private border walls that would cut through its land. Days earlier, a former Republican official in the town warned the sanctuary's director to either leave town or carry a gun. QAnon believers were furious at the sanctuary, claiming it was a front for child sex-traffickers.

A few days before the rally, two far-right activists showed up at the sanctuary. Why, they wanted to know, were the sanctuary staffers helping child traffickers? The sanctuary closed for days out of fear of what the QAnon believers might do. The sanctuary's plight made me wonder. If something as innocuous as a butterfly refuge can be targeted by QAnon, what chance do the rest of us have?

Conspiracy theories have always been with us. But the combination of America's polarized politics and social media helped QAnon surpass the conspiracy theories that came before it, creating a superviral conspiracy theory and even menacing American democracy.

QAnon's growth is a story about how Trump and the Republican Party decided to capitalize on QAnon's growth for their own benefit. The president and Republican leaders could have easily dismissed it a year or two after it began. Instead they decided to tolerate its growth within their party. Republican voters, meanwhile, were too committed to their party to keep QAnon supporters like Lauren Boebert and Marjorie Taylor Greene out of Congress.

The social media companies also helped QAnon's spread. They were too late to crack down on QAnon, only moving years after a fellow tech company, Reddit, took a stand against it. Some, like Facebook, even funneled new recruits to QAnon because it drove engagement for their own businesses. While QAnon is banned from their platforms for now, there's no reason to think the social media companies won't be as slow to react to a new conspiracy theory that goes by another name.

Here's the part where I wish I had a solution for QAnon. But I think grappling with conspiracy theories like QAnon will be almost impossible within the American political system. It's difficult to imagine Republicans participating in any sort of bipartisan government solution to disinformation, whatever that might look like. Republican politicians haven't shown any appetite for alienating QAnon supporters and risking those votes. Worse, Q supporters might replace them, as Greene and Boebert did. Meanwhile, the First Amendment, rightly, makes it impossible to punish people who promote QAnon if they aren't breaking other laws.

There are some more unorthodox ideas. 8chan founder Fredrick Brennan thinks that the federal government should prosecute whoever's behind Q for impersonating a government official. But if it's even possible for the FBI to prove who's behind the Q account, it seems unlikely that QAnon believers would be dissuaded by an indictment conducted by the deep state they despise. One genuine anti-sex-trafficking group has called for fighting Q with immigration reforms and increased services for runaway youth. They say these policies could make it harder for QAnon boosters to exploit actual sex-trafficking victims in their stories. But Q believers aren't swayed by policy white papers—they exist in a fantasy world where children are shipped in Wayfair cabinets and eaten in pizzeria dungeons.

Ultimately, I think the best solution to conspiracy theories comes from building a government that fulfills its citizens' basic needs, so people aren't driven to find comfort in conspiracy theories in the first place. Throughout my reporting, it became clear to me how many people found QAnon because they felt marginalized. While QAnon is a conservative movement, the post-Storm world it promises is far to the left of anything that Bernie Sanders could imagine: the destruction of major pharmaceutical companies, the cancellation of all personal debt, and renters inheriting the property they live in, among other things. QAnon believers sometimes have legitimate critiques of how the world runs, but they decide to blame individual people in a cabal for their problems, rather than the entire economic system. Austin Steinbart–follower Michael Khoury, for example, was driven into QAnon after his application for Social Security disability benefits was denied. He came to feel that the government didn't care if he lived or died. QAnon offered him a way to act on that disappointment.

If people are driven to conspiracy theories because they feel disrespected in their lives, then the solution is to treat all people with more dignity. I believe that anything that broadly improves conditions in the United States, from a universal daycare program to a minimum wage increase, would do more to keep people out of movements like QAnon than any kind of targeted anti-disinformation effort could.

Of course, waiting for single-payer health care in the United States is about as quixotic as hoping for the Storm. Instead, I think responding to QAnon means starting at a smaller level. As I worked on this book, I was struck by how often our institutions, from law enforcement to the mental health establishment, failed QAnon's victims. It's time for them to step up.

More should be done for the people whose lives are shattered by QAnon radicalization. Family members who lose loved ones to QAnon shouldn't have to scrounge through Google searches or email reporters like me to find resources. I should not have been Kasey Mayer's best shot at convincing her sister to leave Steinbart's QAnon "Ranch." Psychiatrists and therapists could do more to learn about QAnon and other conspiracy theories, while the government should offer programs to pull people out of conspiracy theories.

No one may be less protected, though, than the people who are targeted by QAnon. Innocent people find their lives upended because Q becomes fixated on a social media post they made. It's time for law enforcement agencies, including the FBI, to take online harassment by conspiracy theorists more seriously. When Kim Picazio was attacked by QAnon, she had to assemble a small army of researchers just to convince police to enforce a court protective order she had already obtained. Victims without Picazio's resources or tenacity have been left to fend for themselves.

Most of all, I want people in power to seriously consider the threat posed by new conspiracy theories before they reach this point. For too long, QAnon was brushed aside by politicians and too many in the media as an internet curiosity that didn't pose a serious threat—right up until its believers tried to overthrow the government on January 6, 2021.

America's polarized atmosphere guarantees that conspiracy theories will remain a force in our politics, especially as the 2024 election approaches. If it's not QAnon, this strain of totalitarian, violent, conspiracy theory thinking will remain with us.

That movement might be labeled as a resurgent QAnon, or it could go under another name. QAnon itself was just a Trump-themed packaging of older conspiracy theories like NESARA, Pizzagate, and Jewish blood libel. Q's descendants are being shaped right now, waiting for the right moment—a controversial political campaign, or a terrorist attack, or an economic depression—to set them off.

The next time, I hope we'll be more prepared.

Acknowledgments

This book only exists because of the support of my wife, Juliana, who first encouraged me to turn my fascination with American conservatives into reporting of my own. She took on far more than her fair share of work to keep our lives running while I was writing this book, and remains the best editor I know. Juliana: I love you so much.

My parents, Peggy and Bill, have given me more support and encouragement than any son could ask for. My wife's parents, Michele and Steve, and her brother, Ben, have been sources of inspiration and help throughout this process.

Covering the right can be lonely work. It was even more so in QAnon's first days, when few people recognized that it was shaping up to be bigger than a few kooks online. My reporting is indebted to the work of other people who covered this beat from the beginning, including Mike Rothschild, Jared Holt, Brandy Zadrozny, Ben Collins, and Paris Martineau. The hosts of the *QAnon Anonymous* podcast—Travis View, Julian Feeld, and Jake Rockatansky—have also done excellent work on the world of Q.

Cullen Hoback's HBO documentary, *Q: Into the Storm*, broke new ground on Q's possible identities. The operators of several anonymous Twitter accounts tracking QAnon have also played a key role in expanding our understanding of its consequences, doing crucial work compiling videos and tracking court cases.

My agents, Matt Latimer and Keith Urbahn at Javelin, were the first to recognize the possibilities in a book about QAnon. My editor at Harper-Collins, Sarah Haugen, suffered through rounds of edits to improve this book. Rebecca Raskin at HarperCollins and Jordan Mulligan at Harper-Collins UK helped bring the book on board.

I've been blessed to have excellent editors at The Daily Beast, including Tracy Connor, Jackie Kucinich, Matt Fuller, Noah Shachtman, and Sam Stein. I have shared bylines with a number of great reporters on this beat, including Asawin Suebsaeng, Zachary Petrizzo, and Kelly Weill. This book never would've happened without my partners in The Daily Beast's *Fever Dreams* podcast—Asawin, Kelly, and Jesse Cannon—who picked up the slack so I could keep writing.

This book is only possible because of the encouragement from readers and listeners who have supported my reporting: first the subscribers to my newsletter, *Right Richter*, and then on *Fever Dreams*. It's been gratifying hearing from many of you, and I'm thankful for your support over the years.

I fell in love with journalism while working on Georgetown's campus newspaper, the *Georgetown Voice*. I'm lucky enough to still be friends today with many of the people I met there: Chris, Molly, Daniel, Kate, Brendan, Tim, Jeff, Joe, and Henry, all of whom have heard more about QAnon than any reasonable person could ever expect to.

Finally, reporting and writing this book would not be possible without the people whose lives have, one way or another, been torn apart by QAnon. I'm thankful that they trusted me with their stories.

Notes

Introduction: The Storm

1   zip ties in hand: Ryan Reilly, "Armed Jan. 6 Rioter Had Zip Ties during
    Capitol Attack, Friend Testifies at Trial," NBC News, March 4, 2022,
    https://www.nbcnews.com/politics/justice-department/armed-jan-6
    -rioter-zip-ties-capitol-attack-friend-testifies-trial-rcna18733.

2   rogue CIA supercomputer: Will Sommer, "Infamous 'Hoax' Artist Behind
    Trumpworld's New Voter Fraud Claim," Daily Beast, Nov. 9, 2020, https://
    www.thedailybeast.com/infamous-hoax-artist-behind-trumpworlds-new
    -voter-fraud-claim.

6   "The Punisher": Sam Thielman, "How Do You Stop the Far-Right Using
    the Punisher Skull? Make It a Black Lives Matter Symbol," Guardian, June
    11, 2020, https://www.theguardian.com/books/2020/jun/11/how-do
    -you-stop-the-far-right-using-the-punisher-skull-make-it-a-black-lives
    -matter-symbol.

8   seized on the pizza emails: Amanda Robb, "Pizzagate: Anatomy of a Fake
    News Scandal," Rolling Stone, Nov. 16, 2017, https://www.rollingstone
    .com/feature/anatomy-of-a-fake-news-scandal-125877.

9   Welch said later: Adam Goldman, "The Comet Ping Pong Gunman
    Answers Our Reporter's Questions," New York Times, Dec. 7, 2016,
    https://www.nytimes.com/2016/12/07/us/edgar-welch-comet-pizza-fake
    -news.html.

13 purchased a new truck: "QAnon FAA Employee from California Charged
    with Taking Part in U.S. Capitol Riot," Associated Press, Jan. 22, 2021,
    https://ktla.com/news/california/qanon-faa-employee-from-california
    -charged-with-taking-part-in-u-s-capitol-riot/.

14   Boyland died: Ayman M. Mohyeldin and Preeti Varathan, "Rosanne Boyland Was Outside the U.S. Capitol January 6. How—and Why—Did She Die?" *Vanity Fair*, Jan. 5, 2022, https://www.vanityfair.com/news /2022/01/capitol-insurrection-rosanne-boyland-how-and-why-did-she -die.

14   using a bullhorn: "Government's Brief in Support of Detention," *USA v. Jacob Chansley,* Jan. 14, 2021.

15   left a note: "Government's Brief in Support of Detention."

Chapter 1: The Genesis

19   A March 2021 poll: Chuck Todd, Mark Murray, and Carrie Dann, "Study Finds Nearly One-in-Five Americans Believe QAnon Conspiracy Theories," NBC News, May 27, 2021, https://www.nbcnews.com/politics /meet-the-press/study-finds-nearly-one-five-americans-believe-qanon -conspiracy-theories-n1268722.

20   conducted by the American Enterprise Institute: Daniel A. Cox, "After the Ballots Are Counted: Conspiracies, Political Violence, and American Exceptionalism," Survey Center on American Life, Feb. 11, 2021, https:// www.americansurveycenter.org/research/after-the-ballots-are-counted -conspiracies-political-violence-and-american-exceptionalism/.

20   a running poll: "Are You a Supporter of QAnon?" Civiqs, https://civiqs .com/results/qanon_support?uncertainty=true&annotations=true& zoomIn=true.

21   more anime porn: Dale Beran, *It Came from Something Awful: How a Toxic Troll Army Accidentally Memed Donald Trump into Office* (All Points Books, 2019), ix.

21   Nanashii: Beran, 37.

22   trolled racist website Stormfront: Beran, 123.

22   Dale Beran notes: Beran, 124.

Chapter 2: "Ask the Q"

28   Roman Riselvato: E. J. Dickson, "Meet the Parents of 'Qbaby,' Star of the Trump Rally and New QAnon Mascot," *Rolling Stone*, July 18, 2019, https://www.rollingstone.com/culture/culture-news/qbaby-qanon -conspiracy-theory-trump-rally-860526/.

29   "pissing off the crazy": Will Sommer and Asawin Suebsaeng, "Team Trump Wrestles with Its QAnon Problem," Daily Beast, Sept. 12, 2019, https://www.thedailybeast.com/team-trump-wrestles-with-its-2020-qanon-problem.

30   QAnon's "coming out party": Elizabeth Nolan Brown, "At Trump Tampa Rally, QAnon Conspiracists Abound as President Claims You Need ID to Buy Groceries," *Reason*, Aug. 1, 2018, https://reason.com/2018/08/01/trump-tampa-rally-a-hotbed-of-qanon/.

30   complained to a local website: Adam C. Smith, "Florida Insider Poll: 'We've Gone from Being the Party of Jeb, Winning Everywhere, to the Party of Cletus, the Slack-jawed Yokel," *Tampa Bay Times*, July 24, 2018, https://www.tampabay.com/florida-politics/buzz/2018/07/24/florida-insider-poll-weve-gone-from-being-the-party-of-jeb-winning-everywhere-to-the-party-of-cletus-the-slack-jawed-yokel/.

30   DeSantis told a reporter: Steve Contorno, "Ron DeSantis on His QAnon Conspiracy Supporters: 'I'm Not Sure What That Is,'" *Tampa Bay Times*, Aug. 28, 2018, https://www.tampabay.com/florida-politics/buzz/2018/08/28/ron-desantis-on-his-qanon-conspiracy-supporters-im-not-sure-what-that-is/.

32   a rally in Grand Rapids, Michigan: Tom Porter, "QAnon Conspiracy Theorists Turned Out in Force at Trump's Michigan Rally as He Hailed Victory over 'Deep State,'" Insider, March 29, 2019, https://www.businessinsider.com/qanon-conspiracy-theory-attend-trump-michigan-rally-deep-state-2019-3.

33   Frank said: Emily Singer, "Campaign Official Promises to Share QAnon Supporter's Message with Trump," The American Independent, May 26, 2020, https://americanindependent.com/donald-trump-campaign-qanon-kayleigh-mcenany-rally-arizona-phoenix.

34   an Axios report: Jonathan Swan and Zachary Basu, "Episode 3: Descent into Madness," Axios, Jan. 17, 2021, https://www.axios.com/2021/01/17/trump-off-the-rails-descent-into-madness.

39   Straka told the *Washington Examiner*: Jerry Dunleavy, "QAnon Slogan Spoken from Trump Rally Podium as FBI Warns about Conspiracy Theory-related Violence," *Washington Examiner*, Aug. 2, 2019.

39   Dan Scavino posted a meme: David Gilbert, "The Jan. 6 Committee Wants to Speak to Trump's Social Media Guy about QAnon," Vice News, March 29, 2022, https://www.vice.com/en/article/dypjky/dan-scavino-qanon.

41   televised town hall: "Donald Trump NBC Town Hall Transcript October

15," Rev.com, https://www.rev.com/blog/transcripts/donald-trump-nbc
-town-hall-transcript-october-15.

Chapter 3: Q's Priests

42   launched "The Black List": Kenny Malone, "Hollywood's Black List," NPR,
      July 10, 2020, https://www.npr.org/2020/07/10/889708583/hollywoods
      -black-list.

44   On his blog: "Soros' Hollywood Rentboy Exposed," Neon Revolt, https://
      www.neonrevolt.com/2018/10/18/soros-hollywood-rentboy-exposed-by
      -blacklistanon-greatawakening-neonrevolt/.

47   proved to be a surprising hit: Ben Collins, "On Amazon, a QAnon
      Conspiracy Book Climbs the Charts—with an Algorithmic Push," NBC
      News, March 4, 2019, https://www.nbcnews.com/tech/tech-news
      /amazon-qanon-conspiracy-book-climbs-charts-algorithmic-push-n97
      9181.

50   appeared on InfoWars in 2015: Elizabeth Williamson, "Alex Jones and
      Donald Trump: A Fateful Alliance Draws Scrutiny," *New York Times*,
      March 7, 2022, https://www.nytimes.com/2022/03/07/us/politics/alex
      -jones-jan-6-trump.html.

51   allegedly acted as a cutout between Stone and WikiLeaks: Jeffrey Toobin,
      "Roger Stone's and Jerome Corsi's Time in the Barrel," *New Yorker*, Feb. 11,
      2019, https://www.newyorker.com/magazine/2019/02/18/roger-stones
      -and-jerome-corsis-time-in-the-barrel.

52   its leading figures started to grapple for control: Brandy Zadrozny and Ben
      Collins, "How Three Conspiracy Theorists Took 'Q' and Sparked QAnon,"
      NBC News, Aug. 14, 2018, https://www.nbcnews.com/tech/tech-news
      /how-three-conspiracy-theorists-took-q-sparked-qanon-n900531.

53   "I'm sick of all these witches and warlocks": Rebecca Speare-Cole, "Alex
      Jones' QAnon Rant Watched Over 2 Million Times: 'I'm Sick of It!'"
      Newsweek, Jan. 11, 2021, https://www.newsweek.com/alex-jones-qanon
      -rant-viral-infowars-1560394.

53   Robert Cornero: Details on Cornero's life come from *Revolution Q*, his
      self-published memoir released under the name "Neon Revolt." Open-
      source intelligence company Logically connected Cornero to the "Neon
      Revolt" persona in 2021. Cornero has neither confirmed nor disputed the
      identification. I tried to reach Cornero via email, phone calls, and a letter to
      his parents' house, but didn't receive a response.

53   a long-term decline: Neon Revolt, "Revolution Q: The Story of QAnon and the 2nd American Revolution," 2019.

56   discovered Cornero's double life: Nick Backovic, "EXCLUSIVE: Failed Screenwriter from New Jersey Behind One of QAnon's Most Influential Personas," Logically, Jan. 11, 2021, https://www.logically.ai/articles /exclusive-failed-screenwriter-from-new-jersey-behind-one-of-qanons -most-influential-personas.

Chapter 4: Who Is Q?

59   Cicada 3301: David Kushner, "Cicada: Solving the Web's Deepest Mystery," *Rolling Stone*, Jan. 15, 2015, https://www.rollingstone.com /culture/culture-news/cicada-solving-the-webs-deepest-mystery-84394/.

59   claimed he had chat logs: Michael Edison Hayden, "Jack Posobiec Interviewed a Pro-Hitler Disinformation Poster on One America News Network," Hatewatch, July 23, 2020, https://www.splcenter.org/hate watch/2020/07/23/jack-posobiec-interviewed-pro-hitler-disinformation -poster-one-america-news-network.

60   BuzzFeed News declared: Ryan Broderick, "People Think This Whole QAnon Conspiracy Theory Is a Prank on Trump Supporters," BuzzFeed News, Aug. 6, 2018, https://www.buzzfeednews.com/article /ryanhatesthis/its-looking-extremely-likely-that-qanon-is-probably-a.

60   political pranks: "Prologue," Luther Blissett, http://www.lutherblissett .net/.

62   robbed almost immediately: Michael Wilson, "City Newcomer Is Let Down by a Stranger, Then the Police," *New York Times*, Jan. 18, 2014, https://www.nytimes.com/2014/01/18/nyregion/city-newcomer-is-let -down-by-a-stranger-then-the-police.html.

63   Brennan replied: Don Caldwell, "Q&A with Fredrick Brennan of 8chan," Know Your Meme, 2014, https://knowyourmeme.com/editorials/inter views/qa-with-fredrick-brennan-of-8chan.

64   Brennan partied: Adrian Chen, "Gamergate Supporters Partied at a Strip Club This Weekend," *New York*, Oct. 27, 2014, https://nymag.com/ intelligencer/2014/10/gamergate-supporters-party-at-strip-club.html.

65   a linguistic analysis report: David K. Kirkpatrick, "Who Is Behind QAnon? Linguistic Detectives Find Fingerprints," *New York Times*, Feb. 24, 2022, https://www.nytimes.com/2022/02/19/technology/qanon -messages-authors.html.

68　wrote in his memoir: Paul Furber, "Q: Inside the Greatest Intelligence Drop in History," https://paulfurber.net/qinside/.

69　Brennan called for 8chan to be shut down: Kevin Roose, "'Shut the Site Down,' Says the Creator of 8chan, a Megaphone for Gunmen," *New York Times*, Aug. 4, 2019, https://www.nytimes.com/2019/08/04/technology /8chan-shooting-manifesto.html.

70　*Q: Into the Storm*: Cullen Hoback, *Q: Into the Storm*, HBO, 2021.

71　fled the country: Hoback.

71　The linguistic analysis: Kirkpatrick, "Who Is Behind QAnon?"

Chapter 5: Plan to Save the World

73　created her first Facebook account: Leaked internal Facebook document, "Carol's Journey to QAnon," published via Gizmodo's release of the "Facebook Papers," "Read the Facebook Papers for Yourself," https:// gizmodo.com/facebook-papers-how-to-read-1848702919.

74　Facebook had thousands of QAnon groups: Ben Collins and Brandy Zadrozny, "Facebook Bans QAnon Across Its Platforms," NBC News, Oct. 6, 2020, https://www.nbcnews.com/tech/tech-news/facebook-bans -qanon-across-its-platforms-n1242339.

74　Mark Zuckerberg made the decision: Rachel Metz, "Likes, Anger Emojis and RSVPs: The Math Behind Facebook's News Feed—and How It Backfired," CNN, Oct. 27, 2021, https://www.cnn.com/2021/10/27 /tech/facebook-papers-meaningful-social-interaction-news-feed-math /index.html.

75　the community had broken Reddit's rules: Kaitlyn Tiffany, "Reddit Squashed QAnon by Accident," *Atlantic*, Sept. 23, 2020, https://www .theatlantic.com/technology/archive/2020/09/reddit-qanon-ban-evasion -policy-moderation-facebook/616442/.

75　told the *Atlantic* in 2020: Tiffany.

77　cleaning up QAnon: Sheera Frankel, "QAnon Is Still Spreading on Facebook, Despite a Ban," *New York Times*, Dec. 18, 2020, https://www .nytimes.com/2020/12/18/technology/qanon-is-still-spreading-on-face book-despite-a-ban.html.

78　believers rejoiced: Will Sommer, "Fox News Promotes Pro-Trump QAnon Conspiracy Theorist," Daily Beast, March 22, 2019, https://www.thedaily beast.com/fox-and-friends-first-promotes-pro-trump-qanon-conspiracy -theorist.

78 Twitter ire fell: Mike Rothschild, "The Inside Story of How QAnon Derailed a Charter School's Annual Fundraiser," Daily Dot, May 10, 2019, https://www.dailydot.com/debug/qanon-grass-valley-charter-school -foundation/.

79 one Twitter user wrote: Reuters Fact Check, "Fact Check-False QAnon Claims That Oprah Is Wearing an Ankle Monitor During Interview," Reuters, March 10, 2021, https://www.reuters.com/article/factcheck -oprah-ankle/fact-check-false-qanon-claims-that-oprah-is-wearing-an -ankle-monitor-during-interview-idUSL1N2L81CO.

80 the Wayfair sex-trafficking plot: Jessica Contrera, "A QAnon Con: How the Viral Wayfair Sex Trafficking Lie Hurt Real Kids," *Washington Post*, December 16, 2021, https://www.washingtonpost.com/dc-md-va/inter active/2021/wayfair-qanon-sex-trafficking-conspiracy/.

80 she wrote: Contrera.

81 entered the lobby: Eddie Kim, "How 'Save the Children' Became a Conspiracy Grift," *MEL Magazine*, https://melmagazine.com/en-us/story /save-the-children-qanon-child-trafficking.

82 "Pastel QAnon": Marc-André Argentino, "Pastel QAnon," Global Network on Extremism & Technology, March 17, 2021, https://gnet-research. org/2021/03/17/pastel-qanon/.

82 "QAmom": E. J. Dickson, "The Birth of QAmom," *Rolling Stone*, Sept. 2, 2020, https://www.rollingstone.com/culture/culture-features/qanon -mom-conspiracy-theory-parents-sex-trafficking-qamom-1048921/.

Chapter 6: Viral Load

86 vaulted into the QAnon pantheon: Will Sommer, "QAnon's Newest Hero Is D-list 'Vanderpump Rules' Star Isaac Kappy," Daily Beast, Aug. 7, 2018, https://www.thedailybeast.com/qanons-newest-hero-is-a-d-list-vander pump-rules-star.

86 "tainted their adrenochrome supply with the coronavirus": Kyle Mantyla, "Liz Crokin Claims Celebrities Are Getting Coronavirus from Tainted 'Adrenochrome Supply,'" Right Wing Watch, March 18, 2020, https:// www.rightwingwatch.org/post/liz-crokin-claims-celebrities-are-getting -coronavirus-from-tainted-adrenochrome-supply/.

87 Frazzledrip: Jane Coaston, "YouTube Conspiracy Theory Crisis, Explained," Vox, Dec. 14, 2018, https://www.vox.com/technology /2018/12/12/18136132/google-youtube-congress-conspiracy-theories.

88   found a Twitter thread: "Q Is Always Wrong About Everything," Twitter user @PokerPolitics, June 4, 2019, https://twitter.com/PokerPolitics /status/1135811817073270785.

91   fertile ground for conspiracy theories: Samuel K. Cohn, "Pandemics: Waves of Disease, Waves of Hate from the Plague of Athens to A.I.D.S.," *Historical Journal*, 2012, https://www.ncbi.nlm.nih.gov/pmc/articles /PMC4422154/.

91   QAnon activity grew significantly: "The Genesis of a Conspiracy Theory," Institute for Strategic Dialogue, https://www.isdglobal.org/wp-content /uploads/2020/07/The-Genesis-of-a-Conspiracy-Theory.pdf.

92   late nights reading QAnon websites: David Gilbert, "Man Inspired by QAnon and Hopped Up on Caffeine Purposefully Derailed Train," Vice News, April 15, 2022, https://www.vice.com/en/article/7kb38q/man -inspired-by-qanon-and-hopped-up-on-caffeine-purposefully-derailed -train.

93   retracted her findings: Martin Enserink and Jon Cohen, "Fact-checking Judy Mikovits, the Controversial Virologist Attacking Anthony Fauci in a Viral Conspiracy Video," *Science*, May 8, 2020, https://www.science.org /content/article/fact-checking-judy-mikovits-controversial-virologist -attacking-anthony-fauci-viral?cookieSet=1.

93   Mikki Willis: Josh Rottenberg and Stacy Perman, "Meet the Ojai Dad Who Made the Most Notorious Piece of Coronavirus Disinformation Yet," *Los Angeles Times*, May 13, 2020, https://www.latimes.com/entertain ment-arts/movies/story/2020–05–13/plandemic-coronavirus-documentary -director-mikki-willis-mikovits.

93   Willis introduced Mikovits to Zach Vorhies: Anna Merlan, "An Ex-Google Employee Turned 'Whistleblower' and QAnon Fan Made 'Plandemic' Go Viral," Vice News, May 14, 2020, https://www.vice.com/en/article/k7q qyn/an-ex-google-employee-turned-whistleblower-and-qanon-fan-made -plandemic-go-viral.

94   reposted the video: Sheera Frankel, Ben Decker, and Davey Alba, "How the 'Plandemic' Movie and Its Falsehoods Spread Widely Online," *New York Times*, May 21, 2020, https://www.nytimes.com/2020/05/20/tech nology/plandemic-movie-youtube-facebook-coronavirus.html.

95   roughly $100: Geoff Brumfield, "What a Bottle of Ivermectin Reveals about the Shadowy World of COVID Telemedicine," NPR, Feb. 9, 2022, https://www.npr.org/sections/health-shots/2022/02/09/1079183523 /what-a-bottle-of-ivermectin-reveals-about-the-shadowy-world-of-covid -telemedicine.

95 patients complained: Vera Bergenruen, "How 'America's Frontline Doctors' Sold Access to Bogus COVID-19 Treatments—and Left Patients in the Lurch," *Time*, Aug. 26, 2021, https://time.com/6092368/americas -frontline-doctors-covid-19-misinformation/.

96 Steele wrote: Lindsey Ellefson, "Former CIA Officer Who Called COVID a 'Hoax' Dies from Virus," Wrap, Aug. 30, 2021, https://www.thewrap.com /robert-david-steele-covid/.

97 "a mass spreader event": David Moye, "Pro-Trump Speaker Wants to Turn D.C. Rally into 'Mass-Spreader Event,'" HuffPost, Jan. 5, 2021, https:// www.huffpost.com/entry/clay-clark-trump-dc-rally-mass-spreader-event_n _5ff4e12cc5b6ec8ae0b69f57.

Chapter 7: The Wizard of Mattoon

101 wrapped in aluminum foil: John Kelly, "Omega Victims Bought Hope in $100 Investments," Associated Press, Sept. 7, 2000.

101 bought a boat and a Harley-Davidson motorcycle: Pam Belluck, "Wads of Cash, Gossip, then Fraud Charges," *New York Times*, Sept. 2, 2000, https:// www.nytimes.com/2000/09/02/us/wads-of-cash-gossip-then-fraud-charges .html.

101 once been convicted for helping to steal guns: Shane Tritsch, "False Profit," *Chicago*, Sept. 2001, https://www.quatloos.com/FalseProfit.pdf.

102 more than a dozen rare cars: "Vehicles Belonging to Clyde Hood Among Those to Be Auctioned," Copley News Service, May 2003.

102 a banking wheeler-dealer of the highest order: Tritsch, "False Profit."

102 "Keep the Lord's Warehouse full": Belluck, "Wads of Cash."

102 an ice cream shop owner sold her business: David Marchant, "Funny Business," UPI, May 16, 2001.

103 The scam spread across the world: Myron Levin, "Suspect's Arrest Lifts Veil on 'Financial Scam of '90's,' " *Los Angeles Times*, Sept. 3, 1994.

103 Earth's magnetism had delayed the financial transfer: Flynn McRoberts, "Downstate Fraud Had Global Reach, U.S. Says," *Chicago Tribune*, Sept. 4, 2000.

105 a powerful force in American politics and culture: Jesse Walker, *The United States of Paranoia: A Conspiracy Theory* (New York: HarperCollins, 2014), 8.

105 American history is filled: Walker, 9.

105 Thomas Jefferson's opponents accused him: Claus Oberhauser,

"Freemasons, Illuminati, and Jews: Conspiracy Theories and the French Revolution," in Michael Butter and Peter Knight, eds., *Routledge Handbook of Conspiracy Theories* (London and New York: Routledge, 2020), 562.

105 American Protestants reacted to waves of Catholic immigration: Annika Thiem, "Conspiracy Theories and Gender and Sexuality," in Butter and Knight, eds., *Routledge Handbook of Conspiracy Theories*, 297.

105 conspiracy theories about "Slave Power": Walker, 7.

105 summed up conspiracy theories: Joseph E. Uscinski and Joseph M. Parent, *American Conspiracy Theories* (New York: Oxford University Press, 2014).

105 a conspiracy theory is: Jeffrey A. Hall, "Aligning Darkness with Conspiracy Theory: The Discursive Effects of African American Interest in Gary Webb's 'Dark Alliance,'" *Howard Journal of Communications*, Nov. 2006, quoted in Julien Giry and Pranvera Tika, "Conspiracy Theories in Political Science and Political Theory," in Butter and Knight, eds., *Routledge Handbook of Conspiracy Theories*, 152.

105 Barkun writes: Michael Barkun, *A Culture of Conspiracy: Apocalyptic Visions in Contemporary America* (Berkeley: University of California Press, 2014), 3.

106 Shaini Goodwin discovered Omega: Sean Robinson, "Snared by a Cybercult Queen," *News Tribune*, July 18, 2004.

107 possibly disguised as pizza deliverymen: Tritsch, "False Profit."

108 Goodwin came upon the writings of Harvey Barnard: Robinson, "Snared by a Cybercult Queen."

108 NESARA started to mutate: Robinson.

110 "the strong dominate the weak": Anthony Lantian, Mike Wood, and Biljana Gjoneska, "Personality Traits, Cognitive Styles, and Worldviews Associated with Beliefs in Conspiracy Theories," in Butter and Knight, eds., *Routledge Handbook of Conspiracy Theories*, 162.

110 less likely to use condoms during sex: Daniel Jolley, Silvia Mari, and Karen M. Douglas, "Consequences of Conspiracy Theories," in Butter and Knight, eds., *Routledge Handbook of Conspiracy Theories*, 236.

110 support political violence: Uscinski and Parent.

110 A 2013 study: "Conspiracy Theories Prosper: 25% of Americans Are Truthers," Jan. 17, 2013, Fairleigh Dickinson University, http://publicmind.fdu.edu/2013/outthere/final.pdf, quoted in Steven M. Smallpage, Hugo Drochon, Joseph E. Uscinski, and Casey Klofstad, "Who Are the Conspiracy Theorists?" in Butter and Knight, eds., *Routledge Handbook of Conspiracy Theories*.

111 Another survey taken in 2011: J. Eric Oliver and Thomas J. Wood,

"Conspiracy Theories and the Paranoid Style(s) of Mass Opinion,"
American Journal of Political Science (October 2014).

112   Joseph Gregory Hallett: Nick Backovic and Joe Ondrak, "All Hail the
King? How QAnon Is Backing a Conspiracy Theorist's Bizarre Claim to
the Throne of England," Logically, July 22, 2020, https://www.logically
.ai/articles/all-hail-the-king-how-qanon-is-backing-a-conspiracy-theorists
-bizarre-claim-to-the-throne-of-england.

113   most famous millenarian movement: Barkun, *A Culture of Conspiracy*, 9.

114   Sanchez said: Jason Strait, "Few Stake Claim to Millions in Omega Case,"
Associated Press, Jan. 24, 2002.

Chapter 8: Those Who Know Can't Sleep

115   9/11 conspiracy theorist: WCT Newsroom, "Northwest Pilot from Rural
Glyndon Alleges 9/11 Cover-up," *West Central Tribune*, March 9, 2007,
https://www.wctrib.com/news/northwest-pilot-from-rural-glyndon
-alleges-9–11-cover-up.

116   A woman named Judy Johnson became convinced: Mark Sauer, "Decade
of Accusations: The McMartin Preschool Child Abuse Case Launched 100
Others—and a Vigorous Debate on How to Question Youngsters," *San
Diego Union-Tribune*, Aug. 29, 1993.

116   a thermometer: Richard Beck, *We Believe the Children: A Moral Panic in
the 1980s* (New York: PublicAffairs, 2015), 53.

116   a letter: Beck, 9.

117   forced to drink blood: Sauer, "Decade of Accusations."

117   a devilish "goatman": Beck, 79.

117   Geraldo Rivera earned massive ratings: Becker, 181.

118   martial arts star Chuck Norris: Beck, 122.

118   Beck writes: Beck, 272.

119   ended in 1990: Sauer, "Decade of Accusations."

119   At a cost to the government of $16 million: Gordon Dillow and Marilyn
Kalfus, "McMartin: The Pain Lingers," *Orange County Register*, May 20,
1995.

119   One former Miami daycare operator is still in prison: Rael Jean Isaac, "The
Last Victim," *National Review*, Sept. 10, 2018, https://www.national
review.com/magazine/2018/09/10/the-last-victim/.

119   taken by plane to the rituals: Beck, 160.

120   Haleigh Cummings vanished: Eileen Kelly, "10 Years Later: Haleigh

Cummings Disappearance Still a Mystery," *Gainesville Sun*, Feb. 9, 2019.

120   received an official trespassing warning: Kelly.

120   past drug use: Eileen Kelly, "Still a Mystery," *Florida Times-Union*, Feb. 10, 2019.

121   filed by Picazio: "Petition for Injunction for Protection against Repeat Violence," *Kim Lowry Picazio v. Timothy Charles Holmseth*.

121   On his obscure blog: "Petition for Injunction for Protection against Repeat Violence."

121   Using the internet: "Petition for Injunction for Protection against Repeat Violence."

122   Holmseth sent Picazio: "Petition for Injunction for Protection against Repeat Violence."

122   violated the order: "Report and Recommendation," *Timothy Charles Holmseth v. City of East Grand Forks*, U.S. District Court, District of Montana.

124   "Agent Margaritaville": Mack Lamoureux, "Arrest of 'Agent Margaritaville' Hitting Conspiracy Movement Hard," Vice News, Feb. 8, 2021, https://www.vice.com/en/article/v7mj8b/arrest-of-agent-margaritaville-hitting-conspiracy-movement-hard.

126   a mysterious substance called adrenochrome: Tarpley Hitt, "How QAnon Became Obsessed with Adrenochrome, an Imaginary Drug Hollywood Is Harvesting from Kids," Daily Beast, Aug. 14, 2020, https://www.thedailybeast.com/how-qanon-became-obsessed-with-adrenochrome-an-imaginary-drug-hollywood-is-harvesting-from-kids.

126   Thompson explained to him: Hitt.

127   said in a 2021 interview: Blake Montgomery, "'Passion of the Christ' Star Hawks Unhinged QAnon Adrenochrome Conspiracy Theory," Daily Beast, April 17, 2021, https://www.thedailybeast.com/passion-of-the-christ-star-jim-caviezel-hawks-qanon-adrenochrome-conspiracy-theory.

127   his death took on an enormous importance: Kjetil Braut Simonsen, "Antisemitism and Conspiracism," in Butter and Knight, eds., *Routledge Handbook of Conspiracy Theories*, 358.

127   seventy-nine cases of blood libel allegations: Simonsen.

128   killed more than forty Jews: "Kielce Pogrom," United States Holocaust Memorial Museum, https://www.ushmm.org/learn/timeline-of-events/after-1945/kielce-pogrom.

128   were sharing: Brian Friedberg, "The Dark Virality of a Hollywood Blood

Harvesting Conspiracy," *Wired*, July 31, 2020, https://www.wired
.com/story/opinion-the-dark-virality-of-a-hollywood-blood-harvesting
-conspiracy/.

128 He fled: "Protesters Gather at Polk County Justice Center Monday
Morning," KROX-AM, Aug. 26, 2019, https://kroxam.com/2019/08/26
/protesters-gather-at-polk-county-justice-center-monday-morning/.

Chapter 9: The QAnon Kidnappers

130 Jessica pointed out to her mother: "Affidavit for Arrest Warrant," Parker
Police Department, Parker, CO, Oct. 3, 2019.

131 wrote in a report: Douglas County Department of Human Services report,
Jan. 2019.

131 holed up in her apartment: "Affidavit for Arrest Warrant."

132 introduced to her daughter as a "sniper": "Affidavit for Arrest Warrant."

132 bought a gun: "Affidavit for Arrest Warrant."

132 according to her daughter: "Affidavit for Arrest Warrant."

133 turned his truck into an improvised armored vehicle: William Mansell,
"Man Pleads Guilty to Terrorism Charge after Blocking Hoover Dam
Bridge with Armored Truck," ABC News, Feb. 13, 2020, https://abcnews
.go.com/US/man-pleads-guilty-terrorism-charge-blocking-bridge-armored
/story?id=68955385.

134 a man armed with a katana: Will Sommer, "QAnon Disciple Allegedly
Vandalized Catholic Church with Crowbar While Ranting about Human
Trafficking," Daily Beast, Sept. 30, 2019, https://www.thedailybeast.com
/qanon-disciple-allegedly-vandalized-catholic-church-with-crowbar.

134 convinced that his brother was secretly a "reptilian": Will Sommer,
"Qanon-Believing Proud Boy Accused of Murdering 'Lizard' Brother with
Sword," Daily Beast, Jan. 9, 2019, https://www.thedailybeast.com/proud
-boy-member-accused-of-murdering-his-brother-with-a-sword-4.

134 a man tried to burn down Comet Ping Pong: Peter Hermann, "Man
Who Set Fire at Comet Ping Pong Sentenced to Four Years in Prison,"
Washington Post, April 23, 2020, https://www.washingtonpost.com/local
/public-safety/man-who-set-fire-at-comet-ping-pong-pizza-shop-sentenced
-to-four-years-in-prison/2020/04/23/2e107676–8496–11ea-a3eb-e9fc93
160703_story.html.

134 aimless twenty-four-year-old: Ali Watkins, "A Conspiracy Theorist,
Anthony Comello, and a Mystery Motive in Gambino Murder," *New York*

Times, March 22, 2019, https://www.nytimes.com/2019/03/22/nyregion /gambino-comello-mob-boss.html.

134   FBI wiretaps: "Murder of Gambino Boss Triggered Flawed Theories," National Museum of Organized Crime and Law Enforcement, https:// themobmuseum.org/blog/murder-of-gambino-boss-triggered-flawed -theories/.

135   held up one of his hands to reporters: Ali Watkins, "Accused of Killing a Gambino Mob Boss, He's Presenting a Novel Defense," *New York Times*, Dec. 6, 2019, https://www.nytimes.com/2019/12/06/nyregion/gambino -shooting-anthony-comello-qanon.html.

135   data compiled by University of Maryland researchers: Michael Jensen and Sheehan Kane, "QAnon Offenders in the United States," National Consortium for the Study of Terrorism and Responses to Terrorism, 2021, https://www.start.umd.edu/publication/qanon-offenders-united-states.

136   Arrived at McConnell's house: Accounts of Abcug's months on the run are taken from court and police records, as well as a three-hour interview Ramos gave in 2020 to NorthWest Liberty News, an online TV show. Ramos and Abcug didn't respond to requests for comment.

136   Now they planned to lie low with McConnell: "Field McConnell Was Surprised That We Were There," NorthWest Liberty News, https://rumble .com/vcaal7-field-mcconnell-was-surprised-that-we-were-there-joseph -ramos-part-1.html.

138   The FBI's 2019 memo: Jana Winter, "Exclusive: FBI Document Warns Conspiracy Theories Are a New Domestic Terrorism Threat," Yahoo News, Aug. 1, 2019, https://www.yahoo.com/video/fbi-documents-conspiracy -theories-terrorism-160000507.html.

139   harboring a fringe congressional candidate: Osceola Police Dept., "Incident Report #20-010128."

140   Ramos recalled later: NorthWest Liberty News.

142   arrested in Wisconsin: "Complaint," *State of Wisconsin v. Field McConnell*, Nov. 5, 2019.

142   fugitive life came to an end in Kalispell: Robert Garrison, "Parker Woman Arrested in Montana for Conspiracy to Commit Kidnapping," Denver7, Jan. 4, 2020, https://www.thedenverchannel.com/news/local-news/parker -woman-arrested-in-montana-for-kidnapping.

143   Struggled for years with opioid addiction: Hopkins County Jail medical report, March 30, 2020.

144   long-simmering frustrations: Georgia Wells and Justin Scheck, "How a Custody Fight Plus QAnon Turned Deadly," *Wall Street Journal*, Aug. 2,

2021, https://www.wsj.com/articles/when-online-conspiracies-turn -deadly-a-custody-battle-and-a-killing-11617376764.

146   Wray said: Zachary Cohen, "FBI Director Says Bureau Is Not Investigating QAnon Conspiracy 'In Its Own Right,'" CNN, April 15, 2021, https:// www.cnn.com/2021/04/15/politics/fbi-director-wray-qanon-threat/index .html.

Chapter 10: When Dad Takes the Red Pill

154   Reddit's "QAnon Casualties" board: "QAnon Casualties," https://www .reddit.com/r/QAnonCasualties/.

155   who has studied QAnon: Ronald W. Pies and Joseph M. Pierre, "Believing in Conspiracy Theories Is Not Delusional," Medscape, Feb. 7, 2021, https://www.medscape.com/viewarticle/945290.

Chapter 11: The Q Caucus

160   Jade Helm: Dan Lamothe, "Remember Jade Helm 15, the Controversial Military Exercise? It's Over," *Washington Post*, Sept. 14, 2015, https://www .washingtonpost.com/news/checkpoint/wp/2015/09/14/remember-jade -helm-15-the-controversial-military-exercise-its-over/.

160   cosponsored a resolution: Susan Davis, "House Votes to Condemn QAnon Conspiracy Theory: 'It's a Sick Cult,'" NPR, Oct. 2, 2020, https://www.npr .org/2020/10/02/919123199/house-votes-to-condemn-qanon-conspiracy -movement.

160   recorded a video: Allie Bice, "Rep. Kinzinger: 'It's Time' for Leaders to Disavow QAnon," *Politico*, Aug. 16, 2020, https://www.politico.com/news /2020/08/16/adam-kinzinger-trump-qanon-396414.

161   McCain grabbed the microphone: Jonathan Martin and Amie Parnes, "McCain: Obama Not an Arab, Crowd Boos," *Politico*, Oct. 10, 2008, https://www.politico.com/story/2008/10/mccain-obama-not-an-arab -crowd-boos-014479.

164   Pamela Patterson: Will Sommer, "In a First, Lawmaker Cites QAnon Conspiracy from City Council Floor," Daily Beast, Dec. 13, 2018, https:// www.thedailybeast.com/in-a-first-lawmaker-cites-qanon-conspiracy-from -city-council-floor.

164   Matthew Lusk: Will Sommer, "A QAnon Believer Is Running for Congress

and Is Currently Unopposed in His Republican Primary," Daily Beast, April 10, 2019, https://www.thedailybeast.com/matthew-lusk-meet-the -first-qanon-believer-running-for-congress.

165   fleeing across the state border: Will Sommer, "Ilhan Omar's Challenger Is Literally on the Run from the Law," Daily Beast, Feb. 21, 2020, https:// www.thedailybeast.com/ilhan-omars-challenger-danielle-stella-is-literally -on-the-run-from-the-law.

166   Perkins said: Will Steakin and Meg Cunningham, "Republicans Wrestle with Conspiracy-Theory Advocate Winning Senate Primary," ABC News, May 22, 2020, https://abcnews.go.com/Politics/republicans-wrestle -conspiracy-theory-advocate-winning-senate-primary/story?id=70829450.

166   list of QAnon supporters: Alex Kaplan, "Here Are the QAnon Supporters Running for Congress in 2020," Media Matters for America, Jan. 7, 2020, https://www.mediamatters.org/qanon-conspiracy-theory/here-are-qanon -supporters-running-congress-2020.

167   the waitresses were armed: Chaney Skilling, "Armed and Ready to Feed You: Shooters Grill in Rifle Serves Up Barbecue with a Gun on the Side," *Denver Post*, June 22, 2018, https://www.denverpost.com/2018/06/22 /shooters-grill-rifle-waitresses-guns/.

167   Vandersteel asked Boebert: Jim Anderson, Nicholas Riccardi, and Alan Fram, "GOP Candidate Is Latest Linked to QAnon Conspiracy Theory," Associated Press, July 2, 2020, https://apnews.com/article/e21311e35e70 63834222942a1702211b.

167   a lengthy digital trail of support for QAnon: Eric Hananoki, "A Guide to Likely Member of Congress Marjorie Taylor Greene's Conspiracy Theories and Toxic Rhetoric," Media Matters for America, Oct. 15, 2020, https:// www.mediamatters.org/congress/guide-likely-member-congress-marjorie -taylor-greenes-conspiracy-theories-and-toxic.

168   9/11 Truther: Catie Edmondson, "Marjorie Taylor Greene's Controversies Are Piling Up. Republicans Are Quiet." *New York Times,* Jan. 29, 2021.

168   the racism and anti-Semitism at the heart of QAnon: Ally Mutnick and Melanie Zanona, "House Republican Leaders Condemn GOP Candidate Who Made Racist Videos," *Politico*, June 17, 2020, https://www.politico .com/news/2020/06/17/house-republicans-condemn-gop-candidate -racist-videos-325579.

169   McCarthy initially took a hard line: Aaron Rupar, "Kevin McCarthy's Remarkable Flip-flop from 'There's No Place for QAnon' to 'I Don't Even Know What It Is,'" Vox, Feb. 4, 2021, https://www.vox.com/2021/2/4/22 266193/kevin-mccarthy-qanon-marjorie-taylor-greene.

169   listed Watkins in a planning document: Cheryl Teh, "The Trump Team's 22-Page Communications Playbook to Overturn the Election Had QAnon Influencer Ron Watkins Playing a Key Role," Insider, Jan. 5, 2022, https:// www.businessinsider.com/trumps-team-enlist-qanon-influencer-ron -watkins-overturn-the-election-2022-1.

171   won a seat: David Gilbert, "One of QAnon's Earliest Influencers Just Got Elected to South Carolina GOP," Vice News, April 26, 2021, https://www .vice.com/en/article/93ywwv/one-of-qanons-earliest-influencers-just-got -elected-to-south-carolina-gop.

171   Juan O. Savin has organized: Will Sommer, "Jim Caviezel's QAnon Guru Wants to Control Elections," Daily Beast, Oct. 27, 2021, https://www.the dailybeast.com/jim-caviezels-qanon-guru-juan-savin-wants-to-control -elections.

172   a ruse to arrest top Democrats all along: Bob Woodward and Robert Costa, "Virginia Thomas Urged White House Chief to Pursue Unrelenting Efforts to Overturn the 2020 Election, Texts Show," *Washington Post*, March 24, 2022, https://www.washingtonpost.com/politics/2022/03/24 /virginia-thomas-mark-meadows-texts/.

Chapter 12: Baby Q

176   has three criteria: Robert Jay Lifton, *Thought Reform and the Psychology of Totalism: A Study of "Brainwashing" in China* (Chapel Hill: University of North Carolina Press, 2016), vii.

176   "thought-terminating clichés": Lifton, 429.

179   a way station for cabal child-sex traffickers: Tay Wiles, "Conspiracy Theories Inspire Vigilante Justice in Tucson," *High Country News*, Sept. 12, 2018, https://www.hcn.org/issues/50.17/politics-conspiracy-theories-inspire -vigilante-justice-in-tucson.

181   Steinbart's mother: Amen Clinic letter to Steinbart family, March 17, 2020.

189   admitted: "Petition for Action on Conditions of Pretrial Release," *USA v. Steinbart*, Sept. 1, 2020.

191   a sexual relationship with accused Russian spy Maria Butina: Michael Corkery, "Overstock C.E.O. Takes Aim at 'Deep State' after Romance with Russian Agent," *New York Times*, Aug. 15, 2019, https://www.nytimes.com /2019/08/15/business/overstock-paul-byrne-maria-butina-affair.html.

191   Byrne finagled his way into the White House: Alan Feuer, Maggie

Haberman, Michael S. Schmidt, and Luke Broadwater, "Trump Had Role in Weighing Proposals to Seize Voting Machines," *New York Times*, Jan. 31, 2022, https://www.nytimes.com/2022/01/31/us/politics/donald-trump-election-results-fraud-voting-machines.html.

Chapter 13: Q Goes Abroad

195   Q had someone on the inside: Louise Milligan, Jeanavive McGregor, and Lauren Day, "QAnon Follower Tim Stewart's an Old Friend of Scott Morrison. His Family Reported Him to the National Security Hotline," Four Corners, June 13, 2021, https://www.abc.net.au/news/2021–06–14/qanon-follower-old-friend-scott-morrison-stewart-family-speaks/100125156.

197   split into two factions: Emiko Jozuka, Selina Wang, and Junko Ogura, "Japan's QAnon Disciples Aren't Letting Trump's Loss Quash Their Mission," CNN, April 23, 2021, https://www.cnn.com/2021/04/23/tech/qanon-consipiracy-theory-japan-trump-hnk-intl-dst/index.html.

198   QAnon Facebook groups: "Interpreting Social Qs: Implications of the Evolution of QAnon," Graphika, https://public-assets.graphika.com/reports/graphika_report_interpreting_social_qs.pdf.

198   Brazil: Robert Muggah, "In Brazil, QAnon Has a Distinctly Bolsonaro Flavor," *Foreign Policy*, Feb. 10, 2021, https://foreignpolicy.com/2021/02/10/brazil-qanon-bolsonaro-online-internet-conspiracy-theories-anti-vaccination/.

198   raising a Q flag: Mark Townsend, "Fan of Trump and Farage Raises Far-Right 'Q' Flag at His Cornish Castle," *Guardian*, Jan. 11, 2020, https://www.theguardian.com/politics/2020/jan/11/trump-and-farage-supporter-flies-flag-for-qanon-rar-right-conspiracy.

199   marched in front of Buckingham Palace: Ruchira Sharma, "How a Desire to 'Save Our Children' Took People Down the Rabbit Hole into the QAnon Delusion," iNews, Sept. 11, 2020, https://inews.co.uk/news/long-reads/qanon-uk-conspiracy-theory-save-our-children-march-explained-642000.

199   roughly 200,000 QAnon devotees: Katrin Bennhold, "QAnon Is Thriving in Germany. The Extreme Right Is Delighted," *New York Times*, Oct. 11, 2020, https://www.nytimes.com/2020/10/11/world/europe/qanon-is-thriving-in-germany-the-extreme-right-is-delighted.html.

199   adherents of the Reichsbürger: Bennhold.

201 made a startling announcement: Mack Lamoureux, "QAnons Are Harassing People at the Whim of a Woman They Say Is Canada's Queen," Vice News, June 17, 2021, https://www.vice.com/en/article/3aqvkw /qanons-are-harassing-people-at-the-whim-of-a-woman-they-say-is-canadas -queen-romana-didulo.

202 messages to her flock: Daphne Bramham, "The Absurd and Disturbing Tragedy of Romana Didulo," *Vancouver Sun*, Dec. 9, 2021, https:// vancouversun.com/news/daphne-bramham-the-absurd-and-disturbing -tragedy-of-romana-didulo.

202 Didulo herself was detained: Andrew Russell and Stewart Bell, "Self-Declared 'Queen of Canada' Detained by RCMP after Alleged Threats to Health-Care Workers," *Global News*, Dec. 1, 2021, https://globalnews.ca /news/8417379/queen-of-canada-covid-online-threats/.

203 kidnapped a five-year-old girl: Lori Hinnant, "French Child Kidnap Plot Shows Global Sway of QAnon Style," Associated Press, Oct. 5, 2021, https://apnews.com/article/coronavirus-pandemic-europe-kidnapping-health-79761187c5d2767a8a27072a0e2d81ef.

205 replicating the Myanmar coup: Maggie Astor, "Michael Flynn Suggested at a QAnon-Affiliated Event That a Coup Should Happen in the U.S.," *New York Times*, June 1, 2021, https://www.nytimes.com/2021/06/01/us /politics/flynn-coup-gohmert-qanon.html.

Conclusion: Patriots in Control

208 provided security: Alan Feuer, "Another Far-Right Group Is Scrutinized about Its Efforts to Aid Trump," *New York Times*, Jan. 3, 2022, https:// www.nytimes.com/2022/01/03/us/politics/first-amendment-praetorian -trump-jan-6.html.

210 suing her for $1 billion: Tucker Huggins and Dan Mangan, "Dominion Voting Systems Brings $1.3 Billion Defamation Suit Against Ex-Trump Lawyer Sidney Powell," CNBC, Jan. 8, 2021, https://www.cnbc.com /2021/01/08/dominion-brings-defamation-suit-against-sidney-powell .html.

211 Q social media content: Jim Hoft, "BOOTED! Police Escort Leftist Troll Will Sommer from Dallas Pro-Trump Conference—Crowd Cheers the News … Update: Response from Will Sommer," Gateway Pundit, May 30, 2021, https://www.thegatewaypundit.com/2021/05/booted-police-escort -leftist-troll-will-sommer-dallas-pro-trump-conference-crowd-cheers-news/.

212   telling his fans to consume chlorine dioxide: Andrew Jacobs, "Trump
       Disinfectant Remarks Echo Claims by Miracle-Cure Quacks," *New York
       Times*, April 27, 2020, https://www.nytimes.com/2020/04/27/health
       /coronavirus-disinfectant-bleach-trump.html.

212   the Food and Drug Administration warns: "Danger: Don't Drink
       Miracle Mineral Solution or Similar Products," U.S. Food and Drug
       Administration, https://www.fda.gov/consumers/consumer-updates
       /danger-dont-drink-miracle-mineral-solution-or-similar-products.

214   released a secret recording: Will Sommer, "QAnon Hero Michael Flynn
       Secretly Said QAnon Is 'Total Nonsense,'" Daily Beast, Nov. 28, 2021,
       https://www.thedailybeast.com/qanon-hero-michael-flynn-secretly-said
       -qanon-is-total-nonsense.

214   start disguising their support: David Gilbert, "QAnon Is Going into
       Stealth Mode Ahead of the Election," Vice News, Sept. 30, 2020, https://
       www.vice.com/en/article/935pgp/qanon-is-going-into-stealth-mode
       -ahead-of-the-election.

216   encouraged Republicans to follow it: Isaac Arnsdorf, Doug Bock Clark,
       Alexandra Berzon, and Anjeanette Damon, "Heeding Steve Bannon's Call,
       Election Deniers Organize to Seize Control of the GOP—and Reshape
       America's Elections," ProPublica, Sept. 2, 2021, https://www.propublica
       .org/article/heeding-steve-bannons-call-election-deniers-organize-to-seize
       -control-of-the-gop-and-reshape-americas-elections.

216   declared that human traffickers: Vera Bergengruen, "QAnon Candidates
       Are Winning Local Elections. Can They Be Stopped?" *Time*, April 16,
       2021, https://time.com/5955248/qanon-local-elections/.

216   accusing her of being pro-pedophile: David D. Kirkpatrick and Stuart A.
       Thompson, "QAnon Cheers Republican Attacks on Jackson. Democrats
       See a Signal," *New York Times*, March 24, 2022, https://www.nytimes.com
       /2022/03/24/us/qanon-supreme-court-ketanji-brown-jackson.html.

216   NPR poll: Tovia Smith, "They Believe in Trump's 'Big Lie.' Here's Why It's
       Been So Hard to Dispel," NPR, Jan. 5, 2022, https://www.npr.org/2022
       /01/05/1070362852/trump-big-lie-election-jan-6-families.

216   targeted a butterfly sanctuary: Meagan Flynn, "The National Butterfly
       Center Closed Indefinitely. A Fringe Va. Candidate Is Partly to Blame,"
       Washington Post, Feb. 3, 2022, https://www.washingtonpost.com/dc-md
       -va/2022/02/03/kimberly-lowe-national-butterfly-center/.

218   impersonating a government official: Will Sommer, "He Was Partners
       with QAnon. Now He Wants Them Arrested," Daily Beast, April 9, 2021,

https://www.thedailybeast.com/he-was-partners-with-qanon-now-he
-wants-them-arrested.

218   fighting Q with immigration reforms: "Countering QAnon," Polaris
       Project, https://polarisproject.org/wp-content/uploads/2021/02/Polaris
       -Report-Countering-QAnon.pdf.

Index

About the Author

WILL SOMMER is a media reporter for the *Washington Post*. He previously worked as a politics reporter for the *Daily Beast* and as a host of the podcast *Fever Dreams*. His work covering QAnon and other conspiracy theories has been featured in multiple documentaries, including HBO's *Q: Into the Storm*.